The Cambridge Series

for

Schools and Training Colleges

THE MAKING OF

CHARACTER

THE MAKING

OF

CHARACTER

SOME EDUCATIONAL ASPECTS
OF ETHICS

BY

JOHN MacCUNN, M.A., LL.D.,

BALLIOL COLLEGE, OXFORD, EMERITUS PROFESSOR OF PHILOSOPHY
IN THE UNIVERSITY OF LIVERPOOL.

CAMBRIDGE:

AT THE UNIVERSITY PRESS

1912

CAMBRIDGE
UNIVERSITY PRESS

University Printing House, Cambridge CB2 8BS, United Kingdom

Published in the United States of America by Cambridge University Press, New York

Cambridge University Press is part of the University of Cambridge.

It furthers the University's mission by disseminating knowledge in the pursuit of
education, learning and research at the highest international levels of excellence.

www.cambridge.org
Information on this title: www.cambridge.org/9781107425781

© Cambridge University Press 1900

First edition 1900
First published 1900
Reprinted 1901, 1903, 1905, 1908, 1912
First paperback edition 2014

A catalogue record for this publication is available from the British Library

ISBN 978-1-107-42578-1 Paperback

CONTENTS.

PART I.

CONGENITAL ENDOWMENT: ITS NATURE AND TREATMENT.

PREFACE TO SIXTH IMPRESSION.

THIS impression contains three new chapters on *Natural Inequality, The Economy of Human Powers,* and *Punishment.* The chapter on *Capacities, Instincts, Desires* has been expanded by a fuller treatment of Pleasures and Pains; and that on *Development and Repression* by a more adequate discussion of Asceticism. There are also a few lesser additions and some re-arrangements.

PART II.

EDUCATIVE INFLUENCES.

PART III.

SOUND JUDGMENT.

PART IV.

SELF-DEVELOPMENT AND SELF-CONTROL.

PART I.

Congenital Endowment: its nature and treatment.

CHAPTER I.

HEREDITY.

It has been reserved for our democratic generation to give a new life to the fast perishing faith in pedigrees. It writes, it preaches, it talks, it thinks biologically; and with the result among others that the idea of Heredity has been lodged beyond displacing in the mind even of the average man. Thus rooted it has its applications, and of these there are at any rate two which intimately concern the making of character.

The idea of Heredity is generally accepted.

One is that the old familiar metaphor of the pure white sheet of paper, so often in times past invoked in the interests of educational responsibility, must now be decently and finally laid to rest. Psychology knows nothing of absolute beginnings. Everywhere its analysis strikes on existing preformations, and if the old metaphor is to survive at all, it must be by saying that the page of the youngest life is so far from being blank that it bears upon it characters in comparison with

It implies that we cannot in Education begin at the beginning.

which the faded ink of palaeography is as recent history. So that, by general consensus, the first step towards the making of character is the recognition of beginnings that have been already made.

Hence, as further result, the growth of a new educational motive. When a father knows that his boy

And imparts an added interest to educational work. inherits tendencies, none the less definite because possibly hidden even from the eye of affection, there is no loss of responsibility here. There is the enhanced responsibility to be for ever on the watch, as there is with the gardener who watches his seedlings, or the farmer his stock. Just because none of them know what is going to happen, just because the tender plant, animal, child, may at any moment unfold unsuspected tendencies, so must there devolve upon those to whose care they are entrusted the obligation of an unintermitting watchfulness. It is in fact precisely this that imparts to education so much of its fascinating interest. Moulding the clay or hewing the block (well-worn metaphors!) is dull work in comparison. For education, and especially the education of character, would lose half its interest if, as some have fancied, education were everything. It is interesting just because it is not everything, because, in other words, the youngest child is already old in proclivities whose manifestation is often the first sign to us of their existence.

Nor does either this responsibility or this interest limit itself to our dealings with the young. Inherited

Tendencies may be inherited although their manifestation be deferred. tendencies, it is to be remembered, need by no means appear all at once. Like the seeds of an hereditary malady, they may lie latent for many a year, and are none the less inherited though their manifestation is deferred. It is the source of many a surprise and many a disappointment. The "ugly duckling" becomes the swan: the cygnet too becomes the duck. And so it will continue to be, so long as these deferred instincts have to wait upon physiological development, upon favouring environment, or upon simple lapse of time, to bring them at last to light. It is difficult to set limits to this. There are cases of men who seem to develop in comparatively late life belated tastes—tastes for travel or society or art or sport—which persistently struggle through, though they may have been inhibited for half a life-time. We are apt to call such tastes acquired, attributing them to the influences of environment which have been so long at work before they make their appearance. Yet the proclivity may have been there from the first. We may at least suspect it was, because it often seems to survive much discouragement, and because we are often able when it appears to identify it as a family trait long hidden but revealed at last.

Thus far then, it may with confidence be said that the idea of heredity is practically fruitful. It brings this enhanced responsibility, and this added interest into all educational work.

It is another matter when we go beyond this, and ask if what is known about Heredity can justify hopes that we can ascertain, otherwise than by the actual watching of those with whom we have to deal, what their congenital endowment is. And we may reduce this question to its most practical terms by asking if it is of real moment to study stock and parentage, in order that we may better discern the endowment of the child.

The idea of Heredity further suggests the value of a knowledge of stock and parentage.

There seems no reason to doubt that something can be done in this direction. Supposing ourselves able to arrive at trustworthy knowledge of the characteristics not only of parentage but of stock, we stand at an undoubted advantage. For when we detect some trait emerging which we know to have had a masterful influence upon the family history—be it love of adventure, or of money, or of ease, or of fighting, and so forth—we can understand that we are in presence of a proclivity that will tax all our resources. We may thus find an index as to the lines upon which we have to watch and work. It may be granted further that our knowledge of ancestry will bear the fruit of all genuine knowledge. It will sharpen our perceptions by giving us "pre-perceptions." It will enable us, by knowing what to look for, to detect the first tiny shoots of congenital proclivity as soon as they break the soil, and to lay our plans accordingly. In this way knowledge of stock and parentage may work in helpful alliance with observation.

Yet it is safest here not to expect too much. The conviction that every new life inherits much is entirely consistent with the contention that knowledge of stock and parentage, even much fuller and more carefully generalised than seems possible for those whose ends are practical, can furnish but an imperfect clue as to what we may expect to find in the individual boy or girl, even when these are of our own household. This for quite definite reasons.

Yet belief in Heredity need not involve much confidence in the practical value of such knowledge.

In the first place, we are not, in the present stage of controversy, entitled to treat the habits a father or mother has formed during lifetime, be they virtues or vices, as indicative of what the child is to inherit. Too many of the preachers and teachers of our day, over eager to impress Science into the service of edification, have caught at the doctrine that the acquired characteristics of one generation become, by inheritance, the instincts of the next. It may be so. Habitual skill with chisel, pencil, or piano, habitual temperance or immoderation, thrift or prodigality, may thus be transmitted in ways we cannot trace. But we really cannot be said to know. The evidence is inconclusive. We seem powerless to adduce a single conclusive instance. What we actually know is that this whole question of the transmission of "acquired characters" is open, and vigorously argued by Lamarckians and Weismannians. Till they settle their differences, results are too uncertain to be made the basis of responsible action.

For, 1. The transmission of acquired characteristics is still doubtful.

When we pass to the other qualities—the qualities handed on from generation to generation irrespective of the life-acquisitions of individuals—we are in a sense upon surer ground. It will not now-adays be denied that such transmission is a fact. *2. Though other qualities are transmitted,* Even primitive tribesmen recognised it in their flocks and herds; and the reappearance in sons of family traits has long been one of the stock themes of popular remark and conversation. It appears to be scientifically well-established in regard to inherited physical constitution. It need not be doubted in the region of temperament (especially emotional temperament), capacity and instinct.

Yet this fact is of less practical value than might at a first glance appear. It is only necessary to set ourselves to study any given family history to meet the initial difficulty of dis-criminating what is inherent in the stock and transmissible, from what is acquired in the life-time of individuals and (it may be) not transmissible. Even if this difficulty, and it is not slight, could be overcome, the knowledge of what is inherent in the stock could not with much confidence be made the basis of action. For Nature is wayward. Marvellously con-servative though she be in passing on qualities from generation to generation, she yet strangely loves to hide from our eyes her ways of working. Thus the congenital tendencies of a father, though they be pronounced and unmistakeable, *yet the quali-ties of parents need not re-appear in the next genera-tion.* need by no means reappear in the son. They may go under for generations, and only reappear in children's children. Add to this that children may manifest unexpected qualities of their own. For in any given child we may, to an extent not easy to limit, find ourselves confronted by those "sports," those variations small or great from the an-cestral stock, of which so little seems to be known, except that they are many and incalcu-lable. *Children may also exhibit variations from the ancestral stock.* Rare gifts, both of mind and disposition, may thus break the crust of unlikely soils, and inexplicable, lamentable perversions seem to give the lie to the most excellent of ancestries. Not without their lessons. The one surprise tells us never rashly to despair of the progeny even of the worst. The other warns us never to lull ourselves into a careless confidence in the progeny even of the best. Both forbid us, however firm our faith in Heredity, to see a prophecy of the son in the parent. And both remind us that precon-ceptions based on study of stock and parentage may betray us into the fatal errors of foregone conclusions in regard to the young lives we have to deal with.

Nor must we forget that the genealogical tree of every son

And each child possibly inherits a bewildering multitude of tendencies.

of man broadens out, as we ascend it, into a quite limitless host of ancestral kindred. It is not necessary for our argument to ascend very far. Ten or twenty generations will suffice. For even then, precisely as we are firm in the faith that ancestral traits persist, so must our anticipations of the inherited endowment of any individual multiply; if indeed we do not sink bewildered in presence of the number of accumu-lated possibilities of the small final product, in whose veins runs blood, mixed in ways subtler than chemical combination, by the intermarriage of hundreds or thousands of families.

"The blessings of a good parentage," Dr Maudsley assures

Hence it seems safer to base our knowledge of congenital en-dowment upon direct observa-tion.

us, will do more for a man in the trials and crises of life, "in the hour of death," he says, "and in the day of judgment than all that has been taught him by his pastors and masters[1]." The words are, of course, as controvertible as they are sweeping. They obviously carry with them a startling estimate of the influence of what is congenital upon the rest of a man's life. But, even were they true, many

[1] *Physiology of Mind,* p. 367.

A full discussion of Heredity will be found in Ribot's *Heredity* (H. S. King and Co.). Cf. also Lloyd Morgan, *Habit and Instinct,* c. xv.

a large gap in knowledge would have to be filled before they could be made to yield a justifiable expectation that the study of stock and parentage is a trustworthy path to a knowledge of the concrete child. For even if we believed that all that is congenital must be inherited[1], the belief would not dispel the difficulties still to be overcome before we could predict with confidence what the inheritance in a given concrete case is likely to be. And so long as this is so, it would seem the more practical course to look, for our knowledge of the congenital endowment of those we have to educate, less to what we can glean about their ancestry than to what, by direct observation, we can learn about the young lives themselves.

CHAPTER II.

NATURAL INEQUALITY.

THE fact that meets us on the threshold here is inequality. This is only what one might expect. When ancestry is endlessly diverse; when variations, sometimes for better sometimes for worse, appear *Inequality is a fact.* even in households where they are least looked for; when widely dissimilar environments prescribe the conditions, adverse or favouring, under which young lives first look out upon the world, it would be against all reason to expect anything but inequality. And, in this case, what we expect is also what we find. Are not the boys or girls on the same school-bench, are not even the children of a common home unequal—unequal in vital energy, in temperament, in capacities, in instincts? Few and feeble proclivities, torpid feelings that are the despair of the educator lie at the one extreme: at the other, a rich endowment of gift and promise, and a faculty of response that perplexes by its many-sidedness. Between, an almost endless scale. Nor is the full extent of these inequalities

---

[1] A statement not too rashly to be accepted.

manifest all at once in early years. Time the revealer is needed to reveal it. Not all the inequalities that emerge as the years go on are to be set down to education. Far other-

Education reveals the natural inequalities of men.

wise. For whatever be the inequalities of its own making for which education is responsible, it is likewise the revealer of inequalities, congenital inequalities, for which it is not responsible. Assuredly of all doctrines ever fathered by serious thinkers, the dogma of the natural equality of men is amongst the least tenable.

It is, in fact, just because these natural inequalities are so pronounced that it is sometimes taken to be the

The policy of levelling up.

peculiar task of education to level up. The naturally gifted are supposed to be in no danger of neglect, or even to be able to take care of themselves; and it is regarded as the peculiar task of education to redress the inequalities of nature by making average mediocrity, and even conspicuous defect, its peculiar case. Witness the volume of effort that has of recent years been directed upon elementary and technical education, upon provision for the physically and mentally and morally defective, even upon the reclamation of the criminal.

Nor is this movement motived merely by sympathy and compassion. It rests on a surer and more rational

The value of the individual.

foundation. For it is precisely one of the most deeply-rooted characteristics of our western civilisation to have come to convictions as to the worth, the potential worth at all events, not only of the average man but even of the feebler specimens who drop far below the average level. These are not by any means the convictions of theorists only, far less of visionaries. On the contrary they lie deep in the popular consciousness because they have taken root in institutions: in Law, which hedges about by its inviolable circle the weakest and the humblest of the sons of men; in the churches, which, alike in teaching and in action, have always stood for the worth of the individual soul even when in the eye of the world it may be "worthless"; in

organized philanthropic effort, which lavishes care and money
upon the dregs of the population; and, we may add, in
political development which has now for some time been
exalting the claims of the poor, the neglected, the struggling
to their share in the benefits of the democratic State.

These convictions, thus sponsored, may of course be held
on various grounds. They may be an article of a religious
creed accepted on authority; they may be simply intuitions
of the heart and conscience; or they may be justified of
philosophy by a searching investigation into the nature,
capacities and destinies of man. For it stands without saying
that the ascription of this unique value to even the least and
the lowliest is just one of those central problems to which
philosophy is bound to address itself. The solutions of course
vary. They must vary so long as idealism diverges from
utilitarianism and both from naturalism[1]. But be this as it
may, the conviction stands firm as a practical belief which
has become the basis of action in many directions, and of
these education is one.

Its immediate influence here is far-reaching and decisive.
For once it be granted that the child or the man
whose elevation is the object of educational   **Education
recognises the
effort** has this peculiar value, forthwith the   **worth of man.**
whole outlook is transformed. The physical defects, the
undeveloped powers, the stunted capacities, the imperfect
gifts, the poor or squalid environment, in a word all the
characteristics which mark the less favoured amongst life's
children cease to be regarded as merely things to be deplored
and redressed. Instead, they come to be viewed rather as
obstructions which hinder the human spirit from making the
most of its powers—obstructions which, in the name of the
worth even of the "worthless," it is the beneficent task of education to remove. Nor is it a bad description of the province of
education to say that its task is to clear away the obstructions
that thwart and frustrate the forward-struggling spirit of man.

[1] See "The justification of motives to social work" in *Addresses on
Ethics of Social Work*, The University Press, Liverpool, 1911.

This will be clearer when we come in the sequel to see what human capacities actually are, but meanwhile we may

Why has the child stronger claims upon us than the animal?

emphasize the point by asking a simple question : Why has any child, even when far below the average, an unmeasurably stronger claim upon our services than even the highest of the animals? Why is it, unless because we find, even in the least favoured of the human race, that value, actual or potential, for which we may search long and in vain even in the aristocracy of the animal world.   For educational work at its best is never motived merely by social sympathy however strong, but by social sympathy enlightened and intensified by this perception of the worth of all the objects of its care.

Hence indeed it becomes possible to speak of education, and especially on its moral side, as if its whole

Educational effort counter-works the law of "sur-vival of the fittest."

aim was to counterwork the methods of Nature[1]. For if it be Nature's law—and it has been well dinned into our ears by Darwinian biologists for the last half-century—that the strong survive and the weak succumb, Education has not resignedly bowed down before it.   It has made up its mind that the weak must not be suffered to succumb.   Not only has it, in the equal-itarian spirit of a democratic age, directed an unprecedented volume of effort and expenditure to the levelling-up of the average child; it has not forgotten the residuum which, if Nature had her way, would receive short shrift in the struggle for existence.

This line of thought, and action, must not, however, be pressed unduly.   It is a long stride from the

Yet belief in the value of the individual is not belief in the equal value of in-dividuals.

belief that every human life has a unique worth to the notion that all have equal worth—a re-mark which might seem obvious were it not for the fact that, when men are out of heart at the inequalities of human faculty and lot, and ready

[1] See Huxley's *Evolution and Ethics*, esp. p. 32.

to rail at Nature or Fortune for their own short-comings, it
has been customary for preachers and moralists to tell them
that, if they will, they can redress the balance, however un-
favourable, by making themselves second to none in moral
character. Has not the gospel of independence, from the
Stoics to Burns, consoled the honest man with the assurance
that he can be "King of men for a' that"? "Brother, thou
has possibility in them for much," cries Carlyle, "the possibility
of writing on the eternal skies the record of a heroic life[1]."
Nor need the profound and satisfying truth that underlies the
words be disputed. No student of life can miss the fact that
the obscurest lot and the most insignificant bit of work can
be transfigured by the motives that lie behind them. This,
indeed, is precisely one of the reflections which give an
enheartening hopefulness to the whole enterprise of moral
education.

But it would be a fatal blunder to forget, on this account,
that great natural inequalities not only exist but
persist, and to miss the fact that superiorities
of congenital endowment have claims that are
second to none. For is it not rather Nature's
favoured children, the strong the gifted the
promising who most demand attention? And this for more
reasons than one.

It is the best natural gifts that most demand attention.

(*a*) For one must ever remember here that it is precisely
the most gifted natures that we can least afford to leave to
themselves. It is the neglect of the best that produces the
worst: it is the greatest natural gifts, when not taken in hand
by the maker of character, that may work the greatest mischief
both for society and for their possessor. Who can doubt it
when he thinks what the results may be when intense feelings
and fiery passions fasten upon evil or even upon second-rate
ends, or when an imaginative temperament is left to feed itself
upon debased ideals, or when faculty of utterance, by tongue

[1] *Past and Present*, Bk IV, c. viii.

or pen or brush, is abandoned to the vagaries of an energetic caprice?

(*b*) And this result is the more deplorable because it is the best natural gifts that most repay attention. They have most response. If, in a sense, they make their possessor independent of the helping hand, in a truer sense they accentuate the need for it, because they have it in them to assimilate influences to an extent that may well be the envy of their less gifted fellows.

Hence, in presence of inequality, we may say that the task of education is two-fold. On the one hand it

The two-fold task of Education.

must level up. Alive to the reality of human worth, it must do its utmost for the natural capacities of all men, even where promise is at its minimum. On the other hand, it must dismiss the illusion that it can, by any levelling-up, expect to diminish the inequalities between man and man. On the contrary, it must unhesitatingly recognise the claims of the naturally fit, and give them of its

Education does not level.

best. The result will not be levelling. The inequalities after education are probably much wider than those before it. Are children more on an equality or less when they leave a school than when they enter? Are men more equal or less when they leave the University than they were in their schooldays? Few things are so certain as that, however much education may do for the naturally weak as well as for the naturally fit, it is far enough from making for equality either of mind or character.

Nor is there anything in this that is really hostile to the equalitarian spirit of modern democratic thought.

But it is not, on that account, hostile to the democratic spirit.

For though it is in vain for the equalitarian to deny that Nature and Education alike set their seal on inequality, this need not discourage the justifiable and most human aspiration that not only mediocrity but weakness and defect will receive even more than their due. For in no direction is nurture of great powers more justified of education than when it is made tributary to the common good. And who can doubt that, in a community in which, in proportion as individuals were richly endowed by nature, they were trained to be compassionate, just and public spirited, even the weakest would come by his own?

That inequality is thus a fact with which we have to reckon, will appear more evident when we turn to the specific modes in which it appears from the outset. One of these, and it is of far-reaching significance, is Temperament.

Specific forms of congenital endowment.

CHAPTER III.

TEMPERAMENT [1].

TEMPERAMENT is not to be regarded as one element among other elements of human nature. It is rather the result of the manner in which the elements are mixed. So far as analysis can go, it would seem that these elements are various. To say that the soul is alive is to say that, at least in rudimentary fashion, it strives, feels, and knows;

Temperaments differ according to the proportions in which the elements of the soul are mixed.

and that it has already (if such a metaphor be applicable to organic relation) struck that partnership with the body which is not dissolved while life lasts. Nor has the youngest lived a day till each of these elements has already asserted itself in the irresistible tendency, bound up with all life, further to differentiate itself. There are differences between man and man of course; but they are differences, not of ultimate elementary constitution, but of comparative preponderance of elements [2].

---

[1] For suggestive treatment of Temperament cf. Lotze, *Mikrocosmus*, bk. VI. c. ii.

[2] Höfiding, *Outlines of Psychology*, p. 88.

We say sometimes in our haste, "The man has no feeling," "no passions," "no imagination," "no sense." But we cannot really mean it. The worst that can happen is that feeling, passion, and the rest, are in meagre proportion. All the elements are there in subtlest intermixture, and in proportions so various that different persons may so little recognise their common constitution as to eye their next-door neighbours as if they belonged to a different species. Writers used to speak of "the native equality of man": it is truer to say that, by the very constitution of human nature, there are no two men alike.

It is here one might hint that the man of the world has something to learn from the philosopher, at whom he is apt to smile on the ground that, in his generalisations he is blind to the diversities of man from man. *De te fabula.* It is the man of the world who, in his innocence of analysis, is ignorant that, by virtue of the very plan on which it is built, human nature is, by this endlessly varied mixing of its elements, predestined to an endless diversity.

It is the man of the world, not the philosopher, who underestimates the differences of man from man.

Of this mixing of the elements, Temperament is the reflexion. Inwrought in the very texture of the life, it modifies all we receive, and from first to last conditions all we do. It is, so to say, a medium that colours, that suffuses all experience. It is modifiable enough. For every influence that alters the relative preponderance of the elements within us must *ipso facto* alter it. Yet, bound up with the proportions in which our capacities for sensation and idea, for striving and feeling, in all their varied modes have been, by Nature's distribution, intermixed, it can rarely, if ever, by the most coercive of educations, be revolutionised.

From this it follows that we go astray if we seek for the seat of Temperament exclusively in any single element of our constitution. Its secret is not to be found in physiological constitution, nor in those general or organic sensations which so vaguely yet so deeply colour our moods, nor in our emotional susceptibility. These all work : often they work upon Temperament with masterful power. But Temperament is not thus simple. Rather is it like a ten-stringed instrument that vibrates in all its chords, now in this fashion and now in that, as these have been variously attuned.

Tempera-ment is there-fore not due to any single element in human nature.

It also follows that Temperament has many modes. Few elements may be fruitful of many combinations. And when one begins to think how the diverse phases of our mental and emotional and conative life may be multifariously blended and interfused, there is room enough here for the warning, always so needful in psychological analysis, not to travesty the lavish, finely-discriminated varieties of Nature by reducing them to a handful of cut and dried types.

It may also be endlessly varied.

Yet types of Temperament exist, and indeed the four classical types have, in literature and usage, so long and persistently survived the effete physiology which gave them names, that it may be assumed that experience has found it profitable to discriminate them. Diagnosis will at any rate not be fruitless if it suggests ideas as to the manner of their educational treatment.

The four classical tem-peraments.

Thus there is one type whose characteristic it is to be rapidly and easily responsive to all impressions and interests. It is caught by the event or the appearance of the moment ; and, when one has it at its height, it is difficult to know at which trait most to wonder—at its responsiveness or at its fickleness, at its readiness to be interested, or at its readiness to transfer its interest. This is the characteristic temperament of most children, to whose unpreoccupied outlook the world is so interesting a place that they cannot fix their interest for long upon anything in it. But it does not pass with childhood. It lives on in the man or woman who is so excellently fitted to be a pleasant

The " san-guine " tem-perament.

companion and agreeable member of society, whose interests
are many and quick, who does not, because he cannot, agitate
or bore us by absorbing enthusiasms, who, in a word, is something of everything and everything of nothing.   Such is the
so-called "sanguine" temperament.   Its strength

Its strength,   lies in its open and ready receptiveness, and in
the promise these contain of cheerful and fruitful contact with
experience.   Hence we like to see it in children.

and defects.   But then it has the defects of its virtues.   It is
infirm of purpose, and it has a fatal facility for skating lightly
over the deeper experiences.   Not only is it incapable of
heroisms or devotions : it does not seem to miss them.   Left
to itself it would people the world with "ten-minutes emotion-
alists."   Yet, when all is said, such are hopeful material to work
upon.   They come half-way to meet us.   They spare us the
dreary task of awakening interest where none is.

Mode of   And if only they can be yoked to more strenuous
treatment.   fellow-workers, or enlisted in the service of some
great institution, or deepened by hardship and struggle, or
convinced (even though the appeal be in part to their vanity[1])
that something is expected of them, they will not fail of a
creditable ending.   The drawback is that they are so apt to
disappoint the promise of early years.   In the University it is
the youth whose reputation for animated conversation, charm,
general ability, is so brilliant—till the day comes when it is
whispered that Pendennis of St Boniface is plucked : in
Literature it is the versatile author of unwritten books : in
business, the man of many enterprises and few dividends : in
industry, the "Jack of all trades" : in life in general the man of
promise who could "do anything," yet has it not in him, when
his chance comes, to bend himself to one resolute effort.   Is it
to their credit or otherwise that these sanguine types nevertheless remain cheerful to the last, the one thing to which they

[1] Adam Smith goes so far as to say that "the great secret of education
is to direct vanity to proper objects."   *Moral Sentiments,* VI. 3.

seem unable to turn their minds being the fact, so obvious to the onlooker, that they have been tried in the balance and found wanting.

Very different is the sentimental, or as it is usually called the "melancholic" type. Like the sanguine it The "melan-
is sensitive and responsive: unlike it, it has cholic" tem-
neither the open outward outlook, nor the ready perament.
responsiveness to changing influences. On the contrary, it dips deep in moods, and is prone to brood over them even till they touch the dark fringe of morbidity. In certain Its superior-
respects this type is superior to the other. It is ity to the
not the shuttlecock of every new attraction. sanguine.
Whatever it be it is not flighty. From what experience offers, it selects: and what it selects it cleaves to—a direct contrast to the facile appreciations of the sanguine. The depth of its interests moreover is some compensation for its want of flexibility; and whatever future awaits it, it is likely to take life seriously. On the other hand, it is just this Its dangers.
preoccupation with particular experiences that is
its snare, so that many an aspect of the great opening spectacle of life is suffered to pass unheeded away without eliciting a single response. This tendency may have still more serious results. Sentimentality may become the keynote; and emotion which, in less one-sided natures, is the prelude to active ex-pression, comes to be valued so much for its own sake that it quenches the practical impulses it ought to have vitalised. This is at any rate the result in many a case where tempera-ment has found food in literature and art, in music, in poetry, in novel-reading and all the means whereby, with little trouble to ourselves, we can enjoy the luxury of emotion. Hence *Welt-schmerz* in all its modes. Hence the make-believe afflictions of "those good old days when we were so miserable." Hence those other afflictions, not make-believe, which catch up all the promise of life in the absorbing vortex of one rooted sorrow, one baffled ambition, one irreparable mistake.

M.   2

It is such dangers that justify the wisdom of the maxim, so earnestly insisted on by Professor James, never to suffer a single emotion to evaporate without exacting from it some practical service[1]. To the melancholic temperament it will never come amiss. For, normally, emotion is not divorced from action. In children feeling is already on the way to action. All that is needful is that these possible victims of sensibility should be thrown betimes into cheerful and manly companionship, there to be fed upon healthy outward interests whenever their susceptibilities offer an opening; and that they should be reared in homes where energetic, active interests get their due. Not that the spirit ought to be quenched. For the "melancholic" nature has a promise of its own, and much may be done for it, if its emotions find worthy and not maudlin or melodramatic objects. So nurtured it begets the tender and sympathetic heart. This however is no light task; and the melancholic subject will stand in need of watchful and discriminative tendance, where its sanguine counterpart may often be safely left to shift for itself.

Importance of utilising emotion for action.

In both these temperaments the emotional element is prominent, though in the one it is mobile and in the other intense. In the next two there is less of feeling and more of practicality.

Thus of the "choleric" temperament the characteristics are precipitancy and persistence in action. There is strong reaction within some more or less definite range of stimulus. There is also a tendency to persevere in this with astonishingly little distraction from other interests. It is the temperament of the small boy who, like Samuel Budgett, becomes "the successful merchant" from the day when he finds—and sells—an old horse-shoe; of the girl who must needs be a nurse, and begins her duties in the wards of the nursery amongst her dolls; of the youth who *will* go to sea

The "choleric" temperament.

Its practicality.

[1] *Principles of Psychology*, vol. I. p. 125.

from the hour he sees a ship and has the honour of the acquaintance of a real sailor. One must not confuse this with the merely wilful type. For whereas the wilful boy or girl may be capricious and uncalculable, this is the reverse. Nor has it much kinship with the sanguine, though the two, like all temperaments, may be mixed. For there is no risk here of flighty fragmentariness of pursuits. The danger here is obstinate narrowness—the limitation, not to say the mutilation, of character which in later years is apt to mark the man, however successful, who is driven through life by coercive practical proclivity.

Proclivity of course is in itself no evil. Pronounced instincts are the opportunity of the educator : they come half-way to meet him. If only they were always as reasonable, as congruent with circumstance, as good, as they are pronounced ! Here lies the crux. For of all types this is the most refractory. When the parent proposes, it disposes. And where affectionate foresight has been at endless pains to clear the path for some ambitious or respectable career, this "choleric" object of anxiety will not walk in it, but goes his own way. Small wonder if many a parent has asked, and failed to answer the question, How is it to be dealt with ?

It furnishes opportunities to the educator.

Not, one might suggest, by the strong and risky policy of withstanding it to the face. When proclivity is pronounced it may still be modifiable : it may even, if some counter instinct be available, be subjugated. But it is precisely the difficulty that in the choleric type these counter-proclivities are not always to be found. And when this is so, the more hopeful policy would seem to be that of frankly accepting proclivity, and of going to meet it. After all it is a sign of strong life. When Nature speaks clearly we must listen. And a ruling instinct has a way, under flat contradiction, of becoming a ruling passion.

Dangers of attempting to repress pronounced proclivity.

Naturam expellas furca; tamen usque recurret.

2—2

Therefore it is so often the wiser plan, when instincts are thus pronounced, to cast about for the means of finding for them the healthiest and highest development of which they seem capable: for the lad of roving and adventurous spirit, some manly and honourable service: for the boy who must needs drive a bargain, a stool in the best firm, or apprenticeship with the best tradesman available: for the confirmed meddler with household clocks, barometers and water-taps, the workshop bench, and so forth. This may be difficult. It may be out of keeping with family traditions, circumstances, influence, projects. Yet this temperament is worth humouring. For it is perhaps by these choleric types, with their masterful proclivities, that the hardest work of the world is done.

Importance of encouraging strong instincts.

The fourth temperament, even though it be weighted with the unpromising label "phlegmatic," has been regarded by one writer[1] as in a sense superior to all the others. This on the ground that it is a sign of strength not to be flightily led from interest to interest like the sanguine, not to be at the mercy of moods like the melancholic, nor yet, like the choleric, to be mastered by any dominant pursuit. For is it not those natures that are slow to be moved which often astonish the world by displays of the reserved strength that has been slowly funding itself under a "phlegmatic" exterior? It is the very disposition in which Englishmen are so apt to take pride when they flatter themselves that they are not as their more precipitate, flighty, or sentimental neighbours.

The 'phlegmatic' temperament.

It has been regarded as superior to all the others.

This may hold of a certain type of character: and we may believe, further, that such implies a native inertia hostile alike to hastiness of action and emotional disturbance, and still more to quick transfer of interest. It may also be conceded that that type

Grounds for regarding it as indicative of a strong nature.

[1] Lotze, *Mikrocosmus*, Bk. VI. c. ii.

in which there is a barrier that must be broken through before impression stirs emotion, or emotion passes into action, has a strength and stability that others lack. It will at any rate remain remote from the sham practicality, and the sham sympathy that arise from nothing more than weak inhibition. Yet it is too wide a stretch to concede all this, which is in most cases the result of moral discipline, to temperament. Phlegmatic *temperament*, whatever its merits, has the demerit of a stolidity that is the despair of the educator. The other temperaments are at any rate not inaccessible. The phlegmatic subject on the other hand gives us no opening. There may be a world of wealth below the crust. But the crust is, or seems, impenetrable. The man (or boy) neither gives sign of what he is fit for, nor does he respond to our experiments to discover. As the proverb has it, it is not the rearing but the dead horse that is the hardest to drive. Probably the best plan is, placing our trust neither in ideas nor feelings, to weight this type as heavily as we can with practical responsibilities; and to bring him face to face with issues that will squeeze out from him such inert strength as he possesses.

Per contra, it is peculiarly inaccessible.

This simple list might easily enough be enlarged. We might for example distinguish temperaments that are buoyant or depressed, self-confident or timid, explosive or hesitating, headstrong or calculating, docile or refractory and so on. And teachers, from their intimate contact with masses of children, might render fruitful service by devising classifications of their own. For results would here be of more than theoretical interest, inasmuch as a careful diagnosis of types is the first step to clear ideas of the treatment they severally demand.

Possibility of further classifications of the temperaments.

CHAPTER IV.

CAPACITIES, INSTINCTS, DESIRES.

DESPITE the Stoic paradox (by no means false) that he who has one virtue has all the rest, it would be absurd to hold that every one has equal aptitude for every virtue. There are too many of us who admire virtues in others just because we find it so hard to develope them ourselves. All actual moral achievement is, in short, profoundly conditioned even to the end by specific congenital aptitude. This may be expressed by saying that it depends on innate Capacity, and Capacity need only be named to suggest two characteristics that are conspicuously encouraging.

All development is conditioned by innate Capacity.

(*a*) One is that it is capacious : it means capacities. For, by wide consensus, man outstrips the animals just in this, that he comes into the world richly dowered with capacities. How comparatively contracted the development that awaits even the paragons of the animal kingdom : how comparatively limitless—as time-honoured moralising has not failed to remind us—the possibilities that lie hidden in the humblest of cradles.

The capacities are many,

(*b*) The second characteristic is that capacities are emphatically modifiable. For though we must suppose that every single capacity has, so to say, an individuality of its own, and sends down specific roots of its own into human nature, yet our ordinary capacities do not, like those pronounced forms of capacity, the instincts, obstinately resist the modifying influence of man or circumstance. Thus much truth at all events remains to the obsolete doctrine that education can shape its products at its will. For though the evolutionists have upset that doctrine by pointing out that each new life falls heir to a rich dower of capacities which have to be reckoned with, even they make haste to add

and modifiable.

that these capacities are singularly plastic to the educator's hand[1]. And this of course serves for encouragement.

It is important however here to discriminate between at least three meanings which this ambiguous word *capacity* may be made to bear. When we use it we may be thinking mainly, if not solely, of capacities for pleasures and pains, or we may be so stretching the term as to include under it those pronounced and definite proclivities which we commonly call instincts, or we may be thinking also of a third class of propulsions which, on the one hand, lack the definiteness of instincts, while yet, on the other, they are not to be regarded as simply propulsions towards pleasure or aversions to pain.

Three meanings of "Capacity."

Now, if we take capacities in the first of these senses, it is not to be denied that they offer large opportunities for educational action. The inherent attractiveness of pleasure, the inherent repulsiveness of pain are all but ineradicable. Especially so with pain. Our first and last instinct is to shrink from pain. We hate it. If we could, we would banish the very thought of it. And even those, to whose worn-out bodies and souls the pleasures of life have lost their charm, usually have energy left to recoil from pain. In that warfare they never flag. It would seem therefore that, when other resources fail, we can at least reckon upon the effectiveness of appeal to pain.

Capacities for pleasures and pains: their importance.

Nor is it doubtful that memories of pleasures and pains can by association be firmly knit to most things that have to be pursued or avoided alike in the domain of thought and action. The association may be rivetted by the gradual and cumulative results of repetition or, more rarely, by the single memorable experience that lasts a life-time; but however rivetted, it can certainly become indissoluble. To think of *this* action is to shy with instant aversion from the pain that shadows it: to think of *that* action is to be lured by the attendant pleasure that beckons us towards it coercively.

[1] Cf. Lloyd Morgan's *Habit and Instinct*, p. 333.

Even the ascetic, though he will have none of pleasure, knows well how to impress pain into his service, and by its help to scourge human nature into the paths of virtue. To deny all this would be to fly in the face of facts.

Nor need the associations thus established be by any means of express human contrivance. By grace

Pleasure is the concomitant of healthful function.

of Nature, as Aristotle pointed out in the tenth Book of his *Ethics*, man is so constituted that the normal exercise of all his powers brings pleasure as surely as health is accompanied by the glow upon the face of youth, and, no less surely, abnormal function brings its concomitant pain. The law, it is true, may not be absolute. Even deadly poisons may produce effects that are far from painful, and, on the other hand, the high courage that lays down life on the battle-field can hardly (as Aristotle himself admits) be fitly called pleasurable[1]. Yet the generalisation, taken broadly, holds its ground. For Nature helps us here, and by annexing to each line of action its own appropriate pleasures or pains, presents us with additional incentives, these "natural pleasures" to wit, to which, as to well-tried allies, we can make our confident appeal. And, then, if Nature fails us, we can, here as elsewhere, improve upon her. If the natural pleasures of telling the truth and shaming the devil be not enough, we can possibly tip the scale by throwing into it the promised pleasures of reward: if the natural pains of lying seem insufficiently deterrent, we can awaken in the wavering culprit's mind the prospect of what we shall think of him, or do to him if he backslides. Let no one therefore deny that appeal to these capacities for pleasures and pains can be made effective.

It may be well to add that there are good reasons for

Effectiveness of appeal to fear of Pain.

thinking that appeal to fear of pain is the more effective of the two.

(*a*) For, in the first place, there seems to be a greater promptness and definiteness in movements induced

[1] Aristotle's *Ethics*, Bk III. ix. 3.

by fear of pain, even as there are in movements induced by
actual pain. Obedience, for example, may be secured either
by threat or by proffer of reward. Both motives move. But
does the second move with equal swiftness or with equal
definiteness? For, fear of pain prompts quick reactions.
Whence indeed there is only too much temptation to turn
to it. It is so convenient, and not seldom so deplorable,
a short-cut.

(*b*) Again, there is the further advantage, and it is not
slight, that when we work upon fear of pain, we
are less likely to induce mistaken ideas in young
minds as to what is reasonably to be expected
of them. Two lads, we shall suppose, have
been both disciplined to tell the truth, the one
by a diet of threats, the other by a policy of rewards. Neither
of them are admirable: both of them may have nothing higher
than dramatic virtue. But the former will at any rate escape
the illusion that veracity is more than is to be expected of the
sons of men. Else why should deviation from veracity be
punished? Whereas the other may only too easily slip into
the flattering unction that to tell the truth is a positive merit.
Else why should the telling of the truth be rewarded? It is
obviously easy, here in this second case, to lower the youthful
standard. To enforce the plain duties of life by threat of
punishment may, of course, produce a slave. But the slave
will at any rate escape the pernicious sophistication that to do
one's bare duty is to deserve reward.

Comparative value of appeal to pleasures and pains.

(*c*) It may be added that there seems to be one way in
which pain, and the fear of it, can be made peculiarly effective. This discloses itself in dealing
with those cases where good proclivities and
promising instincts may be present, present
even in force, but may be inhibited by some
obstructing weakness or vice which disastrously blocks their
path. And the point is that, if pain can only be applied to

Punishment can release good proclivities by inhibiting bad ones.

stamp out the bad, it may work wonders by releasing the good.
We see this often in the larger scene of life, where, in natures
sound enough at the core and even rich in promise, some fatal
infatuation, some unworthy passion, some stain of vice, some
dash of worldliness, some yielding to ignoble ease, is withered
to the roots by the wholesome bitter blight of disillusionment
and suffering. The result is a changed life. People sometimes
call it a moral conversion but it is better described as a moral
emancipation.

The same thing happens on a lesser scale in the life of
school or home. There are boys enough with sound instincts
and proclivities for good who may nevertheless be careless, or
unpunctual, or truants, or practical jokers, or mutineers, and so
on. Their faults may not go deep, they may at any rate be
only parasitic; but they may, to an extent the culprits little
dream, inhibit the growth of character quite out of proportion
to their intrinsic heinousness. Hence the possibility of cure
by punishment. For if timely punishment can only be so
directed as to kill the parasitic failing or vice, and to bring
home its true significance to the culprit, the good that is in

It is not the
worst cases
that most
justify the
ministry
of Pain.

him will have at the very least a better chance of
struggling outwards into fuller life. For it is
not the thoroughly bad cases, not the cases
where there is little good and much evil, which
are most amenable to the ministry of pain. If
the discipline of pain is ever salutary, it is where it can be
made an ally of the good in its struggle with obstructing evil.

Nor ought it to be forgotten that there are other ways of

Appeal to
anticipated
pleasures and
pains is not
the only way
of utilising
pleasures
and pains.

impressing pains and pleasures into the service
besides by appeal to anticipated results. It is
entirely possible to make the thought of a good
action pleasurable here and now, and yet to say
little or nothing about the results in the way of
pleasure that are to be reaped from its performance. A man may live for posthumous fame, the thought of

it may be so pleasing as to nerve him to unflagging effort, and yet it stands without saying that this pleasant thought of post-humous fame is not an anticipation of any pleasure that he can enjoy. So in other things. A schoolmaster may succeed in making it a pleasure to his pupils to read *Vergil*, and yet do nothing to create the somewhat fatal impression that the end of all study of the *Aeneid* is pleasure. The moralist may make the thought of a duty to be done a pleasing thought, and yet say never a word to foster the expectation that the duty done will yield a harvest of pleasure. Who will deny that the thought of some act of sacrifice, even though it be the path to certain suffering, may nevertheless fill the mind with a lofty and inspiring joy? So in lesser things. It is good that the work of life should be made cheerful and pleasant. But there are other ways of securing this besides the awakening of those anticipations of pleasure to come which play so large a part in the doctrine of the Hedonists.

And yet when all is said—and one does not forget the goodly company of Hedonists from Aristippus to Mill and Spencer—it must be affirmed, and quite decisively, that the place to be assigned to these capacities for pleasures and pains in the making of character is far from paramount.

For it is not the capacities for pleasures or pains, but the instincts, that furnish the educator with immea-surably his greatest opportunities. To seek out the instincts we deem good, and to tend them with untiring solicitude: to watch for the in-stincts we deem bad, dangerous or useless; and to use the good instincts to oust the bad—this is great part of moral education[1]. For when life is young it struggles ever forwards. Its heart is set upon the things that interest it for no other reason than that they satisfy its instinctive propulsions. And its powers of foresight and discrimination being still all undeveloped, it never pauses, and indeed it cannot pause, to disentangle pleasure-giving quality from the concrete attractive-

Yet the educator's best opportunities are found, not in them, but in the Instincts.

[1] Cf. pp. 52 and 88.

ness of the concrete object that evokes the ruling passion of the hour. Simply, the object draws the instinct upon it, and in truth it draws it with attraction so powerful that it is the commonest of experiences that a strong instinct is not to be thwarted by the pains, far less by the warnings of pain, which it encounters in its headlong pursuit.

> "We wander there, we wander here,
> We eye the rose upon the brier,
> Unmindful that the thorn is near,
>   Among the leaves !
> And though the puny wound appear
>   Short while it grieves[1]."

Even in later years, long after the idea of pleasure or pain has disentangled itself from the context of life, the instinctive love of adventure, or of sport, or of acquisition, or of books, even of philosophy, may obstinately refuse to be checked in conscious immoderation, either by the warnings of the wise, or by the castigations of experience. What then are we to expect of the years when foresight has still to be learnt, and when young and eager eyes are turned, not self-wards to pleasures or pains, but healthily outwards upon the rich store of interesting things which the world has to offer to the uncalculating hungers and thirsts of instinct? For although, refusing to be numbered amongst that small minority, the haters of pleasure, we may with utmost frankness accept the fact that human nature loves and longs for pleasure-giving things, we may not, without a fatal lapse, forget that pleasure-giving quality is but one among the attributes of the things we instinctively covet. And though we hardly need to be reminded that it may come to play a main part in the lives of some of us in later years, to begin with it is not so much as known to exist until instinctive proclivity has already driven us upon the objects that yield it. The utilitarians have long

The propulsions of Instinct are strong and uncalculating.

---

[1] Burns, *To James Smith.*

striven to convert the world to their dogma that all desire
is in its essence desire for pleasure. Seizing upon the fact
that, by Nature's law, pleasure is the usual sequel of all
healthful function, they have falsely converted   All desire is
the sequel of activity into activity's initial aim.   not desire for
They have misread the truth that all desire is   pleasure.
desire for pleasure-giving things into the falsehood that all
desire is desire for the pleasure that these things give. This
is an inversion of the order of Nature. We do not eat, it is
to be hoped, for the pleasure that eating brings; or love our
parents for the pleasure of so doing; or stand by our friends
for the pleasure they afford us; or pursue the arts and sciences
for the pleasures of study. No, we turn to these objects first
of all by instinct or by habit, and then the pleasure follows;
and, not seldom, follows all the more surely just because it
was *not* our initial aim. So true is this, especially of earlier
years, that one cannot but suspect that if these Hedonists had
turned their analytic eye upon the ways of their own children,
they might have convinced themselves that the manifold
cupidities of young lives are as lamely accounted for by their
attitude to pleasures and pains as are the instinctive propulsions
of the animal world. "In many instances," says Darwin, "it is
probable that instincts are persistently followed from the mere
force of inheritance without the stimulus of either pleasure or
pain....Hence the common assumption that men must be
impelled to every action by experiencing some pleasure or pain
may be erroneous[1]."

Hence it follows that when the artist in character, be he
parent, teacher or moralist, finds himself face to   The main
face with the question, "To what in the nature   educational
of boy or girl do you propose to make your   appeal ought
                                                     to be, in early
main appeal? Is it to capacities for pleasures   years, to the
and pains, or is it to instincts?" the answer is   instincts.
that, if he is not to fling away his opportunities, his vote

[1] *Descent of Man*, p. 105 (2nd ed.).

must go for the instincts. For, as the greatest of the Greek moral philosophers so clearly saw, never will a virtue be so deeply rooted in the character, as when it has its beginnings already implanted by Nature in those proclivities which are ours "from our very birth[1]."

This may become clearer when we see more precisely what these instincts are[2].

Their salient characteristics at all events are well known.

Instincts are tendencies to movement, of more or less complexity (involving as they do the cooperation of the whole organism). They are prompt in response to stimulus almost with the promptitude of reflex action. They are strikingly persistent in asserting themselves: and above all they are definite. In the animal world the chick hardly out of the shell strikes, with amazing precision, at the particle of grain, the bee makes for the flower, the kitten, carnivorous from infancy, pursues its predestined mouse. And so in the human world; the child unhesitatingly satisfies its hunger and thirst, or closes tiny hands decisively on its first toy, or begins its prolonged tyranny over the domestic animals, or imitates the whole small circle of its acquaintance. Nothing is more surprising than the organised complexity of the reaction in proportion to the slightness of stimulus. For stimulus here is like a trigger; it liberates forthwith a discharge in the way of movement of an amazingly definite and well-concerted character. The proclivity is as explosive as it is determinate. And yet there has been no previous education in this astonishing performance. This is the old trite marvel. Without schools or masters, in a scene all new to them, these untaught experts of nature

Characteristics of the instincts. complexity,

promptitude,

persistence,

definiteness,

"explosiveness,"

independence of Education.

[1] Aristotle, *Ethics*, Bk. VI. c. xiii.
[2] Cf. Lloyd Morgan, *Habit and Instinct*, pp. 4 et seq. and 327 et seq.; and James, *Principles of Psychology*, c. xxiv.

pick and choose with more than the promptitude and infallibility of old experience. No wonder that biologists have
sometimes tried to see in these performances the work of
"lapsed intelligence." For had intelligence expressly designed
and presided over this mechanism that is more than mechanism, it could not more happily have compassed its ends.

This is the more remarkable in that these ends are not
foreseen. Instinct inverts the proverbial phrase; In what sense
instead of seeing roads before they are made, it the instincts
makes roads before they are seen. For all that are blind.
is needful is that the immediate object be presented, be it
food, warmth, shelter, object of possession, attractive example,
or what not: forthwith it is pursued. *Blindly* pursued, we
say; meaning, not of course that the creature does not see the
immediate object. It sees it, usually with miraculous sharp-
sightedness. But it does not see it *in the light of what is going
to ensue upon its appropriation*—a fact, we may remark in
passing, of which the human race has not been slow to avail
itself when it baits traps and devises decoys for even the
intelligent aristocracy of its "poor earth-born companions and
fellow-mortals." At first, man's instincts are hardly more than
this. With no foresight, still less with calculation of results,
and less still of hedonistic results, children eat, drink, play,
imitate, trustfully seek the face of man, or timidly shun it,

"For 'tis their nature too[1]."

Hence that excellent definition of Instinct:—"the faculty of
acting in such a way as to produce certain ends
without foresight of the ends, and without pre- Instinct de-
vious education in the performance[2]." fined.

[1] A little Highland boy, caught *flagrante delicto*, was once rebuked by
a Church elder for furiously riding a stolen pony on Sunday. "Do you
know that it is very wrong, my little man?" "Oh," was the impenitent
reply, "I must do this whateffer." There spoke the genuine voice of
instinct.

[2] James, *Principles of Psychology*, vol. II. p. 383.

To this general account of Instinct it remains to add certain characteristics of especial educational importance.

Characteristics of especial educational importance.

1. The first of these is that the instincts are many.

This statement however is no sooner made than it needs qualification, and indeed some may think that it needs contradiction. For has it not been said upon high authority, and is it not widely accepted, that man stands apart from the animals precisely because *his* instincts are few? Much capacity and few instincts —so runs the accepted analysis.

1. Human instincts may be regarded as many,

It may be granted at once that, if "instinct" be pressed to its more rigorous and more strictly biological meaning, this last statement is the true one. Certainly man has not many instincts that exhibit in full measure the promptitude or the definiteness of animal endowment. In admitting this, it is however of importance to reaffirm, in harmony with the distinctions drawn above, that there are in man many proclivities which cannot be rightly regarded as capacities for pleasures or pains (however true it be that pleasures and pains are inseparable retainers upon them). Like the instincts these proclivities are innate and untaught. Like the instincts their look is outwards upon their objects not inwards upon anticipated pleasures or pains. Like the instincts, they imply no foresight of the ends. And like the instincts, though in feebler and more wavering fashion, they come out to meet our efforts when we hit upon the objects which, by Nature's adaptation, are fitted to evoke them. Now, of course, if we prefer it, we may refuse to call these proclivities "instincts." It does not much matter what we call them, if we recognise that they exist, and that they are of the utmost practical importance. But in view of the fact that they have so much in common with instinct, and are therefore to be sharply distinguished from

if we somewhat stretch the meaning of the word.

capacities for pleasures and pains, it will be practically convenient to class them along with the instincts strictly so called. And we shall then be able to follow Professor James in saying, as against the commonly accepted view, that the instincts of man are many[1].

2. A second point is that human instincts, thus understood, lend themselves to education, for the simple reason that, because of certain features, they cannot be safely left to themselves.

2. Instincts invite intervention;

(*a*) One such feature is that they are transitory. They ripen at a certain time of life, and thereafter, if they be not taken up and transmuted into habits, they decay and dwindle. Hence if they be good and promising, the importance of taking them in hand, and hence the penalties of neglecting to take them in hand, at the right time. Professor James has put the point so convincingly as to make any other statement of it presumptuous[2]. "If a boy grows up alone at the age of games and sports, and learns neither to play ball, nor row, nor sail, nor ride, nor skate, nor fish, nor shoot, probably he will be sedentary to the end of his days; and though the best of opportunities be afforded him for learning these things later, it is a hundred to one but he will pass them by and shrink back from the effort of taking those necessary first steps the prospect of which, at an earlier age, would have filled him with eager delight....In all pedagogy the great thing is to strike the iron while hot, and to seize the wave of the pupils' interest in each successive subject before its ebb has come, so that knowledge may be got and a habit of skill acquired—a headway of interest, in short, secured, on which afterward the individual may float. There is a happy moment for fixing skill in drawing, for making boys collectors in natural

(a) because they are transitory.

---

[1] James, *Principles of Psychology*, vol. II. p. 393; and Lloyd Morgan, *Habit and Instinct*, p. 327, "The first fact that strikes us is how far what is innate is, in the hereditary endowment of man, in excess of what is instinctive." et seq.

[2] James, *ibid.*, vol. II. p. 401.

history, &c....To detect the moment of the instinctive readiness for the subject is, then, the first duty of every educator."

The wisdom of this is incontrovertible. It finds confirmation alike in the fulness of the life in which no strong and healthy instinct has looked in vain for timely nurture, and in the forlorn spectacle of those whom we sometimes see struggling belatedly in later years to cultivate pursuits or pastimes for which the auspicious educational hour has long passed. It was well said by Froebel that every period of life has claims of its own upon us, and is not to be abridged unduly by the raw haste that hurries after the next step in development. For if we starve instincts when they ought to be fed, the result is more than a thwarted and unhappy youth. It is an impoverished manhood.

(*b*) Add to this that, even whilst they have their day, these instincts are *intermittent* in their promptings.

(b) because they are intermittent in their promptings.

For their alliance with the feelings is intimate— so intimate that it is far from easy to discriminate them from the expressions of the emotions. Hence they are only too prone to lie at the mercy of our moods.

" I feel the weight of chance desires,"

says Wordsworth[1], confessing the weakness of a being, however favoured, who still lives upon the bounty of Nature. For life does not adjust its demands upon us to humour our moods. He would be a sorry citizen who acted only when he felt the strong glow of patriotism or benevolence; a poor student who never turned to his books save when the spirit moved him. If the work of life is to be done we must have something steadier and more calculable than instinct to go upon.

(*c*) A further shortcoming of instinct remains. Even the most definite, in other words even the most

(c) because they are morally indeterminate,

instinctive of our instincts, may still, so far as its *moral* direction goes, be *indeterminate*. Man is not born to virtue as the sparks fly upward,

---

[1] *Ode to Duty.* " Me this unchartered freedom tires,
  I feel the weight of chance desires."

nor does he unfold the qualities of a character by the same predestinate necessity wherewith the plant expands in the sunshine[1]. In man, even within the domain of one and the same instinct, there is a possibility of widely different developments. When a child, for example, has an overmastering instinct of acquisitiveness, who will prophesy the sequel— thrift or avarice? When he has an unmistakable hunger for praise, is it to end in vanity, or in a just "love of the love of other people," of which vanity is the counterfeit? When all his instincts are to give, is his to be the future of the good-natured prodigal, or of the generous friend of charities, who holds his fortune as a trust? And is there not for every instinct a like parting of the ways?

Hence the transparent infatuation of the cheap advice, "Trust to your children's instincts." By all means let us study their instincts, and watch them, and tend them. In them, as we have asserted, lie our opportunities. Let us *not* trust them. For this is to forget that the only kind of instinct that is really to be trusted is that educated instinct we call a virtue.

and therefore not to be trusted.

(*d*) All this is further confirmed by the fact that, as years pass and development proceeds, instincts assume higher forms that still more manifestly invite the educator's hand.

(d) and because they

It has been already suggested that human instincts are by no means so certain and unhesitating as those of the animals. The truth is that, as one generation succeeds another, there is so much variation in human circumstance, and by consequence adaptation becomes so progressive, that the tendencies which the progeny inherit and pass on have something less than the confidence of those of creatures who have, since long before Adam delved, been faithfully repeating the actions of their progenitors. It is a precious fact for their development. If our children moved

involve hesitancy

[1] Cf. Aristotle, *Ethics*, Bk. II. c. i.

upon the objects of their desires with all the certainty of clockwork (or chickwork) they would not give us openings. Fortunately they do not, and, as result, their hesitancy carries at once appeal and opportunity for intervention.

This invaluable hesitancy is moreover all the greater be-

and conflict, unknown to the animal world.

cause the instincts, being many, often conflict with one another. Thus the gregariousness which draws man to his fellows may conflict with that instinct of fear that eyes a strange face with uneasiness, if not with aversion : or the greed that grasps at every new object may conflict with the distrust that looks fearfully round in novel surroundings : or the vanity that courts the gaze of all eyes, with the bashfulness that would sink into the earth ; or the friendliness that prompts little boys to exchange gifts, with the jealousy or the combativeness that impels them, five minutes later, to fight their first battle. The fact is so familiar that it has been used to point to a well-known contrast :—

> " The blackbird amid leafy trees,
> The lark upon the hill,
> Let loose their carols when they please,
> Are quiet when they will.
> With Nature never do they wage
> A foolish strife ; they see
> A happy youth, and their old age
> Is beautiful and free[1]."

And the moral implied is, of course, that we hapless human

Man cannot really envy the happiness of the animals.

beings, clouding our present good by the uneasy hope or regret for something else, might well envy this calm undistracted life of the brutes. Is it too prosaic a comment to suggest that if the brutes be enviable upon this score, it is because of their poverty ? If their lives are a harmony it is because their native endowment carries in it so few possibilities of dissonance.

[1] Wordsworth, *The Fountain.*

They have comparatively few conflicts with themselves because they have comparatively few instincts. In man it is otherwise. The distractions, the unrest of his life, is proof of the fulness of his endowment. As Professor James puts it[1], he has so many instincts that these block each other's path, thereby creating bewilderment and distraction. Better that it should be so. For these warring pro-clivities suspend action. They create an interval, unknown to the creature of swiftly satisfied unerring instinct, between the excitement of stimulus and the reaction upon it. It is a pregnant interval. For with it comes the possibility that the impetuousness of youth, else headlong and heedless, can be disciplined to look before and after, and to make its first tentative essays in De-liberation and Choice[2].

Importance of the interval between stimulus and reaction.

Hence it comes that as development proceeds, human instincts disclose features which make it difficult to speak of human *instincts* at all. Instinct passes up into higher forms. For as man begins to learn from his experience, and not least from his blunders, his propulsions cease to be "blind." Possibly

Instincts, ceasing to be 'blind,' be-come desires.

this holds even of some of the animals. When a trap closes upon some wild creature it probably realises, at least for some little time to come, that it has made a mistake: and anglers at least may indulge the supposition that an experienced trout which has suffered much at their hands, has visions of ulterior discomfort if it yields to rise at a fly. But whereas trout or rabbit or other victim may be again befooled in a day, the man learns from his experience. It would be flattery to say he cannot forget. But he does not forget so easily, and some experiences even once brought home, he never can forget. The result is momentous. The early, sanguine, instinct-prompted attack upon reality[3] suffers a check from which it

---

[1] *Principles of Psychology*, II. 393.

[2] Cf. Höffding, *Outlines of Psychology*, p. 326.

[3] Cf. *ibid.* p. 132.

never recovers; and the unsuspecting confidence of the mere
life of instinct passes, not to return. It is thus that man
profits by even very youthful experiments in living; thus that
he is educated to look beyond the immediate object upon
which "blind" instinct terminates; thus that he begins to
acquire that faculty of foreseeing ends which is the sign that
Instinct has become Desire[1].

　　This opens up possibilities. For this consciousness of ends
has not hard and fast limits to its development.
Insatiability of human desire. Well was Desire called by the Greeks in-
satiable (ἄπληστος). For as reason gains in
grasp, and as the horizon which it sweeps is for ever enlarging,
the soul voyages on to unpathed waters and to undreamed
shores. New ends rise before it, and of none can it be said,
"This is the last": and as each takes shape under the
moulding influences of man's device, desire and aspiration
reach out after it with a seemingly exhaustless vitality, practically exhaustless in the race, and for the individual only
exhausted by the hungry span he calls his life. In nothing
does man more conspicuously part company with the animal
kingdom from which he has emerged. When instincts arise
in animals, they satisfy them. The instincts
Desire, un- like animal appetite, is progressive. recur: they satisfy them again. And so from
generation to generation they round the same
small monotonous circle of their lives. Not so
with Desire. Not all the treasury of Nature, nor all the
ingenuity of human resource, can suffice permanently to still
its cravings. Hence that consciousness of unrest that dis-
quiets and often torments even those who lead full lives,
from Carlyle's "infinite shoeblack" upwards[2]. Hence too the
tragedy that sometimes ensues when the resources, be it of
a rich stupid household, of a luxurious, ill-educated city, of

----

[1] Cf. Spinoza's definition of Desire. "Desire is Appetite with consciousness thereof," *Ethics*, Part III. Prop. ix. Scholium.

[2] Cf. *Sartor Resartus*, Bk II. c. ix. Cf. the lines on the unrest of
human life which George Herbert quaintly calls "The Pulley."

a materialistic civilisation, are not qualitatively adequate to
the cravings of a progressive nature, and set themselves to
appease desires that are capable of higher things by multiplying lower satisfactions.

> "In his cool hall, with haggard eyes
>   The Roman noble lay;
> He drove abroad in furious guise
>   Along the Appian way.
> He made a feast, drank fierce and fast,
>   And crowned his brow with flowers,
> No easier nor no quicker passed
>   The impracticable hours[1]."

Hence the truth of the saying that man's unhappiness
comes of his greatness. Some of it at any rate unquestionably
does. For we must never think of the desires as if they and
their objects were simply given by grace of Nature, and as if
nothing were left for Reason to do but to find the means for
their satisfaction. On the contrary, desires emerge, from their
earliest beginnings, in so intimate a fusion with imagination
that they would not be what they are, nor would their objects
so much as exist, if intelligence were not already inwoven in
their essence. In this lies the secret of their progressiveness.
For it is the distinction of the human soul that it can not only
discover new and ever new objects to satisfy its cravings; if
discovery fails, it is not daunted. With a resourcefulness of
which the history of civilisation is witness, it calls the constructive imagination to its aid and invents an endless wealth of
ideal ends which become the objects of its passionate pursuit.
Nor has it hesitated, from the days of the old mythologies to
those of latter-day creeds, to project these visions of unfulfilled
desire into a future life in which it might find the fruition that
is denied to it on earth.

Cynics sometimes declare that the brutes are temperate,
sober and happy as compared with man. So they are. And

[1] Matthew Arnold, *Obermann.*

indubitably had man remained a brute, he would have escaped many a vice and much suffering.   But it would have been at
And this fur- the cost of surrendering those progressive desires,
nishes grounds of which his excesses are the dark shadow.   And
of hope. it is just this progressiveness of Desire that is
the opportunity, the hope, and, if he fail to find it adequate
nurture, the judgment of the maker of character.

CHAPTER V.

THE ECONOMY OF HUMAN POWERS.

WITH given congenital endowment as material to work
upon, the task of the educator is manifestly two-
A two-fold fold.   He must so nurture the capacities and
task. desires as to increase to the utmost the quantum
of psycho-physical energy, and he must so direct and distribute
this energy as to secure the best economy of life's resources.

To the first of these enterprises there is, doubtless, a limit.
Even some of the most strenuous and aspiring
(a) Increase spirits that the world has ever seen have been
of vital energy. forced to recognise that there are tasks beyond
their strength.   It may be when they have had to learn that
their "brother ass," the body—as St Francis called it—is an
inadequate instrument for executing their plans and projects;
or it may be when a just estimate of their powers has compelled
them to narrow their range of thought and action far within
their wishes; or it may be when they are constrained to see,
with a half-envious admiration, in men of greater force of
character, realities of moral achievement which they cannot
hope to rival.   And the same lesson—is it needful to say it?—
may be much more easily learnt in the school of experience by
the multitude of lesser men who swell the rank and file of the

moral world. There are, in short,—for we need not labour a
point that so closely borders on a platitude—many degrees of
possible force of character, even as there are manifestly many
degrees of possible bodily vigour.

Not that it is so easy in the one case as in the other to
accept the limits. For when we pass from body
to soul, and especially to the moral and religious
life, we are often surprised, and even startled by
an unexpected rise in the currents of the spirit.

*Are there
limits to in-
crease of moral
energy?*

It is always difficult, and perhaps rash, to say of any man, even
though he may seem a feeble specimen of humanity, that he
cannot do this or that, when the "cannot" refers to moral and
religious possibilities. What a man has it in him to do and to
be is a thing not known to any mortal, not even to himself.
For, as Aristotle long ago pointed out, there is no way of
judging what are the potentialities of the soul except from
their actual manifestations. And if it be matter of experience
that energies of unsuspected force—some sudden awakening of
instinct, some sudden flooding of the tides of desire, some
sudden intensification of effort and resolve—do really emerge
in many lives, it is nothing but reasonable to read such things
as so many warnings against the rash supposition that we can
discover final limits to the development of moral or religious
energy in any given case. Even Spinoza, that foe of the
popular belief that the Will is free, has declared that we do not
know what the body can do[1]. Still less, we may add, would it
become us to dogmatise as to what the soul can, or cannot, do.
For, whatever be the ultimate truth as regards the limits of
moral energy which must needs encompass human nature, if
only by reason of its finitude,—a large and obscure question on
which we cannot enter here—we must certainly not fall into
the fallacy of regarding force of character as if it were as
definitely limited as the horse-power of an engine. Who is

[1] *Ethics*, Part III. Prop. ii. Scholium, "For what the Body can do
no one has hitherto determined."

there who will be bold enough to say, when he sits down in a quiet hour to review his life, that he has put forth all the spiritual energies of which he was capable? Who will venture to deny that millions of our race have come and gone,

**The poten-
tialities that
are never used.** possessed of faculty which they have never used, and of potentialities which have been smothered by an apathetic or cowardly inertia? Nor are our moral prophets to be dismissed as vain dreamers who would beguile the world by illusory appeals and barren exhortations. They are within their right, because they are in touch with experience, when they tell their fellow-men, be they laggards or leaders, that they have in them "possibilities for much." It would be the hardest of tasks for any theory, even for a theory that would reduce human nature to a higher kind of mechanism (as some theories do), to rule out as a futile figment the unexhausted potentialities of the human spirit.

This question however—the abstract question of the limits to increase of psycho-physical energy—is not one that can longer detain us here. It is beyond our scope. Nor indeed is it necessary to pursue it further in order to justify educational effort in working, by every resource at its disposal, for the increase of mental and moral force. For two reasons.

**In practice
there is wide
scope for in-
creasing the
energies of the
soul.** *Firstly*, because it is not likely to be denied by anyone that, in all normal cases, the vital energies can indubitably be nurtured into a stronger and fuller life. As our thoughts pass from the infant in the cradle to the man, even the most ordinary man, in the plenitude of his strength, we might well marvel, were it not that the facts are so familiar, at the continual miracle of ordinary development. And, *secondly*, because, be the limits to this development what they may, it remains beyond dispute that in the actual children with whom we have to deal in educational work (unless they be conspicuously abnormal), the actual lags so far behind the possible

that neither parent nor teacher, neither voluntary effort nor public authority, need disturb themselves by the fear that their occupation will be gone in making the weak strong and the strong stronger. That limits might be reached if we went far enough, need not be denied : that we have ever gone far enough to reach them would be the most gratuitous of illusions.

Increase of energy is, however, but one aspect of moral education. For it is not lack of force, of one kind or another, that is perhaps the main cause of moral shortcoming : it is rather waste, through (b) Distribution of energy. wasteful economy of available forces. Even on the higher levels of character it is safe to say that no man is so perfect that his actual powers could not be, by better distribution, turned to better account. And if this be true of the best, what are we to say of the mediocre and the worst? What are we to say of the vices, that prodigal "expense of spirit in a waste of shame"? And, far short of the vices, how vast is the sum of human faculty that The waste of human powers. is lavishly squandered upon nothing worse than a mistaken plan of life, a flighty and fickle choice of interests, a drifting acquiescence in conventional ways, even a desultory pursuit of pleasures. It is facts like these that help us to understand the ethical thinkers who were also the educational teachers of Greece. For it is not the moral dangers due to torpor or inertia that meet us most in the pages of Plato and Aristotle. For these thinkers are agreed that the ruin of the soul of man comes of the very strength and vitality of its powers, and above all of those many and masterful appetites which for ever threaten to burst the bonds of restraint, and which, if left without the guiding and controlling hand, will surely disintegrate the character and precipitate that anarchy of the city of Mansoul which is Plato's synonym for the depths of vice and misery. Small wonder therefore that *The Republic* is a passionate plea for "Justice." For "Justice," in the large Platonic sense, is Plato's conception of moral salvation.

nothing but that right and harmonious and rational distribution of human powers in which—if this great thinker is to be believed—lies the whole secret of man's salvation. Nor when the mood of pessimism is upon him, is it the lack of forcefulness he dreads; it is the failure of direction or the misdirection of perverted forces.

And yet these wasteful violations of a right economy of life's resources, however lamentable, are not wholly discouraging. They do not necessarily imply that human nature is cursed by a canker of original sin which nothing short of a miracle can eradicate. We may even pluck a kind of desperate hope from the eloquence of the moral disasters which follow the perversion of human powers. The hope is that the making of character can follow the path of directing human energies into the ways that are virtue and out of the perversions that are vice. And the encouraging point is that to this enterprise there open up so many, because such life-long opportunities. For long after many human powers have reached their maximum, and even when many energies have begun to fail, it remains entirely possible to devise a better economy of life's resources. No stage of life is too late for turning more to the things that matter, and turning away from the things that matter less or not at all, or for concentrating the energies upon the ends and interests, be they intellectual, moral or social, which are most worth caring for. For it is thus that, by a wise economy of his powers, the man of character may go on making more of life even to the end of his days.

The actual waste of powers may, however, furnish grounds for hope.

But let no one fancy that this can be done unless some preparation for it has been laid in earlier years. Sometimes it happens that the victim of a bad upbringing or a wayward life awakens to a sense of the poverty of the aims on which he has been wasting his years, and sets himself to change his

But this depends on the direction of energy from earliest years.

plan and live for better things. He may succeed. For changes
of character that take the form of changes of direction of will
and effort are commoner, at least in later life, than the more
difficult transitions from apathy and inertia to vigorous activity.
But if success is to be assured, it will not be by mere remorse
however keen, nor by mere resolves however good. For
change of life means change of moral valuations; and moral
valuations are not made in a moment. They come by slow
and gradual growth. They are the product of the years during
which, from childhood onwards, the desires, sentiments, tastes,
habits, attach themselves, with ever firmer grip, to the ends
and interests which have been eagerly and steadily pursued in
the days of life's apprenticeship. This is the educator's opportunity. It is for him, by directing the rising currents of life's
stream into the right channels, to prepare the way for those
sane and sound moral valuations which are the surest of all
securities for a good economy of life's resources. Nor will the
gain of this appear only in development, for development is
also the path to discipline and repression.

CHAPTER VI.

DEVELOPMENT AND REPRESSION.

As human nature is constituted, all development involves
repression. The natural man left to himself   Development
would speedily make the discovery that harmony   involves
was not the law of his life. The multiplicity   repression.
and the conflict of his proclivities would teach him that the
appetites to which he gives the rein have their sacrifices as
well as their satisfactions. Far more is this the case later on.
For if social life, with all its institutions from the Family

onwards, is a contrivance for multiplying wants and satisfactions, so that the civilised man's poverty would be the
savage's wealth, this has its obverse.   Why is it, asks Carlyle,
that every considerable town, though it cannot boast a library,
can show a prison?   Why is it, we might further ask, that
every citizen who walks its streets carries in himself a prison—
a prison in which under watch and ward lie those criminals of
Mansoul whom he dare not amnesty?   Why is it, if it be not
that, as nurture supervenes upon nature, Repression is the
very shadow of Development?

There is, however, here a notable difference between rival
plans of education.   For though every plan,
even that which sent St Simeon Stylites to his
loathsome pillar, involves development as well
as repression, the relative proportions of these
two aspects may vastly vary.   We need not now
perplex ourselves with the question what is the
just proportion, or indeed if, in a world where
ascetics and sybarites seem to have so much to learn from
each other, there is any absolute proportion to be found.
Enough for our present purpose to point out certain aspects
in which the more repressive systems labour under marked
and even fatal disadvantages of a practical kind.

*Though all
educational
systems
include both
development
and repres-
sion, the rela-
tive propor-
tions vary.*

Not that the ascetics are by any means without a case.
Convinced, by a large experience, of the dire
possibilities of sin and vice, they strike at the
heart of the evil in a way which, it must be
granted, is thorough.   They attack temptation
by removing its objects; and not only those objects which on
the face of them are vile and infamous, but many others—
wealth, for example, or social intercourse, or art, or recreation—
which, though in themselves neither infamous
nor vile, might yet by possible perversion become
stones of stumbling and rocks of offence.   To
sweep these objects out of life, or to flee from the life that

*Ascetic
systems have
reasons behind
them.*

*The way of
safety.*

offers them—this to them is the way of safety. Convinced, also, that it is through the encouragement and multiplication of wants and cravings that human life becomes fatally dependent upon externals, the command and control of which may lie quite beyond the reach of the will, they urge the policy of minimising desires and interests, of refusing to "give hostages to fortune," and of finding rest and moral independence in a life that is content with the few great simple satisfying and enduring

The self-sufficingness of the simple life.

things which are, at all times and in all places, within the grasp of the human spirit. Hence from the days of the ancient Cynics to the latter-day Gospel of Wordsworth, the hortatory pleas for the simple life—the simple life which stands secure upon itself, and which has seldom failed to exercise its fascination in epochs when the greed for luxuries and the cult of worldliness have left their votaries rich only in dissatisfactions and disgusts. Nor does one need to be an ascetic to see that it may seem a doubtful policy to fill the heart with cravings for objects for which it may hunger long and in vain, or which it may appropriate only to find that they are to the last degree precarious. Least of all if it be true—and to ascetics of all shades it is a profound truth—that it is the simplest, and most attainable and enduring things that are the best.

Nor can it be denied that there is inevitably an ascetic element in every life, if life be work. If we sometimes say of the favourites of Fortune who have "grasped the skirts of happy chance," that

The work of life demands Renunciation.

they have enjoyed all the world has to give, this is not true at any rate of those by whom the work of the world is done. Life is not built upon that plan. Ruled from end to end by the iron law of specialisation, the price for work well done is surrender of much. The careers of craftsman, merchant, lawyer, doctor, politician, student, inexorably demand their respective sacrifices; and most of all, of course, in proportion as they are pursued with the single eye and the dutiful spirit.

For life means choice, and choice, on its negative side, means renunciation. "Ten years ago," wrote Cobden from Wales, "before I was an agitator, I spent a day or two in this house. Comparing my sensations now with those I then experienced, I feel how much I have lost in winning public fame." Nor is it doubtful that many who have won lesser as well as greater things than public fame, could, from a life-long experience, re-echo the words.

Nor is it to be overlooked that, in a materialistic age and a pleasure-loving civilisation, asceticism is, to say the least, the safer extreme—if only one were sure that it would be most laid to heart by the children of luxury who need it most, and least or not at all by the children of light who need it not at all.

And yet, when all is said, asceticism is not the best path to development. It is not even the most effective plan for securing that repression to the need for which it is so keenly alive. To put the matter paradoxically, repressive or ascetic systems are not sufficiently positive to be effectually negative. They are not generous enough, or tolerant enough, of the proclivities they encourage, to enable them to deal effectively with those they would repress. For when we wish to subjugate an appetite, it is not enough simply to check it, however harshly. All the locks and bolts of mere repression will not suffice. Rather must we seek till we find and can foster some other desire in the presence of which the obnoxious appetite may find it hard to live. How, for example, may we best deal with congenital timidity? Impatience, derision, scorn, threatened disgrace—is it by these? Or is it not rather by striving patiently to awaken a passion for some person or some cause, for love of which even the timid may stand up like a man? So with greed of gain, or of praise, or of pleasure. Flouts and sneers, however cutting, warnings of consequences, however impressive, are after all

Yet ascetic systems are not sufficiently positive.

Passion must be used to oust passion.

but under-agents, and not for a moment to be given the first place, so long as there is any hope of arousing an interest in men or things strong enough to outrival and displace these baser passions. This is the meaning of that phrase "the expulsive power of a new affection." For evil appetites and passions do not yield most readily to direct assault. Passion must be evoked to cast out passion. And if once heart and mind be filled with strong positive interests, the rest will come of itself. For these wholesome incentives will, ever increasingly, occupy the soul, and, if only they be skilfully fostered, will strike up alliances with one another, till the promptings we wish to get rid of will gradually be ousted from their squalid or knavish tenancy. For development and repression are not two things, but one; all genuine development already carries in it repression of much.

It is precisely here, however, that the more repressive systems fail. Suspicious of human nature, they frown upon so many natural desires that they **The weakness of asceticism.** fatally narrow the range of positive appeal. Fearful, and not without reason, of the world, the devil, and the flesh, they purge human life so effectually that they are impelled to draw their positive incentives from an ever-diminishing store. They are driven to this because were their powers equal to their plans, they would cut up by the roots not only those desires which are actually fruitful of evil, but all desires which might, by possible perversion, become a snare. Hence ascetic systems are inevitably driven in two directions. On the one hand, so far as their methods are positive, they build upon a few exceptional motives, love of God, passion for souls, self-sacrifice, if not self-immolation, absolute devotion to a Church or a Brotherhood : on the other, they make wholesale use of Pain as an instrument of repression.

It is not necessary to disparage either of these resources. It is exceptional motives that make exceptional men ; but then, being exceptional, they are not to be counted upon in

ordinary mortals, in whom they are so apt, to borrow a phrase
of Ruskin, "to be inconstant almost in proportion to their nobleness." It may be possible to
rear a chosen religious or political Brotherhood
upon them; but they will hardly suffice for the
daily diet of the rank and file. The ordinary incentives, it is
true, being ordinary, may call for no particular admiration.
What are they but the love of kindred and the charities of
home, the kindliness of neighbourhood, the desire to keep
what is honestly our own, the enjoyments of comfort and
modest luxury, the maintenance of our good name, the cheerful
intercourse of social life? But they will rise in our estimation,
when we learn by experience their power to supersede motives
that are not ordinary only because they are extraordinarily
frivolous, base or vicious.

The strength and weakness of exceptional motives.

Nor, passing to the second resource, need it be disputed
that Pain is a powerful instrument. This has
been already granted[1]. We may freely admit
that it may become, in wise hands, as Aristotle
calls it, nothing less than "a rudder of education[2]."

Pain, as an instrument of education.

Yet we must not expect too much from it. In itself it
makes for death, not for life. It nurtures
nothing. It is negative, inhibitive: and its
value will depend upon the independent strength
and worth of the tendencies which it releases. It does not
nurture them: it only gives them play. Add to this that it
means cost. Always, by its very nature, it tends to lower
general vitality. Has it not even been defined as a consciousness of lowered vitality? And though this fact may be
hidden by the extraordinary energy of the particular aversions
it inspires, it brings with it no positive compensation for the
expenditure of vitality on which it thus mercilessly draws.
Which of us cannot recall cases, cases of lives, weak in all
things except the rigour of their asceticisms, which have been

But its results involve cost.

[1] p. 24 *et seq.*   [2] *Ethics*, Bk x. i. 1.

so effectually disciplined by pain that there is nothing before
them but chronic depression of soul?

It is the weakness of ascetic systems, whether they come
in the guise of Cynic, Stoic, Anchorite, Monk, Puritan, that
they are apt to alternate between these two expedients. In so
far as they are positive—and it is a libel upon them to say
they are only repressive—they would people the world with
saints, devotees and fanatics: this failing, they would turn it
into a House of Correction.

These alternatives, however, are happily not exhaustive.
We may pursue another and a very different   The strongest
course of policy. We may distrust human nature   argument
                                                    against
less. We may see in men's desires promise, not   asceticism is
menace. We may reject the violent dualism   found in the
                                              reasonableness
that sets inclinations and duties in implacable   of less repres-
hostility. We may believe that the life that has   sive systems.
found satisfaction for many a desire which lies under the
ascetic ban attains a fuller realisation even for our most spiritual
and rational part. We may follow the philosophy that, as
result of its analysis, declares that, whatever be the appetites
that seem to link the man to the brute, there is even in
these, and how much more in desires of which the brute is
incapable, the infusion of a spiritual and rational element
which lends itself to direction towards higher satisfactions.

Nor can it be granted that the ascetic ideal opens up the
best path to that moral independence and self-   For asceti-
sufficingness which it so justifiably exalts. If a   cism does not
                                                       ensure the
man can be rich in his own soul, as the ancient   truest self-
Cynics averred, even when he is a beggar in all   sufficingness;
besides, it is desirable to withhold our tribute of imitation till
we see what his spiritual riches really are. We must satisfy
ourselves that he who prides himself on possessing his own
soul and nothing else has left himself a soul worth possessing.
For there are limits where self-mortification begins to pass into
self-slaughter. An ascetic, let us suppose, vows poverty, and

of course he escapes thereby the sordid vices that cluster round money.   But he also shuts out the possibilities of the virtues of commercial honour, of liberality, of munificence.   A puritan turns his back upon Music and the Drama, and doubtless he escapes the snares of dilettantism thereby.   But he also qualifies himself to fail to rejoice in Beethoven and Shakespeare.   The way of safety becomes the path to spiritual starvation.

Similarly with the alluring "independence" of the simple life.

nor the securest independence.   Grant that it is no vain dream of enthusiasts. Grant that it may be noble, carefree, secure and strong.   "Give me health and a day," says Emerson, "and I will make the pomp of emperors ridiculous." Yet there is another and a better way.   For it is not the life of few resources, however elevated and pure, that is the most truly independent.   It is rather the life of the man who has been able to gather up into his will and sympathies the many and varied interests which a civilised social life offers in rich profusion, and who thereby stands strong against the world, because where he is blocked and baffled in one direction, he has the resourcefulness that can find much else that makes life worth living[1].   For aloofness is not independence.   Independence comes through dependence—that kind of dependence which makes the individual sympathetic, sociable, many-sided, and resourceful.   For it is fallacious to infer that, because some desires are corrupt, and all desires corruptible, the desires in general must be cut up by the roots.   For this is to fling away, like ignorant and impatient craftsmen, the very instruments which Nature puts into the educator's hands.   The wiser mind, which is also the more tolerant and hopeful mind, will rather set itself with anxious care to seek out those desires of which we believe that most can be made, and lay our plans to find for them their appropriate and timely nurture; in the reasonable hope that those who have been thus taught to find themselves capable of much good will become less capable of

[1] Cf. p. 252.

much evil. Sensual, mean, frivolous, vicious desires will still arise to thwart, and sometimes to destroy, our work. The best of educations cannot obviate this. But the hope is that, when they come, their objects will no longer possess their malign attraction. And this, not so much by any success we may have had in associating pains and penalties, sufferings and disgusts, with their indulgence, as because fulness of wholesome life, and the hopeful struggle forwards after many a cherished and justifiable satisfaction, will furnish a strong security against descent upon the lower appetites. In other words, we must hold fast to the more practical policy of repressing the desires that need repression by developing the desires which, in the light of a more generous ideal, demand development.

CHAPTER VII.

HABIT AND ITS LIMITATIONS.

The desires need direction. IF, then, repression is best secured by development, it follows that the main part of education is its positive side; and the next question is how to proceed. Nature herself here gives us the clue. For it is the shortcomings of Nature that furnish the opportunities for education. We have seen where the weakness lies. The instincts (or desires) are transitory, intermittent, and indefinite in the double sense, firstly, that they always lack something of the certainty of animal instinct, and, secondly, that even when pronounced, they are morally indeterminate. A human being who had nothing more would be doomed to failure on the very threshold of morality. He would be unequal to the ordinary constant monotonous demands of natural, still more of social, environment. If he is ever to grow to virtue, the transitory must become the permanent, the intermittent the persistent, the indeterminate the definite. The "weight of chance desires" must be thrown off, and the individual must come to confront the world with a stable and calculable inner life of his own.

For there is a world of difference between the life that is the mere satisfaction of desires and the life in which the satisfaction of desires has been made tributary to the making of a character. Two youths may start together on life's race, and, to begin with, there may be little to choose between them.

Both may be eager-hearted, sanguine, hungry for satisfactions. But, when twenty years have passed, how complete may be the contrast. For the one may have lived for nothing more than the passions and the pursuits of the hour; and, if he has done no more than that, he will be no better, possibly

Much satis-faction of desires may do nothing for moral character.

he may be greatly worse, in character than he was in his schooldays. He will have had many experiences of course, and he may even pride himself upon them; but it is entirely possible to have had much experience and to have little morality. The other, we shall suppose, has had a happier lot. His desires have not been left to work their wayward will. His experience has not been barren of all except experience By the directing hand of parent and teacher, and by enlistment in the service of men or institutions that stand for ends worth living for, his desires have been made tributary to a plan of life, and his progressive experiences have brought him, as the years ran their course, to confront the world with something of a compact and persistent self. This is no fancied contrast. It is verified in ten thousand instances in which all the promise of youthful desire proves "empty and in vain" (to use the words of Aristotle) because the so-called satisfactions of the years have left the soul as undeveloped and as void of self-control as it was at the beginning of life's race[1].

Hence the need for habits.

And of the question he put, How is this disaster to be avoided? the first part of the answer is that the desires must be transformed into habits.

This transformation is, at any rate in its more superficial aspects, no mystery. Since Aristotle wrote the Second Book of the *Ethics,* the ethical teachers of the world have been repeating that virtuous habits are formed when natural desires are

Habits are formed by appropriate acts.

guided to appropriate acts. No human tendency is developed by empty wishes, unless it be the tendency to indulge in empty

[1] Cf. Plato's *Gorgias*, especially the simile of the "leaky vessels," pp. 493-4.

wishes; and the better the wishes the worse the failure. For, in Aristotle's memorable simile, the prize is given to the man who has won it in dust and heat; not to the spectator for his strength and beauty, however great they be. This is indeed the law of every aptitude: it finds its illustration in every art—from those ordinary handicrafts, to which the Greek moralists are so rich in reference, up to the greater art of Life. For men are not cunningly devised machines which go unaltered in structure till they wear themselves out into old lumber. They are alive, and it is the fundamental property of living structure that by acting it modifies itself. Physiologists tell us

The Soul, like the Body, grows to the modes in which it is exercised. that our nervous and muscular systems "grow to the modes in which they have been exercised[1]." Do we not know it? Do not our every day neighbours carry, even in their outward man, the visible signs of their vocation, the sure hand,

the light step, the rounded muscle, the light touch? The same law holds of the soul, of which the nervous system so often serves as a helpful diagram. *It* to be sure is not visible; it has not even, except in a metaphorical sense a "structure" at all, and by consequence it is infinitely harder to conjecture what it is that is going on in it when a habit is forming than it is even in the sufficiently baffling domain of physiology. Yet the fact is there, be its secret history what it may. Our souls, like our bodies, "grow to the modes in which they are exercised." It is by striving to act that our desires come to a fuller, more persistent and more definite development. And, as Aristotle long ago declared, it is by the repetition of actions that the corresponding desires are organised into habits.[2]

When we say "actions," however, it is well to bear in mind

[1] Carpenter, cited by James, *Principles of Psychology*, vol. I. p. 112. It will be obvious that my debt to Professor James' chapter on Habit, as well as to that on Instinct, is great. From admiration to appropriation there is but a step.

[2] *Ethics*, Bk. II. c. i. 8.

that the word is not to be construed too narrowly. It is not those outward and overt performances, such as we can most easily compel, that really form the habits we call virtues. It is never to be forgotten that—unless we are prepared to say that Soul is Body—it is the repetition of psychical states that are the causes of the formation of moral habits.

The actions that form the moral habits are not merely outward.

The psychical state no doubt may have its physiological concomitants. For, so far as our knowledge goes, it would seem that this is always the case. Yet if the psychical states, or to be more specific, if the strivings of desire be not induced, the moral habit will not be formed, not even though we could compel the whole physical side of the performance, including the most secret neural and muscular movements. When therefore we adopt the familiar statement that habits come of repeated actions, it is clearly to be understood that the actions cover, as main element, the psychical side of outward performance.

This may be an obvious, but it is not an unimportant reminder. There is many a parent who deludes himself into the comforting belief that when he has secured the persistent performance of outward acts, he is on the certain path to the forming of habits in his children. And of course he will have done something towards the formation of bodily habits.

Practical importance of inducing actions which appeal to natural proclivity.

But his progress towards the formation of virtuous habits may be meagre to the last degree. Virtuous habits are never thus to be mechanically wrought in from without. There have been extreme thinkers who have held that outward behaviour has so little to do with the moral life that even gross misbehaviour is of trifling moment. It is but a distorted version of the fact that the significance of an action in building up the character is insignificant, unless the action have behind it a corresponding activity of the soul's life. The actions whose repetition is really of moment are those which elicit those strong stirrings of native capacity and instinct for which it is the business of education to be for ever on the watch. Two children, for instance, may repeatedly imitate the same example. How different the result, if in the one case the imitative acts are the monkey-like aping of mere outward performance, and in the other the congenial expression of a strong instinct which was but waiting for the example to liberate it into vigorous life. This is but one illustration of a general law. For nothing is more vital in this forming of habits by acts than watchful study of the material we are dealing with. It is only then that the acts we enjoin will do their required work, not simply because they are repeated, but because at each repetition they evoke and confirm inherent capacity and instinctive striving.

Importance of studying our concrete material.

This difficulty of adapting enjoined act to inherent proclivity is however vastly simplified for us by the fact that young life is not given to be secretive. It is, on the contrary, frankly, untiringly, even inconsiderately demonstrative. And by consequence it gives us much to choose from. "Herein lies the utility of the restlessness, the exuberant activity, the varied playfulness, the prying curiosity, the inquisitiveness, the meddlesome mischievousness, the vigorous and healthy experimentalism of the young. These afford the raw material upon which intelligence exercises its power of selection[1]." Not, of course, to begin with, the unaided intelligence of the young themselves; but the wisdom of older heads, whose business it is to select from these exuberant movements, and by encouragement to impart to those selected the stability of Habit.

The educator's task here is mainly one of selection.

When this is done, the advantages which follow are so familiar as to need but the briefest statement. With each repetition the act becomes easier. As the grown man walks and runs without a

Advantages of well-formed habits :—

[1] Lloyd Morgan, *Habit and Instinct*, p. 162.

trace of the stumbling efforts of the two-year-old, so does he, with the acquired facility of "second nature," fulfil the moralities which once needed all the incitements and restraints of watchful discipline. (a) Action becomes easier.
This does not mean that life on the whole will become easier. It becomes more difficult for most as the years go on. But if we are able to grapple with new difficulties, it will be because old ones have become easy.

Closely bound up with this is the further advantage that, as a habit grows, conscious attention upon its conditions is minimised, and thereby made available for other purposes. The knitter, the (b) Conscious attention is economised.
musician, the fencer, the bicycle rider all know this well. Why this should be so is far from obvious. *A priori*, it might even be expected that, by every repetition of a more or less conscious act, the act would become more conscious. But the fact is otherwise. When the habit is sufficiently formed to subserve its purpose, consciousness retires from the scene like an artist whose task is done[1]. This, however, does not imply that the habit has become wholly a thing of physical automatism. It would be a lame conclusion to prolonged moral effort that a habit became a mere thing of nerves and muscles. The fact is that the psychical roots of the habit are not cut but only buried. Let but the most automatic of habits be inhibited, perhaps by outward interference, perhaps by inward temptation: the commotion of soul that ensues is proof sufficient that the feelings and desires that lie behind are abundantly alive.

Nor is it to be supposed that this unconsciousness of habits robs their possessor of the sense of security that comes of the knowledge that habits have been formed. In forming habits the individual is making a moral tradition for himself. (c) In forming habits each man makes a moral tradition for himself.
He has ever at hand the consolation that, as it takes

[1] Stout, *Analytical Psychology*, vol. i. p. 265.

many an act to make a habit, it likewise takes many to break one. "Can the just man act unjustly?" asks Aristotle[1]. And it is no idle question. For though of course the justest of men may, in the hour of temptation, yield to do the unjust thing, and seem by the grievous lapse of a moment to demolish the painfully won virtue of many a year, the just habit within him will not so easily fall before assault. It will remain to part the injustice of the just by a great gulf from the congenial frauds of the reprobate.

From this simple account of habit there follow applications.

Applications. '1. Begin early.' Some of these are so trite as to need few words. Thus it is the tritest of maxims, to begin early; and this partly for the simple reason that early years are the years of plasticity, partly also because there are then as yet no old habits with which the new have to establish a *modus vivendi.* Hence those seemingly boundless possibilities of childhood which have led some with Wordsworth[2] to view the growth of habits as a passage into bondage. It is as well to remember, however, that it is possible to begin too early. In the creation of a habit of physical endurance, for example, or a habit of thrift, nothing is easier than to fall into the errors of premature grafting. For all strong and stable habits must have, as we have seen, instincts at their root, and it often needs time, freedom, and indulgence, to bring the young to reveal the instincts that they offer to us for treatment. Parents in a hurry do well to find patience in the knowledge that instincts are often enough "deferred[3]."

2. Some reasons why growth of habits is not to be forced. Equally trite is the maxim that growth cannot here be forced. An obvious reason is that Habit comes of repetition, and repetition takes time: a less obvious, that between the repetitions, must come intervals not to be abridged. For it would seem

---

[1] *Ethics,* Bk. v. c. ix. 16.
[2] *Ode on the Intimations of Immortality.*
[3] See p. 2.

that habits are forming not only in the periods when the formative acts are being done. Something goes on likewise in the intervals between the acts. How often in the physical habits—skating, shall we say, or bicycling—we leave off with the unwilling certainty that no more progress is to be made then and there—only to discover, when we make our next essay, that we seem to have improved in the interval. Whence the staggering paradox, cited by James, that we learn to swim during the winter, and to skate during the summer[1]! There may of course be nothing here more occult than recovery from fatigue. For the failures of fatigue may bring a knowledge of how a thing can be done which the vigour of restored powers enables us for the first time effectively to utilise. But there may be more. Secret adjustments and adaptations may still be going on in what we call intervals of rest. It is possible that something similar may take place in the growth of habits not physical. Be this as it may, there is room enough for the familiar reminder that habits grow by the imperceptible accretions of many days. And this, not only because the persevering youth may, as Professor James so cheerily remarks[2], "wake up some fine morning to find himself one of the competent ones of his generation," but also because, if he do not take heed to his steps, he may find himself, before he is aware, in the strong grip of some stealthy vice.

It is less incontrovertible that, in habit-forming (and habit-breaking), preference should be given to a strong and decided initiative. For this of course is what every advocate of the gradual well-devised initiations of a moral hygiene would dispute. They have their reasons. They can argue that average human nature is not to be counted upon for strong initiative either of feeling, impulse, or resolve. They can point to the dangers of reaction under burdens beyond the strength, and denounce

3. The strong versus the gradual initiative.

[1] *Principles of Psychology*, vol. I. p. 110.
[2] *Ib.* vol. I. p. 127.

with justice the masterful impotence of the "strong-minded" parent or teacher who will abate nothing of his demands to suit the individual case.

Yet the central fact remains that, in all cases where there is pronounced proclivity to appeal to, the policy of strong initiative has decisive arguments in its favour. It enlists in its service a volume of feeling, and, in adult years, an effort of resolve; and it ensures decided self-committal in respect of circumstance, thereby "burning its boats" and taking securities against a backward step. From early rising to moral or religious conversion, this second point is more important even than the first. The most glowing feeling, the most powerful desire, even the most energetic resolve have often enough found reason to welcome as needed ally this sheer difficulty of turning back. Hence the public pledge, the secret vow, the withdrawal from the world, the rupture of ties, and all the manifold devices for discounting infirmity of purpose by rendering return upon our steps a practical impossibility.

Arguments in favour of the strong initiative.

A fourth maxim is "never if possible to lose a battle[1]." And none can be sounder. For it is always to be remembered that a single lapse involves here something worse than a simple failure. The alternative is not between good habit or no habit, but between good habit and bad. For, as Professor Bain points out, the characteristic difficulty here lies in the fact that in the moral life rival tendencies are in constant competition for mastery over us. The loss of a battle here is therefore worse than a defeat. It strengthens the enemy, whether this enemy be some powerful passion, or nothing more than the allurements of an easy life. It has worse effects still. For if by persistence in well-doing we all of us create a moral tradition for our individual selves, so do we by every

4. Bain's maxim; "never if possible to lose a battle."

---

[1] Bain, *Emotions and Will,* "The Will," c. ix. Cf. James' comments, *Principles of Psychology,* I. p. 123.

failure hang in the memory a humiliating and paralysing record of defeat.

To these maxims Professor James would have us add the somewhat ascetic counsel "to keep the faculty of effort alive in us by a little gratuitous exercise every day." That is, as he explains, "do every day or two something for no other reason than that you would rather not do it, so that when the hour of dire need draws nigh, it may find you not unnerved and untrained to stand the test[1]." It is advice which may not come amiss to those whose lot is cast in circumstances where there may be going on, all unmarked, the slow sap of an easy and leisured life. The rest of the world may perhaps be excused from acting up to it, till they have done justice to the opportunities for acting against the grain which experience provides with an embarrassing and never-failing bounty.

5. **Professor James' ascetic counsel.**

It is hardly needful, in conclusion, to descant upon the stability of life to which the observance of such maxims as these will seldom fail to lead. The lives of nations furnish endless proof how customs and ceremonies may come to enjoy an almost consecrated life, even in face of all the solvents of rationalising theory and criticism. It is not otherwise with the lives of individuals. "It is not possible," says Aristotle, "at least it is not easy to overthrow by theories what has been from of old engrained in the character[2]."

It is time however to turn the other side of the shield, and to read there that Habit has its perversions and its limitations.

Habit has its perversions and limitations.

1. In the first place it is a double-edged instrument. For the reasons given, it can make virtue secure; but it may take the wrong side, thereby making vice incurable. Every reader of Aristotle must remember that upon his view there is a class of persons who have made themselves, by habitual

1. **It cuts both ways.**

[1] *Principles*, vol. I. p. 126. [2] *Ethics*, Bk. x. ix. 5.

profligacy, morally "incurable[1]." And though there are those
hopeful enough to believe that the word incurable ought to be
expunged from the vocabulary of morals, even they must admit
that what is sometimes called a moral "conversion" is, by law
of habit, but the beginning of the long task that has to lay
stone to stone in the rebuilding of a dismantled life.

A second possibility—need the familiar warning be repeated?—is that Habit may easily end by
producing the rigid and wooden type that is
unequal to the demands of life. Life of course
brings its changes, and the day comes when
experience presents new situations. It may be
when a boy leaves home for school, or school for college, or
goes out into the world, or it may be simply one or other of
the hundred lesser variations of which even a monotonous lot
has its share. The pathetic fact is that often enough, just in
proportion as he has been trained up not wisely but too well
in the habits of a sequestered home, the model youth may
lamentably fail[2]. Nor will he ever be equal to the demands of
an environment that changes even in repeating itself, till among
his habits he can number "the habit"—if it be not a contradiction so to call it—"of constantly rehabituating himself[3]."
This holds not only of the passage from old virtues to new.
It holds within the sphere of every single virtue. It is not
courage, for example, to be habituated to face, however sted-
fastly, only a given kind of danger. At best this is a wooden
Courage, compatible with lamentable failure in the hour of
emergency. Genuine Courage must include the flexibility that
turns and adapts itself to novel circumstance.

2. It may prove fatal to "the habit of rehabituating oneself."

3. It may also blunt the sensibilities. It is easy to pass from these considerations to the further possibility that Habit,

---

[1] *Ethics*, Bk. VII. vii. 2.

[2] Cf. the suggestive passage in Plato, *Republic*, Bk. X., 619 C, where
the weakness of the virtue of "habit without philosophy" is exposed.

[3] Cf. Guyau, *Education and Heredity*, p. 50.

uncorrected by the "habit of rehabituation," may blunt the sensibilities and blind the intelligence.

In a sense it is not to be lamented that Habit blunts the sensibilities. It was said of a great surgeon that with him pity as an emotion had to cease in order that pity as a motive might begin. And we may generalise the remark to the full length of the statement that few of our duties but would suffer, if we tried to live from day to day in full emotional consciousness of all that they involve. Not that we have become automata, as indeed we know when the inhibition of habitual duties shews that latent feeling still burns ; but simply that in order to get work done, it is needful to secure some measure of calm in the soul.

But there is another side,

> "It is to spend long days
> And not once feel that we were ever young,"

not to feel it, because we have become case-hardened. It is here that Butler's analysis is so substantially sound[1]. When impressions issue in action, he says, our aptitudes for acting are increased : when impressions are passive, that is, do not issue in action, they gradually issue in insensibility. This, to be sure, has been questioned. Granting that the indulgence of these sentimental passive impressions weakens the practical tendencies, they do not, so runs the criticism[2], diminish the susceptibility to the sentimental pleasure. But is it the fact that sentimental pity, for example, softens the heart even to sentimental pity? Does it not rather wear itself out, till it passes into the apathetic end, not to be disguised though it may still repeat, from the lips outwards, the over-worn sentimental phrases ; if indeed it do not throw off all disguise, and pass into the sneer

The nemesis of sentimentality.

---

[1] Butler's *Analogy*, Part I. c. v.
[2] Bain, *The Emotions and the Will*, p. 458 (3rd ed.).

of the cynic? It is thus that habitual indulgence in sensibility issues in insensibility.

The same result may happen in the case of every habit. Acts done at first with a beating heart or a moistened eye, may come to be done without the stirring of a pulse; and this not because feeling is latent but because it is as good as dead. Hence not unnaturally Feeling and Habit have been set in antagonism, and Habit branded as a kind of death in life[1].

It is of even more serious moment that the acquired facility

Habit may, further, blind the intelligence.
to act in familiar ways, which ought to leave the mind free to deal with unfamiliar difficulties, may easily beget the indolent habit of acting without thinking at all. No result could be more fatal. Moral action, it is never to be forgotten, is by its very nature immersed in circumstance. There are conditions of time and place, of manner and aim. And these are so far from being fixed once for all that, in the changeful scene of human activity, they vary endlessly with the man and the occasion. Hence the need for that perpetual rehabituation without which, as we have seen, Habit will degenerate into a stupid automatism. But such rehabituation will never come where there is not the wakeful, alert intelligence that is quick to read the changeful face of circumstance, and to note the peculiar requirements of the particular emergency. This is

Importance of uniting good habits and
what Aristotle saw so clearly. No one has insisted more emphatically that the moral indeterminateness of natural desires must be superseded by habits: and no one has seen with more unerring perspicacity that this is never enough. The habits he magnifies are in truth not genuine virtues at all unless, as "habits of deliberate choice," they carry in them the resourceful vitality

---

[1] Cf. Wordsworth, *Ode on Intimations of Immortality* :

"Full soon thy soul shall have her earthly freight,
And custom lie upon her with a weight,
Heavy as frost, and deep almost as life!"

that can meet and adapt itself to new situations. For it is not the crowning merit of Aristotle to have seen that virtue is habit. This is perhaps the lesser part of his message. More pregnant far is enlightened judgment. his doctrine that, in any fully developed character, Habit must be found side by side with a sound practical judgment. For though of course there is a long probation during which our actions are chosen for us by those who are wiser than ourselves, this cannot go on for ever. The time comes when the individual must face his own problems and find his own solutions, and this he will never do, unless to the habits that run in the ruts of use and wont he have added that sagacity, shrewdness, practical wisdom, sound judgment (call it what we may) which is nothing less than the crowning virtue of a good character[1].

It follows that the man of habits, however excellent these be, may still be far enough from being what can be fitly called a man of character. In two respects especially he may fall short. His habits, The man of habits and the man of character. severally good, may lack the organic unity and the just relative proportion which are among the touchstones of character. It is not enough to give the young good habits: the habits must be co-ordinated in view of the functions which the man has to fulfil in the social economy, and built into a character that is permeated by the unity of coherent plan and purpose. And, as a second shortcoming, the man of habits may still be without that practised good judgment, in the absence of which no one need hope either to face successfully the complex changefulness of life's problems, or even to carry to their full development the habits that have been given him in the days of his tutelage.

Thus there are three main requirements to be satisfied before moral character can come to its full maturity. The first is good habits rooted in strong and promising instincts: the

[1] Hence the importance of reading Bk II. of the *Ethics* in close connection with Bk VI.

second, that co-ordination of habits that fits the man for his life's work : the third, the sound judgment which enables its possessor, when the days of leading strings are at an end, to stand alone and confront the world in his own independent strength.

Three main requisites of a good character.

It will be our task in the sequel to see how these requirements can be satisfied. And the first step in this direction will be to pass in brief review before us the leading influences, natural and social, under which congenital endowment finds its discipline and nurture.

PART II.

Educative Influences.

CHAPTER I.

ENVIRONMENT.

It is an impossible task to discriminate sharply between what is congenital and what is due to environment. Environment begins to operate with the beginnings of life, nor does it cease to operate, not for an instant, as the days become months and the months years.

The penetrating influence of environment.

> "Our bodies feel where'er they be
> Against or with our will."

So do our souls. And, this being so, it is inevitable that, though we watch never so narrowly, many an effect upon soul as upon body will be wrought unobserved. Even the keenest-eyed and most vigilant of parents must never flatter himself that he knows all, or nearly all, that is happening to his boy. We can see this sometimes in the fate of " experiments " in education. Really, such ventures are not experiments at all : the distinctive requirement of experiment—the thorough knowledge and control of the conditions operating—is not satisfied. For, as the influence of environment is ceaseless and the opportunities of observation intermittent, the results that happen are not the results expected. Nor need we wonder if the experiment so-called often enough in its upshot astonishes none more than the experimenter.

Hence the risk, to which recent physiological and psychological analysis has done much to open our eyes, of rashly setting down as congenital much that is really due to the silent and secret action of external circumstance. When, for example, a boy exhibits what seems an inborn aptitude for his father's trade, or reproduces with precocious fidelity the traits of his father's temper, these things need not be ascribed to the hand of Nature. Capacity and the response to stimulus that capacity implies, this of course must at very least be there. But this much given, the rest may well be due to the simple fact that the boy has first seen the light in a home upon which paternal trade or temper has set its mark. A late master of Balliol used to make merry over certain contemporaries who saw Heredity in the fact that the sons of deans themselves became deans, there being of course other, less occult, reasons why sons walk in the footsteps of their fathers.

Foremost among these is the fact that the experience and the achievement of the elder generation store themselves up in the environment. They leave their impress upon the habitual pursuits and atmosphere of the home, upon its ideal of duty and its ideal of pleasure, upon its choice of friends and its standard of living; and thereby come to act with masterful effect upon the young soul which lives and moves and has its being in their presence. It is thus that family tradition is carried on, it may be for generations. There is of course a given temperament, capacity, and proclivity to work upon. Yet these, it is to be remembered, are modes of endowment which do not, which in truth cannot, exist, where there is not already an environment under whose influence they are, from the very dawn of life, undergoing modification. This is especially true of those deferred instincts which postpone their appearance till later years. They

[margin note] "Social heredity" exercises a powerful influence from the first.

are not to be regarded as acquisitions. But neither can we doubt that the manner and energy of their appearance, when the day for that comes, must be influenced by the action and reaction between organism and environment which has been going on in the years before they found expression. What happens here conspicuously, happens in less degree in the instincts and capacities that are not "deferred." Bare instinct, mere capacity, are things unknown, creatures of analysis. The actual fact is always proclivity and environment in living relation one to the other. The point is practical. When the child reproduces the parent, and especially when he does so with a baleful fidelity to what is bad, it is only too easy to lay the blame on "original sin." But the *damnosa hereditas* is not always, perhaps it is never wholly, the gift of Nature. It comes from the remediable defect of the slipshod home, the barren or vicious example, the sour pasture of a miserable lot. No one nowadays will say that circumstance is everything. Are figs of thistles or flowers of thorns? But circumstance—"social heredity" as some have called it, "tradition" as others have it—this is there from the first. And every discovery that analysis makes as to the extraordinary secretness and subtlety of its action must feed the hopes and nerve the efforts of all, and especially of parents, with whom it rests to make it or to mar it.

The recognised influence of "social heredity" is a ground for hope.

Similarly when the passivity of early years has been left behind and character has entered on its long life-history. For character and environment are not to be set in antithesis, as if a developed character became less receptive to the influences of the world of men and things. It is quite otherwise. For however rich a man may be in those inward resources which raise him above the changes and chances of life, the greatest of all these resources is that he has learnt the secret of opening his heart and mind to the plenitude of what the natural, and social, and

Receptivity increases as character developes.

spiritual environment has in its gift. It is not childhood, in its narrow passivity, but manhood in its enlarged experience, that realises the magnitude of the forces amongst which it moves.

It is just this, indeed, that has opened up to Education a wider scope and a larger ambition. For the educators of our race no longer limit themselves to that direct influence of mind on mind and character on character which is their more immediate concern.

Hence Education, in its wider aspects, includes social organisation.

They have not read Plato and Aristotle in vain. Convinced, as these conscript fathers of education were convinced, that character will never reach its full stature unless it has found a favouring environment, they are coming to realise the extent of the task that lies before them—the task of organising, and if need be of reforming, the social system, so that each new life may pass under the beneficent, constraining hand of those institutions, from Family on to State and Church, whose influences are co-extensive with the whole of life. The work of Education, in the large sense of the word, is but half-done unless each new comer finds welcome from an environment prepared throughout for his reception. For Family and School are but the first forms of that larger hearth to which, cold and indifferent though it often seems, the human spirit must always look for warmth and nurture.

CHAPTER II.

BODILY HEALTH.

THE influences of Nature and of Society are inextricably interwoven in their action upon the members of a civilised community. The difficulties of sharp cleavage meet us (as we shall see) if we try, with Spencer, to part the reactions which are natural from those that are human and social. Nor is it to the barbarian but to the civilised social man, who has drank deep of the spirit of poetry, romance or art, that the Nature of the nature-worshippers reveals the magic of her mystic messages. But as usage has long set its seal on the distinction, it may be permissible, for exposition's sake, to follow it.

Natural and social influences are interwoven.

It is not necessary here to attempt to do justice to all the great natural influences which act upon temperament, instinct, and habit. Climate, for example, and geographical conditions, the succession, the rigour, the mildness of the seasons, the relative length of day and night—these all profoundly modify man's life and development. But, for the most part, we must take them as we find them. They are not within control and, in a practical enquiry like the present, it is enough to bear in mind that such influences operate; and to pass on[1].

Many natural influences are beyond the scope of our enquiry.

[1] For fuller treatment of these cf. Lotze, *Mikrocosmus*, Bk VI. c. ii.

It is very different however when we turn to the conditions of bodily health. Hygiene and therapeutics prove them to be emphatically within control, indeed they are so generally considered to be so that persons not a few live for little else. As to the manner and limits of such control, it is for writers upon Hygiene to speak. It must suffice here, touching but cursorily on a large subject, to specify some general aspects in which moral development is conspicuously conditioned by physical health.

Moral development is conditioned by bodily health.

(1) This is so, in its most obvious aspect, because good health is a prime condition of practical energy. For energetic constitutions enjoy an advantage that goes far beyond the mere superior ability to do what others cannot. This may give them their political or economic value. But, ethically, the gain lies in the fact that it is by energetic action that men make themselves. They do this when by their actions they form the corresponding habits: but they do it even more because it is substantially through action far more than through instruction that they come to identify their lives with diverse social ends and interests. Thus Spinoza's almost fierce denunciation of ascetic contempt for the body turns upon the conviction that the well-nurtured body is the organ of all true development, because it brings its possessor into varied practical relations with experience. On his view to macerate the body is thus to starve the soul[1]. Hence too the wisdom of the Carlylian dictum that, if any man would ever know "that poor Self of his," the first step is to find his work and to do it. Otherwise he will never realise a self that is worth the knowing.

For (1) Health is a condition of practical energy.

Importance of varied contact with experience.

So, conversely, with lack of energy. Idleness, says proverbial wisdom, comes to want. But its worst want is not the

[1] *Ethics*, Part IV. Prop. XLV. Scholium, with which cf. XXXVIII. and XXXIX.

empty purse : it is the soul atrophied for lack of the spiritual wages that never fail the strenuous life. What holds of idleness holds likewise of physical languor and weakness. We may not impute these as a sin, thereby "beating the cripple with his own crutches"; yet we must just as little refuse to face the fact that a weak or sickly body is a grievous moral disability, in so far as by narrowing the range of contact with life it stunts the character.

The nemesis of idleness.

(2) Similarly when we turn to moral endurance. Thus, when some trial falls upon anyone we love, one of the best things to wish for him is good health and well-strung nerves. And this, not for the obvious reason that he will then not break down in health, nor yet for the less materialistic reason that he can always find a manly anodyne in intense and absorbing physical exertion, but for the better reason still that physical strength minimises the risk, never absent when the wheels of vital being run slow, that trial and shock may cut short the life, even of a brave spirit, before the virtues of endurance have had time for their maturing. Hence the folly of indulging the natural recklessness of bodily health in the dark days of trial. Well has Rousseau said that the weaker the body is the more it commands. It commands in the hour when we cannot face our willing work, or when we wince like cowards under demands that shake the unstrung nerves, or when it makes us, in spite of resolutions, morbid, irritable, wrong-headed in our estimates of men and things. And, as the same counsellor adds, it is the strong body that obeys. For the body will be best subjugated, not by hair-shirt or scourge or any other of the like devices which too often thrust the physical life into prominence in the very effort to repress it, but by enlisting the fulness of manly strength in the service of some cause or person, which will tax it to the uttermost.

(2) Health gives opportunity for the virtues of endurance.

The weak body commands.

The strong body obeys.

Hence the strength of the ethical argument for physical educa-

Ethical
argument for
physical
education.

tion. If we are apt to have misgivings about the long hours and days given in boyhood and youth to the strenuous idleness of sports and games, we must not think too exclusively of the immediate results. We must think of the heavy drafts which arduous vocations make in after years on bodily vigour and endurance, of the habitual cheerfulness that follows health, and not least of that sense of insurance against whatever the future can bring which comes of the consciousness of calculable physical fitness. Plato startles us in his educational ideal by assigning two and a half of the most precious years of life to the exclusive pursuit of "gymnastic[1]." If it seem a costly tribute to the body, it is to be borne in mind that it is prompted by the principle "Body for the sake of Soul," and finds its justification in the strenuous service to be exacted by the State of its citizens in later years.

(3) Health is
a condition of
sound judg-
ment.

(3) Add to this that bodily health is also a condition of all soundness of practical judgment. The best of health will not of course ensure wisdom. Not all wise men are robust, nor are all robust men wise. Yet the connection is intimate.

> "Spontaneous wisdom breathed by health,
> Truth breathed by cheerfulness,"

says Wordsworth[2], in a familiar couplet whose full significance is perhaps not always understood. For though health and cheerfulness may not bring wisdom, they afford securities against unwisdom in some of its most familiar forms. For our errors of judgment, as may be more evident in the sequel[3], are not due merely, or even mainly, to positive blindness to the conditions

---

[1] Between 17 and 20—just the time most valuable for forming intellectual tastes and habits. Cf. *Republic.*

[2] *The Tables Turned.*

[3] Cf. pp. 164 and 206.

involved. They come rather from a distorted emphasis, a false perspective in regard to conditions that are well within our horizon. We realise this when we come to ourselves. "How could I have thought it? How could I have said it?"— this is what we say when we regain our balance—that balance that is so hopelessly upset when our nerves are shaken, and our sensibilities morbid. For, by subtle organic influence, the morbid state of body dulls a susceptibility here, and exaggerates a susceptibility there, till we lose, and often know we lose, the power of seeing things as they really are, and as they come to be seen by ourselves when health returns. Nor can it be denied that, even the salt of the earth may thus on occasion be betrayed, by nothing more dignified than physical exhaustion or irritability, into judgments peevish, uncharitable, precipitate; and thereby put to the blush by their worldly neighbours in whom the placid good health that goes with an easy-going life has kept the balance true.

Hence the futility of attempting to argue a victim of Hypochondria into a healthy view of life. He may listen to us and, after a fashion, understand us. For our words are his words. But the facts as they image themselves in our minds are not the facts as imaged in his.

Hypochondria is not to be argued with.

> "Alas, the warped and broken board
> How can it bear the painter's dye,
> The harp of strained and tuneless chord
> How to the minstrel's skill reply[1]?"

This is the gravest injury that weak or shattered nerves can inflict upon us. Pain, exhaustion, even forced inactivity, are lesser evils. For this clouding of the judgment troubles what, in adult years, is the very well-head of moral action. Sometimes,

[1] The lines are the more impressive as coming from Sir Walter, who was little given to the putting on of sadness for the pleasure of it.

no doubt, there are compensations here. Persons of weak health are often anxious, and anxiety begets foresight; and thus, by habitual foresight, they may safeguard themselves against mistakes. Yet this is at best a poor substitute for the even-balanced healthy outlook that goes so far to keep the judgment sound. Better to render such compensations unnecessary by setting to work betimes to secure the healthy body, remembering that, in all treatment of a composite being like man, the most powerful moralising influences are not always those that are directly moral.

Yet we must not press these truths unduly. Though Dr Johnson once declared that illness makes a man a scoundrel, the retort is that illness, and indeed all bodily weakness, may become strength when seized as a spiritual opportunity. There have been men—Erasmus, Montaigne, Heine—who, with a levity more touching than fortitude, made humorous capital out of their own diseases and sufferings, in a fashion which puts the Johnsonian dictum to confusion. Nor could mankind, in presence of all the slings and arrows of disease and decay, afford to surrender even one of those consolations which have taught physical weakness the secret of moral strength. Physical suffering can beget its own virtues, of which fortitude is one. A weak body is, sometimes at any rate, the condition of a deeper and a more refined moral insight; and though long-continued delicacy of constitution is only too prone to the pitfall of a valetudinarianism that is fatally self-centred, it may sometimes induce a discerning sympathy with the sorrows of others which robust and bustling persons do not always feel.

On the other hand, bodily weakness may be a spiritual opportunity.

Yet when all is said such things are still of the nature of compensations. They do not touch the central fact that he who would form a well-developed character must stand far aloof from the ascetic superstition, rooted in a false psychology, that the death of Body is the life of Soul.

There is no materialism in this. It is the reverse of materialism to believe that the moral life is not so resourceless as to be unable to find sufficiently high service for the body at its best. We have already glanced at Spinoza's pregnant remark

Attention to physical education is the reverse of materialism.

that we do not know what the Body is capable of[1]. We may now go a step further and, following Aristotle, declare that we shall never know, till Body is recognised in its true significance as instrument of fully developed Soul. For materialism consists, not in frankest recognition of matter, but in the assignment to it of a spurious supremacy or independence. There can be no materialism in utmost emphasis upon physical education, so long as "Body for the sake of Soul" is, as it was with Plato, the presiding principle of educational action.

[1] *Ethics*, Part III. Prop. II. Scholium, "For what the Body can do no one has hitherto determined."

CHAPTER III.

MR SPENCER'S DOCTRINE OF NATURAL REACTIONS.

IT is beyond dispute good that the young should learn by

The effi-
cacy of natu-
ral reactions
must be recog-
nised.

personal experience how the things and persons they encounter may be expected to behave towards them. Much education must, whether we will or not, remain of this kind. Children cannot be "followed, hourly watched, and noosed[1]." In all early life, in life altogether, we struggle forwards more or less blindly. We leap before we look. And if we learn to do otherwise, it is in large measure by our blunders, and the "reactions" which these entail. It is by tears that the first tiny shoots of foresight, deliberation and choice, are watered. As Burns has it:

> "Though losses and crosses
> Be lessons right severe,
> There's wit there you'll get there
> You'll find no other where."

The gain does not end in the specific experiences. Gradually there will grow up the prudential habit of mind which, as years go on, will help its possessor to steer his course in life. And all along will come, as unsought bonus, an intimate and unforgettable knowledge about the properties of things and beings that burn, cut, sting, tear, bruise, bite, kick, strike and so forth.

[1] Cf. Wordsworth, *Prelude*, Bk. v. 238.

This is the fact which Mr Herbert Spencer urges with uncommon force and varied illustration in his well-known chapter upon "moral education[1]"; and it would be graceless to withhold gratitude for the service he has therein rendered. The chapter will remain a protest against education by arbitrary penalties, against aimless meddlesomeness, against the cruelties of Draconian methods, against the too common illusion that nothing is needed but word of command, or diet of precept. And if we may regard as even remotely typical the parent, for whose existence Mr Spencer vouches, who when his boy was carried home with a dislocated thigh "saluted him with a castigation," it might even earn the thanks of the Society for the Prevention of Cruelty to Children.

Value of Mr Spencer's views on moral education.

It is necessary, however, to define more precisely what this doctrine means. Manifestly enough it is perhaps the most uncompromising plea for "natural reactions" ever written. But there is a difficulty in understanding exactly when it is that a reaction is to be called "natural." Thus there are instances adduced in which children fall, or run their heads against tables, or lay hold of the fire-bars, or spill boiling water on their skins. In these, the reactions follow without any human intervention. There are other instances again in which children who "make hay" on the nursery floor suffer by having to restore their little chaos to order, or small boys who tear their clothes in scrambling through a hedge incur the surely formidable penalty of being set to mend them. In these the reactions would certainly not happen, did not nature find instruments in nurses or mothers. Then—though now we have passed to "later life"—we read of the idle apprentice discharged into poverty, the unpunctual man who proves his own worst enemy, the

There is, however, difficulty in discriminating "natural" from social reactions.

[1] Spencer, *Education*, c. III. All the quotations from Mr Spencer are from this chapter.

extortionate tradesman who loses his custom, the inattentive doctor who destroys his practice. Finally, we have the graver offences—lying, for example, or stealing—with which nature, apart from human intervention, is so incompetent to deal that she calls to her assistance two allies, the first, parental disapprobation, the second, indemnity, which, says Mr Spencer, "in the case of a child may be effected out of its pocket money."

Now it is of course permissible for any writer to call one and all of these reactions "natural." There is a wide sense in which all human society may be included in Nature. It was so regarded by the Greek philosophers. And Burke echoes them, speaking to the pregnant text, "Art is man's nature[1]." If this view were adopted, natural reactions would simply be such as conduct would draw down, not only from Nature ordinarily so-called, but also from a well-constituted Social System. This however is not the doctrine of Mr Spencer. True to his well-known laissez-faire convictions, he would have us minimise human intervention to the uttermost possible limit, and by consequence welcome reactions as "natural" in proportion as they verge towards "the true theory and practice of moral discipline" as illustrated by the burns, scalds, or bruises which the external world never fails to inflict on those who violate her laws. How far this doctrine is sound we shall shortly see. The present point is that it is certainly not allowable to cite in support of it the reactions that overtake the slack tradesman, the incapable doctor, the idle apprentice, or even the small boy who is to be set to mend his own clothes. All these involve the intervention not merely of human beings, but of human beings instinct with ideas of moral desert and moral discipline, which are wholly

The "natural" reactions of Mr Spencer's doctrine involve a minimum of human intervention.

---

[1] *Appeal from the new to the old Whigs*, Works, vol. III. p. 86.

absent in the burns, scalds, and bruises which Nature administers.

The same point will appear if we examine the place assigned to Disapprobation. No one can doubt that it may have immense influence: no one is likely to quarrel with Mr Spencer for invoking it against the graver offences. But its value must of course depend upon the source from which it comes. The disapprobation of the parent who castigated his child for dislocating his thigh was presumably not of much value. It was of less value than the bite of a dangerous animal. What more evident than that Disapprobation can carry *moral* discipline, only when it has behind it ideas and sentiments as to the real well-being of the child who is by it to be disciplined. Mr Spencer sees this. He urges parents to aim at such reactions as "would be called forth from a parent of perfect nature." This is excellent. The difficulty is to reconcile it with the Spencerian faith in Spencerian "nature." To leave our boys and girls to nature's teaching is one thing: to consign them to parents so fully charged with moral ideas as to be even on the way to perfection, is another. For this is moral education as the other is not.

Is parental disapprobation a natural reaction?

It is moreover far from clear that these "natural reactions" merit the overwhelming confidence reposed in them by their advocates. Be it granted that they have their own advantages. It has been freely admitted that they bring knowledge of how things or persons will behave, and that they foster the prudential habit of mind. And to this it may be added that there may be gain to temper both of child and parent. The child is not alienated, as he sometimes is when the parent is punisher: and the parent, by standing aside to let Nature wield the tawse, preserves his equanimity. It is when we read that these reactions are "proportionate to the transgression," or, in more concrete

Natural reactions (thus understood) do not merit the confidence reposed in them.

statement, that "it is not ordained that the urchin who tumbles over the doorstep should suffer in excess of the amount necessary," that one is staggered by the boldness of the assertion.   A little lad forgets his overcoat—is it proportionate that he should have an inflammation?   Another is tempted on to ice—is it just that he should all but, or altogether, drown?   Two small boys climb a fence; one tears his knickerbockers, the other is impaled—which is the "ordained" reaction?   The truth is that the days of an *a priori* trust in Nature are past.   Her ways are too well known.   Merciless and prodigal of life in her dealings with the animal world, "red in tooth and claw with ravine[1]," there is little ground for believing her to be otherwise disposed towards man, who to begin with is among the most helpless of all the animals.   As a matter of fact she seems to aim in a hundred ways at his extinction, in which indeed the ghastly records of infant mortality shew that she too often succeeds.   Precautions may of course be overdone, and parental nervousness may need the reminder that children who run no risk will develop no self-reliance.   But the manifold precautions that hedge about the young in every good home are too large and persistent a fact to be set down to a nervous and groundless distrust.   Even Mr Spencer sees this.   "During infancy," he writes, "a considerable amount of absolutism is necessary.   A three-year old urchin playing with an open razor cannot be allowed to learn by the discipline of consequences; for the consequences may be too serious."   Indeed they may; and one may venture to believe they often are, even when the years are more than three times three.

It is an even graver point that Nature's reactions are often so slow and stealthy that they come too late.   For

Marginal notes:

For (a) they are *not* proportionate to the transgressions.

Ruthlessness of Nature.

---

[1] "Tho' Nature red in tooth and claw
With ravine, shrieked against his creed."

In Memoriam, LVI.

Nature is a hard dealer. When she has a certain stock of wisdom on sale, she usually exacts the uttermost farthing as the price of what we are wont to call, not without reason, "our dearly bought experience." "If you do not run when you are well," *and (b) Nature's reactions are often too slow and stealthy.* says Horace to the sluggard, "you will have to run when you have got the dropsy." It may be said that this—this learning only after the heavy hand of Nature has fallen—is no more than the adult backslider deserves. But can we face it as the proportionate punishment of heedless youth? Are there no records of health lost through unwitting neglect of Nature's laws; or of light-hearted idleness laying up for itself a dreary reckoning; or of insidious gradual lapse preparing the way for some catastrophe; or of "simple pleasure foraging for death." It is no sufficient offset that the lesson, even if it come too late, is learnt. It is never enough in education, any more than in the productive arts, to look simply at results. We must look at product in relation to its cost. For though of course the wisdom that comes too late *Results are to be estimated relatively to cost.* to the individual may be passed on to the world, enforced by all the bitter emphasis of unavailing regret, this can hardly be regarded as good economy. Burns once wrote down in verse some "Advice to a Young Friend." It is throughout the pith of sense. But nothing in it is more suggestive, or more pathetic, than its closing words.

> "In ploughman phrase, God send you speed
>   Still daily to grow wiser;
> And may you better reck the rede
>   Than e'er did the adviser."

Is it presumptuous to add that there are two great arts, both bound up with education, of which Mr Spencer appears to underestimate both the importance and the difficulty?

(*a*) One of them is the art of securing the confidence of those we would influence. Mr Spencer sees the importance

of confidence.   Without it, disapprobation—the disapprobation that is a main element in dealing with graver
offences—would fail of its effect.   But he invites
criticism when he tells us how confidence can be
won.   A child, for example, wishes to play
with fire.   Well, reflects the mother, "the
mother of some rationality," "he is sure to burn himself
sometime."   And so she first warns him, and then—lets him
burn himself; with the reservation (for which we may be
thankful) that serious damage is to be forcibly prevented.
The lesson is twice-blessed.   The child not only learns that
fire burns, but that his mother is his best friend.   Not thus
simple is the winning of confidence.   It is an art of many
resources—of patient affection, of habitual kindliness in little
things, of ready and sincere sympathy with youthful plans
and projects, of firm and tolerant guidance in graver matters;
and, must we not add, of the watchful care, parent of gratitude, which intervenes to avert, or to soften, the consequences
of folly or blindness.   Mr Spencer's device is at best but one
resource, and not the best resource, among many.

Is confidence best won by allowing children to learn from natural reactions?

(*b*)   The other art that receives but scant recognition at
Mr Spencer's hands is the art of punishment.
It is an art that has tested the powers of the
greatest minds, sometimes in contrasting, sometimes in reconciling, its various aspects as reformatory, retributory, and deterrent.   Its difficulties are undeniable.   Nor are they lessened
when its main concern is with the small offenders of nursery
or schoolroom.   For in this case it is complicated at a stroke
by considerations of moral desert and moral effect, which
must needs be largely ignored by the jurist or the political
philosopher.   This indeed is just what Mr Spencer is so quick
to perceive; and it is part of his argument that human blundering has so manifestly punctuated attempts at the administration of punishment that we had better for all time to come

Over-con-fidence in natural re-actions implies imperfect re-cognition of the art of Pun-ishment.

devolve the difficulties upon "nature." The policy has an attractive simplicity, even when we reserve the responsibilities of parental disapprobation and imposition of indemnity. Nor need one withhold a tribute to the sanguine optimism of the faith that young lives, left alone, will struggle on to victory.

But, then, are the credentials of Nature so unimpeachable that we can, with light hearts, resign to her a task so difficult? Are we to set alone upon the judgment-seat a Power who, in her inexorable decrees, seems often so coldly indifferent to all *Are the credentials of Nature sufficient?* those ideas of merit, desert, responsibility, repentance, sin, crime, frailty, which punishment, in human hands, has had to confront? And is the human race indeed so resourceless that it must needs despair of controlling and directing the immense fact of human suffering so that it may be made tributary to individual and social reformation[1]? Nor ought it to be forgotten, in this connection, that there is such a thing as moral discipline through pity and forgivingness. It is sometimes those who, in youthful blunders and follies, have found pity who in after years can bestow pity; and those who have been forgiven, even without indemnity, who are likely to manifest that forgiving spirit for which we may look long and in vain in Nature. Grant that Nature can heal as well as hurt. Grant that the natural forces that make for life, health and joy are strong enough to triumph in the long run (though at grievous cost) over those that make for suffering, decay and death, it is still no part of Nature's plan to remit by jot or tittle the penalty she exacts for violated law. Even if we believed her to be just—which is not easy—it does not lie in her power, as it does in that of man, to temper or supersede justice by mercy.

Taken altogether, Mr Spencer's doctrine sets excessive store upon the value of acquired foresight of consequences. At very most this is a part, and in the young certainly it is

[1] Cf. p. 148.

far from the most hopeful part of education. Least of all is it
sufficient when the reactions are repressive, as
for the most part they are in Mr Spencer's
chapter. There is a wiser and more sympathetic
way. It is to seek out and to find the promising
instincts, the healthy proclivities, the forward-
struggling tendencies, and by all means in our
power to feed and foster these; so that child or youth may
be emboldened to give them play with something of a buoyant
and uncalculating confidence[1]. This is what no diet of "natural
reactions" can ensure; if indeed it do not tend to create a
wary and calculating spirit which, when it comes early in life,
is fatal to the wholesome self-abandonment of the years when
the eyes are fixed far more on the objects of pursuit than
on the pleasures and pains these objects are likely to bring.
"All education," says Guyau, "should be directed to this end,
to convince the child that he is capable of good and incapable
of evil, in order to render him actually so[2]." This is a policy
which will not obviate blunders, disappointments, failures.
And the "reactions" alike of Nature and Society, will not
fail to bring these home. But even then, the hopeful plan
is to encourage those who fall, to rise and struggle forward,
to rally the good that is in them, and, even to the limits
of pious fraud, to convince them they are capable of better
things.

It is a more hopeful plan to foster promising instincts than to develop foresight of consequences.

[1] Cf. p. 52.
[2] *Education and Heredity*, p. 24.

CHAPTER IV.

WORDSWORTHIAN EDUCATION OF NATURE.

It is not profitable to fall to asking what Nature can do for us of herself. Nature never has us to herself. It is, up to the last confines of our knowledge, the social man, and, for our present subject, the civilised social man she has to work upon. This applies even to the gospel of Wordsworth. For although that greatest of all the apostles of the education of Nature—in that revolt against

Belief in the influence of Nature is intensified by the fact that man must be social to appreciate Nature.

the over-elaboration and conventionality of society which he shared with Rousseau—has often enough thrown the natural into antithesis to the social; and though, in verse never to be forgotten he has told us in "Lucy" how Nature can set herself to "make a lady of her own," these things must not be pressed unduly. In all that he tells us, in *The Prelude*, of his own childhood and youth, the influences of social and natural surroundings are not antagonistic to each other, but interfused and cooperant. It is of the child as nurtured in home and social circle he has to speak, and of what the ministry of Nature can do for it. It is precisely this, in truth, that makes this ministry of Nature a greater thing. It would be a poor tribute to Nature to insist that man has to be born into solitude and savagery in order to profit by her influence. The

greater proof of what she can do lies in what her ministry may
be to those whom homes and social nurture have fitted to
receive it.   And indeed it is for this reason that the love of
Nature is so far from being a youthful illusion that fades with
the years, that it can become a life-long passion, never stronger
than when man has learnt to feel and to think by contact with
his kind.

These influences begin long before the presence of Nature

**Early in-
fluences come
unsought.**
is sought for the sake of any deliberately pursued
charm such as the phrase "love of Nature" has
come to suggest to adult and self-conscious
minds.   "The child's world," as Dr John Brown so truly said,
"is about three feet high."[1]   The greater aspects of Nature do
not enter into it; or if, in some vaguely felt fashion they do, it
is still as no more than the little-heeded background for
childish interests, amusements and sports.   These are its
world.   None the less, even then, the unobtrusive influences
of earth, sea, and sky do their work.   They pass imperceptibly
and unsought into the soul.

> "...out-door sights
> Sweep gradual gospels in."[2]

And, as each season brings its own wealth of varying aspects,
the emotional life is vaguely but powerfully stirred.

**And especi-
ally feed the
life of Feeling.**
"From Nature doth emotion come, and moods
Of calmness equally are Nature's gift.
This is her glory."[3]

Hence the natural delight in the sunshine, the joy in the
crisp freshness of the morning, the wonder and fear at flood,

---

[1] "Children are long of seeing, or at least of looking at what is above
them; they like the ground, and its flowers and stones, its 'red sodgers'
and lady-birds, and all its queer things; their world is etc." *Horae Subse-
civae*, vol. II. p. 5.

[2] Mrs Browning's *Aurora Leigh*, Bk. I. (this Book of the poem is of
educational as well as literary interest).

[3] *Prelude*, XIII. 1.

storm, or darkness. Such impressions of course, for many
a year, come only to go. They are quickly lost among
more palpable, homely, and habitual interests. Nor have
they any direct moral significance whatever. But they recur,
and as years go on, they feed into ever fuller strength the
life of feeling. Here Nature vies with imaginative literature,
art and religion as one of the perennial sources of emotional
life. Nor is her power to move the heart ever so needful as
in an age when the urgent practicalities of material progress
and the absorbing and sometimes arid intellectualities of
science and criticism have all too much withdrawn attention
from the culture of the emotions.

For this awakening of the life of Feeling tells in two directions. In one direction, because it is of the
nature of all emotion to be diffusive. Even **The emotions**
thus aroused
when aroused by definite objects, it does not **are diffusive,**
and create a
absorb itself in these. It tends to disturb the **fuller life.**
whole man, in body as well as soul. And it
does this the more, when emotional disturbance is great, and
the objects that awaken it still vaguely apprehended and only
half-defined. This is what happens in these natural influences
of early years. Their intimations do not fail in energy, though
they fall short in clearness. Strong feelings of delight, or fear,
are there; but there is little power as yet of discerning whence
they come. And as all emotion struggles to discharge itself
in some direction, the result is a flooding of springs of vitality
which find overflow in many directions. This at least is
Wordsworth.

> "For feeling has to him imparted power
> That through the growing faculties of sense
> Doth like an agent of the one great Mind
> Create."[1]

It creates that fuller life that is ready to express itself in many
modes.

[1] *Preluae,* II. 255.

But as time goes on, a second result ensues. Discrimination, and more definite association, gain
And come to be attached to simple and enduring objects. upon the vaguer elemental life of mere feeling. The emotions come to attach themselves to definite experiences and definite objects, and above all to objects that are simple, attainable, and enduring. This is what Wordsworth has in mind when he declares that

> " Nature never did betray
> The heart that loved her."[1]

Nature does not betray us, because the objects she so prodigally offers have nothing of the fragility or illusiveness that blight so many of the resources of man's invention. We of course may come short. Habit, against which these apostles of Nature are ever at war, may dull the sensibilities and blind the eyes, and preoccupation with frivolities or cares may close the ways of influence. But Nature is not to blame for this.

> " The morning shines,
> Nor heedeth man's perverseness."[2]

And as often as these scales, scales of our own making, fall from the eyes, Nature is the same great Presence as ever, still offering to us, with unwearied bounty, her " temperate show of objects that endure."[3]

Such influences, moreover, may enjoy a further, and not
Such experiences have a further, and not less important life in memory. less potent life in memory. This comes sometimes by simple association, as when some similar experience summons from the buried past " the immortal spirit of a happy day " spent on hill or shore. But sometimes too, it comes, and to those who are city-pent perhaps it comes oftenest, by law of Contrast, as when the roar of the traffic of streets sends the mind to the memory of solitudes "where great mornings

[1] *Tintern Abbey.*
[2] *Prelude*, XII. 31.
[3] *Ib.* XIII. 31.

shine, Around the bleating pens," or, as when the prose poet
of revolution lifts our minds from the slaughter of barricades to
the vision of ships far off on the silent main. Wordsworth
goes further still. For in the lines (too familiar
for quotation) in which he tells how his mind
has often turned to wood-wandering Wye, in
recoil from "the fretful stir unprofitable and
fever of the world," he makes the bolder claim that the
reawakened emotions of such memories

> "may have no trivial influence
> On that best portion of a good man's life,
> His little nameless unremembered acts
> Of kindness and of love."

Can such
memories in-
fluence the
moral life?

They may, when the spirit has been otherwise impelled in
such direction. For all heightening of emotion in a disciplined
character tends to seek its outlet more especially through those
ways of expression that have become habitual and congenial.
But the more sober claim is that the recall of all experiences of
natural piety can enrich our lives with a sense of possession
that is inalienable and self-sufficing.

> "Bid me work but may no tie
> Keep me from the open sky"

says one who well knew Nature's resources[1]. The words will
find an echo in the hearts of all who, however humbly, have
come to know and to love Nature. She never did betray
them. For, at very least, she hangs the walls of memory with
pictures that flash upon the visionary eye with a satisfying and
restorative joy.

> "To make this earth our heritage,
> A cheerful and a changing page,
> God's bright and intricate device
> Of day and season doth suffice."[2]

[1] Barnes.
[2] Louis Stevenson, *Underwoods.*

There are two ways at least in which this may powerfully
influence after-years.

(*a*)   Inward resource may bring that "self-sufficing power
of solitude"[1] which is peculiarly favourable to a
calm, cheerful, and reflective outlook upon life.
This will not, of course, be always so.   Has not
Wordsworth himself told us, in a masterpiece of
epitaph, how dissatisfied pride and ambition may, despite a
golden promise, find only a bitterer embitterment in the sweet
seclusion of the wilderness, and a deeper sadness in scenes of
beauty poisoned by the stings of a disappointed egoism[2]?   Such
must find their anodyne in cities, not in solitude.   Yet we
must not generalise from an instance like this.   That inability
to be alone with Nature which is so common, is a sure sign
of spiritual weakness.   It needs counteracting, and few counter-
actives are better than those actual and remembered delights
which Nature has in her gift.

*Love of Na-
ture fosters
self-sufficing-
ness;*

(*b*)   A second gain is that love of Nature, early awakened,
gives direction to the pleasures and recreations
of later life.   It is of course not in the fields of
pastime that the virtues grow; or at most it is
only the lesser virtues that grow there.   Yet it is hardly doubtful
that the kind of life an ordinary family leads, and the friendships which its members form, are as much determined by
the accepted ideal of recreation, as by the accepted ideal
of morality.   In this way, from the shaping of household or
individual ideals of pleasure, indirect results may come to
which it is not easy to set limits.

*and influences
ideals of
recreation.*

To this it must be added that love of Nature
tends to develop a healthy, care-free, outward
outlook upon things, which is of peculiar value

*It also
fosters a
healthy out-
ward outlook.*

---

[1] Cf. *Prelude*, II. 76

> "And I was taught to feel, perhaps too much,
> The self-sufficing power of Solitude."

[2] *Poems*, vol. I. p. 44. (Moxon.)

in days when city-life is more and more with us. And it does this perhaps most of all, when it strikes alliance with that interest in the animate and inanimate world which the field naturalist knows how to foster. For the young who are city-born and city-bred run risks. Daily sight or rumour of much that is forbidding and deplorable may make them case-hardened to poverty and misery for the rest of their lives. Or perhaps, and all the more if they belong to pitiful and public-spirited homes, they may too soon be brought compassionately face to face with folly, squalor, and vice, and thereby begin to be prematurely vexed with social problems that are still far beyond them. There are no doubt counter-actives. And the city of course can furnish many of its own. Has it not its games and pastimes, its parks, museums, libraries, and pageants, its rushing tides of many-coloured industrial and commercial life? Yet we may welcome these without neglecting that interest in the green earth, and in its feathered and four-footed tenantry, which is seemingly instinctive in most children, and can indubitably by right nurture—by country holiday, by love of garden, by skill with pencil or brush, by the fascination of natural history—be fostered into a lifelong resource.

Nor is it to be supposed that in turning thus to Nature, we turn away from man. Exclusive preoccupation with society is not the way to know it best. Men seldom understand human life better, or more deeply realise its meaning, than when they can break the bonds of city habit, and stand aside for a season in wholesome and whole-hearted surrender to interests that seem to have little to do with the ways of men and cities.

> "One impulse from a vernal wood
> May teach you more of man,
> Of moral evil and of good
> Than all the sages can."

And though the prosaic mind would no doubt have us pause

to ask how an impulse can bring all this so enviable knowledge, there is reason in the rhetoric none the less. Even if all the woods that ever were greened speak nothing to us of either good or evil, they yet bring us more than we seek from them. Their influences can wean us from the anxious, or frivolous, or sordid, or prejudiced, or paltry thoughts, which so often in the life of the world rise like exhalations to distort our moral perceptions. For, as these roll aside in our seasons of retreat, we begin to see the facts of life and experience in a truer perspective. There are times when it is not teaching that we need, though it were the teaching of all the sages. It is rather the power truly to see what we have been told a thousand times. And this is what Nature can do, as often as she withdraws the veil woven by our own troubled and agitated hearts.

Wordsworth asks us to believe more than this. Bred himself in the lap of Nature, he came to see, with a true insight, that human life, especially the life of shepherds and other men of the wilderness, has a glamour thrown around it by the scenes amidst which its work is done.

Wordsworth's belief in the value of approaching Man through Nature.

> " First I looked
> At man through objects that were great or fair." [1]

And he was deeply convinced that it was by thus approaching life with a prepossession to look on "the golden side of the shield," that in the long run there would settle down a truer because a more hopeful and more sympathetic view of human nature.

To many this has appeared far-fetched and fanciful. And it may be admitted that the side of the shield on which we first look is that which is presented by the kind of life that goes on in the Home, whether this be in heart of city or heart of country. We need too the reminder that the life that is enfolded by dales and hills, as Wordsworth himself knew well, may be

---

[1] *Prelude*, VIII. 215—339.

far from idyllic, and indeed not morally better than that which struggles and sins under "the smoke counterpane" of a great city. And, in any case, it is not through Nature that man is, or ever can, be approached by the vast majority. Yet a truth remains. It may be a lifelong gain to boy and girl to have formed their first notions of life and work from what they have seen in country places. For, just as the simpler, more primitive, and elemental life of the Ballad appeals to the young imagination more than the later and more elaborated literary product, so with the homely epic of humble life that is for ever repeating itself under the sunshine and the rain in the work of field and fold. Cheerful toil as the condition of livelihood, the well-earned rest of toils obscure, the honest independence that looks the world in the face, and all the changes of the ordinary lot—it is no fancy that these stand out, and can be seen in the life of the country, as they never can amidst the mechanism and organisation, the class estrangements and the sheer mass of the more developed but less comprehensible avocations of the city. They are more obviously of the very substance of the lives of those who pursue them : they are more attractive by far in their surroundings ; and, as simple matter of fact, they appeal with incomparably greater force to youthful interest and sympathy. And so long as this is so, there must be gain, despite all qualifications, in approaching life "on the golden side of the shield."

Substantial truth of the Wordsworthian view.

There remains a further point, less easy to define. Our great prophets of Nature are realists to the core. They are sworn foes of "the pathetic fallacy" that sees in the external world the mere mirror of human moods and passions. And accordingly they have ever insisted that "half-revealed and half-concealed" there lies in visible appearances a revelation of Ideas, and of God in whom all Ideas find their source and unity.

The claim that Nature reveals Ideas must be admitted.

This high doctrine is not to be lightly brushed aside as

misty metaphysics[1]. At very least it cannot be doubted that there lies in Nature a store of imagery through which imagination can make ideas, and not least moral ideas, both clear and vivid.

> "Ye breezes and soft airs,
> Whose subtle intercourse with breathing flowers,
> Feelingly watched, might teach Man's haughty race
> How without injury to take, to give
> Without offence; ye who as if to shew
> The wondrous influence of power gently used,
> Bend the complying heads of lordly pines,
> And, with a touch, shift the stupendous clouds
> Through the whole compass of the sky."

But there is more than this. Even an unlettered mind may see Power in the flooded torrent, Peace in the sheen of silent and sailless seas, Evanescence in the leaves of the forest. And though it remains true that such impressions work more through the emotions they excite than through the conceptions they convey, there is more in such experience than mere feeling. There are distinguishable modes of feeling suggestive of diverse modes of being. And when these experiences repeat themselves, it need not be doubted that, if only they evade the dulling influences of habit, they may carry "intimations"—to use a Wordsworthian word—of Ideas that have a veritable objective existence.

On the other hand we must be cautious of crediting Nature

But we may not credit Nature with a revelation of moral values. with a revelation of moral laws and moral values in any ordinary sense of the words. In those hours when Nature speaks to us, our responsive attention is due, in large part, to an aesthetic appreciation which has comparatively little to do with the moral life. And is it not part of the charm of the breezes and

---

[1] As, *e.g.* by Macaulay; cf. Trevelyan's *Life and Letters of Macaulay*, II. 283, "There are the old raptures about mountains and cataracts; the old flimsy philosophy about the effect of scenery on the mind, etc."

soft airs and vernal woods that they so beguile us, that moral distinctions are for the time forgotten, and moral problems cease from troubling?

> "Whoso
> Affronts thy eye of Solitude shall learn
> That her mild nature can be terrible,"

says Wordsworth. But it is only in figure that Nature shines upon the saint and scowls upon the sinner. Not to her need we look for that definiteness of guidance, that sifting of the instincts in the service of an ideal, that deliberate nurture of the habits, all of which lie upon the very threshold of morality. For such things we must turn to Society.

Nor need this conclusion be modified even if we include in the influences of Nature that education by means of those examples of the animal world, which have for ages been made to furnish forth the veiled homilies of parable and fable. The debt is not to be repudiated. Grant that anxiety has learnt something of the care-free spirit from the fowls of the air, and industry and prudence found confirmation in the economy of ants and beavers. Yet such things can only profit when, in the light of other experiences, we have already come to know what are virtues and what vices. The whole animal world taken together can tell us nothing of this. Even its aristocracy, if seriously weighed in human scales, is far from respectable. It is the very poverty of their endowment that fits them for examples, because it makes the few qualities they have so salient. And though it is a well established law of animal life that the "fittest" survives, there need be nothing in the fitness of the survivors to invite our *moral* approbation; seeing that "the fittest to survive" appears to mean the fittest to prevent its neighbours from surviving. It is not really to learn from them that we need turn to the animals. It is to pity and sympathise, to protect them from

Nor is much weight to be attached to the moral examples of the animal world.

7—2

human cruelty, to save them from each other, and to find delight for ourselves in watching their laborious, or sportive, or cunning, or incomprehensible ways.   Certainly the animals do not set themselves up as examples, and it would perhaps be too much to impose on them a thing so obviously beyond the majority of the human race.

CHAPTER V.

FAMILY, SCHOOL, FRIENDSHIP.

PHILOSOPHERS have concerned themselves with the "origin of society"; but when one comes to think of it, the origin of solitude would really be the more natural enquiry. For from first to last man is a "social animal." It is through the nurture and discipline which society furnishes; it is through the sphere of action which it provides, that he can alone develop his powers. From the moment he crosses the threshold of life he passes irrevocably under social influences.

It is man's nature to be social.

Hence psychologists have, with good reason, come to speak of "social heredity[1]." In a sense this is not heredity at all. For the phrase is not meant to suggest any direct transmission of qualities, be they natural qualities or acquired, from parent to offspring. It simply formulates the fact that, as the members of one generation after another pass away, they do not leave their successors to begin the world afresh.

Each new life enters into a social heritage. "Social heredity."

---

[1] Cf. p. 70.

Their work does not perish with them.   On the contrary it is
conserved and stored up in such modifications, small or great,
as they may have succeeded in effecting in their environment;
so that neither arts, nor institutions, nor customs and traditions,
nor language and literature, are left precisely as they found
them.   Into this ever-growing and ever-changing social heritage
each new life comes; and by it is powerfully wrought upon,
from the moment when it emerges on a world thus long and
elaborately prepared to receive it.   Doubts and perplexities
enough may arise (as we have seen) in regard to other modes
of heredity.   But analysis does not throw doubts upon this.
For the deeper analysis goes, the more convincingly does it
disclose the ways in which, through imitation and adaptation,
the growing life adjusts itself to given environment, and feeds
upon this inherited pasture.   Much that might on a first view
seem congenital, much that might too rashly be assumed to be
hereditary in the stricter sense of the word, may find a simpler
explanation in this early, penetrating, and constant action of
society.

It manifestly follows that this conception of social "heredity" tends to emphasise educational responsibility.   It gives a new depth to the conviction
(never far from the reflective observer) that boy
or girl is from earliest years profoundly modified
for good or for evil by the kind of home the parent prepares
for his family, and by the wider social conditions which the
citizen takes his share in providing for the sons and daughters
of his country.   And though of course the congenital endowment that is Nature's gift remains a fact of the first magnitude,
a grasp of what "social heredity" really means will go far to
dispel the indolent assumption, refuge of irresponsibility and
pretext for neglect, that congenital endowment, however strong,
will ever educate itself[1].   For it will reveal the extent to which,

"Social heredity" and educational responsibility.

[1] Cf. p. 35.

from birth and even before it, society intervenes, and lay bare
the fact that many a so-called "natural reaction" could only
befall a being who lives and moves and has his being in a
community. This is a truth to which the very rebels of
Society—the satirists, cynics, solitaries—cannot but choose,
even in their own despite, to bear their witness. They may
denounce society, or abjure it. But none the less they will be found, upon closer scrutiny, to owe that very moral strength and so-called independence which fits them to stand up against society, to the social influences in which they have been cradled and reared. Poets have sometimes seen in the "travelled boulders" of geology the symbols of solitariness. Yet even these will disclose to the scientific eye the tell-tale lineaments that record the days when, ice-berg borne, they tossed upon vanished seas.

Even the anti-social spirit is dependent upon social influences.

Now of course the instruments through which society
thus sets its seal upon its members are many, too many for
enumeration. They are, in truth, as many as are social
institutions, and the manifold means by which these set their
stamp upon their members. But some are salient. And of
these first in time, first also some would add in importance, is
the Family.

The Family.

We must be especially careful not to limit what the Family
gives to what is done consciously and of set purpose by the parent. There is room for this no doubt; and indeed there is so much room for it, that it has become a common-place that the education of children by parents brings, as unsought bonus, the education of parents by

The influence of the Family is wider than what is done of set purpose by the parents.

children   But the vital matter is not the home as parents
make it in seasons of edification, when their consciences are
on the alert: it is the home as it normally is in its habitual
preferences, its predominant interests, its settled estimates of
persons and pursuits, its ordinary circle of as-

For it de-
pends upon
the ideal of life
which the
home habitu-
ally exempli-
fies.

sociates, its standard of living, its accepted
ideals of work and of amusement.   For it is
not only from the family, but with the family
eyes, that we all begin to look out upon the
world.   And if this first outlook is to see the
things for which men live in something like their true perspective, and not as distorted through the deluding medium of the
home that is idle, frivolous, sordid, grasping, quarrelsome, or
sentimental, this will be due far less to what is done of express
educational design, far more to the ideal of life which the
Family consistently embodies.   For it is only thus that the
scale of moral valuation which the Family has wrought into
its life will be likely, as the years go round, to reflect itself
in the habitual feelings, estimates, and actions of its members.

    This kind of influence is moreover peculiarly effective

Ties of natu-
ral affection
prepare the
way for
influence.

because it is made easier by the tie of natural
affection.   Without this, and the trustful confidence which goes with it, comparatively little
can be done.   And many a parent in whom the
qualities which win it have been lacking, even though he may
have been masterful and reasonable, has been compelled to
realise his impotence.   Yet, normally, the parent has a manifest
advantage.   That confidence which a stranger has to gain with
difficulty, he finds either ready to hand, or at most less arduous
to win.   This is a double gain.   It prompts a spontaneous
trustfulness which opens the ways for influence, and, as lesser
adjunct, it invests a father's or a mother's disapprobation with
a power to restrain and chasten such as cannot be found when

love and trust are absent. In this the Family is pre-eminent. No teacher however kindly, no public authority however paternal and mild, can rival it here. And if this be lost, whether by aloofness of parents, or wreck of family life, or by decay of the family as an institution, one of the purest springs of moral influence will be frozen at its source.

It is a further advantage that the parent is beyond all others in a position to adapt his treatment to the individual need. For when father or mother, **Parents can, further, peculiarly adapt their treatment to the individual need.** as is their wont, think their own progeny unique, it is no good policy roughly to disillusionise them. Better admit ungrudgingly that their idols are unique; as indeed they are, in the sense that they stand in need of individual watchfulness and care. This is already recognised in matters physiological, even in the homely details of diet and hygiene. And are we to suppose that it ought to be otherwise with the promising or menacing instincts, the besetting weaknesses, the tone or the twists of temperament, even the oddities, which so manifestly diversify the children of a common home; and which cannot possibly have justice done to them when there is not the ever watchful eye, the ever helpful hand.

Hence there is never so much room for the influence of the Family as when public education is organised on a great scale, and when public authority **Hence public authority can never supersede the Family.** strives in vain to become paternal. It is an idle fear to fancy that such things can supersede the functions of the Family. Is it needful to remember how much of the concrete individuality of even the average child slips through the inevitably wide mesh of forms of organisation which must needs deal with their material roughly and in the mass? Nay, it is precisely when education is organised by public authority that there is more need than ever of a place where the individuality of the child, upon which Rousseau and

Pestalozzi and Froebel laid such passionate stress, may with the discerning eyes of anxious affection be studied, cared for, tended, restrained, developed. For the family has much to give that is not to be found elsewhere. Natural affection is not its only lever. There are common joys and common sorrows: and, as time goes on, there come the cementing memories of a common past. There is disinterested delight in the projects and the successes of kith and kin, and gratitude for benefits which leave no uneasy sense of indebtedness. Not least there is that sincere and ready recognition for which we all crave, and which we can seldom find in equal measure elsewhere.

To this we must add that these influences broaden out, like a circle in the water, far beyond the family pale. They plant the seeds of the social virtues. For it is the substantial nurture of the affections within the home that first gives its members genuinely developed affections to carry beyond it. " No cold relation is a zealous citizen," says Burke[1]. The words are perhaps too absolute. For it is one of the requirements of fact that, in any scheme of moral growth, we must find room for the exceptional type that loves kind more than kindred, even to that perilous and paradoxical extreme of "hating father and mother." Yet for Burke's aphorism and for all like sayings, there remains the substantial justification that from kin to kind is the normal path of the development of the human affections.

The Family as seed-plot of the social virtues.

It is just here, in truth, that individualistic thinkers have set themselves a problem needlessly insoluble. Victimised by the fallacies of abstraction, they have treated the individual as the social unit, and have exhausted their resources in explaining how out of self-seeking, if not mutually hostile human atoms, the strong and oftentimes self-

Individual-ism must be qualified by the fact that Family life is natural to man.

[1] Reflections on the Revolution, *Works*, vol. II. p. 320.

sacrificing social sympathies can be developed. They might have spared themselves much ingenious labour. Their social atom is an abstraction. It is the family, not the atomic individual, that is the block with which, as a matter of fact, we have to build. Those whose lot social heredity has cast in even an ordinary family will find themselves, when they come to years of reflection, already far upon the beaten track that leads to the wider social sympathies. And when we consider how early all these home influences begin, when the soul is still plastic, generous, unsuspicious; and how uninterruptedly they may continue right on through youth, it is not wonderful that the family has been regarded as, in moral education, the most indispensable of all instruments.

It cannot, however, do everything. And in particular it cannot secure for its members adequate variety of development. When the inmates of a household mix little with the world, when, for example, boys or girls do not go to school or to the University, or when they are not stimulated by variety of pursuits, we know the result. However excellent they may be, they depressingly suggest that they have been turned out according to pattern :— *Limits to the influence of the Family. It cannot secure adequate variety of development.*

> "The vicar's daughters look so good,
> We think that they are made of wood.
> Like rests for hymnbooks there they stand,
> With each a hymnbook in her hand[1]."

Is it needful to recall the familiar warning that "home-keeping youth have ever homely wits"?

The family may also easily fail in adequately enforcing discipline. It aims high : the obedience and subordination it would secure must be both prompt and willing. And

---

[1] Miss Kendall's *Dreams to Sell.*

aiming high, it often fails, sometimes in one direction, sometimes in another. Thus there is a type of
parent who knows nothing of authority but the
word, and it may be the blow, of command,
and a corresponding type of child whose attitude
is fear and resentment. Discipline suffers here
from one extreme; as in opposite cases it may suffer, or vanish,
under a foolish lenience. The latter is perhaps the commoner;
and one may venture to suspect that there are many sons and
daughters even of excellent homes who never understand the
meaning of an authority that is not to be called in question, till
they meet it, as they certainly will, in the school or in the world.

There may be a more serious failure still. For experience
too manifestly shows how readily a household,
united within its own limits, may be perverted
into an ugly monopoly, reckless, intolerant,
jealous of all beyond it, thereby admirably
blighting the growth of those wider sympathies
it ought to foster. It is so easy to condone a
collective selfishness, when every participant may claim to be,
after a fashion, zealous for others' advancement. Clearly this
is not the nursery of the public affections. Nor, unhappily, is
it possible to shut one's eyes to the pitiful fact that in every
considerable community there are families, families in name,
in which even corporate family selfishness would mean a moral
reformation. Yet even when the worst is said, the average
family is at least good enough to encourage the hope that it
can be made better, and thereby come to be, in ever fuller
measure, alike preparation and supplement to the education of
school and after life[1].

It may, also, have defects as a disciplinary authority.

It may further create a corporate selfishness fatal to the wider sympathies.

[1] If Plato is to be believed there is a kind of love, a love to kith and
kin, to which a man may compel himself, and which even the heartlessness
of parents cannot alienate. See the remarkable passage in the *Protagoras*
346 which ends, "But the good man dissembles his feelings, and constrains

The School.

Though the School, especially the preparatory school, is sometimes said to be but a larger family, this is not usually the impression conveyed to the new boy by his future playmates. It is not desirable that it should. For it is to the School we look to bring to the front an element of self-help, competition, and emulation, which the Family can but poorly provide. The illusions of innocent self-conceit, which the pardonable partialities of home so readily feed, have little mercy shown to them here. And though the rough scrambles of competition may reck little of justice or desert, they grow their own crop of hardy qualities, courage, self-reliance, respect for one's fellows, and the spirit in which to take rebuff or defeat. The one needful qualification is that the competitive spirit be not suffered to kill the motives that are more direct. In any valuation of the competitive spirit, it is imperative to bear in mind that after all there is little real connection between the desire to beat a rival and the doing of a duty. We may go further and add that not only is the competitive motive thus collateral: it has also, despite all its superficial effectiveness, a fatal weakness. For it is the direct love of the thing to be done that really wears best, because it can face the day when these collateral incitements of rivalry may be no longer forthcoming. Whereas the competitive spirit in all its forms is tainted with the blight that it stakes persistence in a given line of action upon a stimulus that is external to the end of the

The School as sphere for growth of self-reliance and self-help.

The competitive spirit: its value and weakness.

himself to praise them; and if they have wronged him and he is angry, he pacifies his anger and is reconciled, and compels himself to love and praise his own flesh and blood." (Jowett's trans.)

action itself. This however is but a qualification. It leaves untouched the fact that, in a society like our own, industrial and commercial to the core, the competitive spirit will have heavy drafts made upon it in after life. And, this being so, we can ill afford to suppress, even were this in our power, these strenuous rivalries of schoolroom and playground.

It is a further advantage of the School that, as soon as they cross its threshold, our small men begin to pass under the heavy yoke of Public Opinion. This the Family cannot supply. For effective public opinion there must obviously be an effective public; and as everyone knows, this is not long of constituting itself in any considerable school.

School also furnishes the first experiences of public opinion and the reality of the social judgment.

There are all the needful elements: the unwritten traditional code with its unwritten enactments as to cowardice, tale-bearing, sneaking, lying, "good form," or as to the points wherein authority is to be respected and the points wherein it is to be outwitted. And behind the code there are its "sanctions," in whose enforcement this little republic knows nothing of the hesitancies and compunctions which sometimes impede the administration of the larger and more responsible justice. Hence it comes that even those who may learn little else will not fail to learn at school the reality of the social judgment.

Here too are the beginnings of the great twin forces of comradeship and leadership. This one stands out and leads. By native gift, by experimented prowess, he is the intrepid and resourceful initiator and organiser of projects, pastimes, mischiefs; and the lesser rank and file, in instinctive "hero-worship," fall into line and follow with the loyalty to which it is a point of honour to stick to comrades through thick and thin. Need it be added that in most schools there is the further hero-worship, verging upon apotheosis, of the master. For though it is a common experience that it is only in the

It likewise develops the twin influences of Comradeship and Leadership.

retrospects of later days that we come to do justice to what our schoolmasters have done for us, we do not wait till then to clothe them in attributes, sometimes mythical, sometimes happily not mythical, in which boyish enthusiasms insist upon finding the ideal objects of their generous admirations.

Here indeed enters one of those responsibilities of the schoolmaster which is not to be evaded. For though one may hope that there are few teachers of youth who self-consciously erect themselves into examples, this cannot alter the fact that as examples they will certainly be regarded. Not perhaps because of what they say, or even what they do, when the eyes of their youthful constituents are upon them in official hours and duties, but because of what they really care for in their habitual walk and conversation. It is their valuations, even when they remain unspoken, that tell; and they tell with a contagious and penetrating force. There is no escaping this, and if anyone doubts it, we need only refer him to Socrates, who of all men strive to teach as one *not* having authority and succeeded thereby, against his will, in exalting himself all the more in the eyes of disciples who vied with one another in walking in the Socratic way of life. The work of the teacher, it has been said, is only scaffolding. It is not his prime concern to be a paragon, or to hypnotise his charges into a blind following of his example, but to prepare them for the coming of the day when he has to stand aside, and they have, intellectually and morally, to stand or fall in their own strength. In this sense he works for his own self-effacement. But it does not follow that he can therefore efface himself from the first. He cannot. And if he tries, it will only be to make the discovery, later or sooner, that all the instincts of youthful imitation and the ineradicable principle of example are fighting on the other side [1].

> The peculiar moral responsibilities of teachers.

[1] The late Professor Laurie, who knew the teacher well, does not

Beyond all this there are certain quite specific points where the school can act with peculiar effectiveness. It is a kind of revelation of the importance of punctuality and order, of the meaning and value of organisation, of the existence of an authority which, though it does not rest upon compulsion, will not hesitate to compel, and of the fact, which dawns somewhat gradually upon the youthful mind, that work, even when uncongenial, is a thing to be expected and exacted of the sons of men.

Further lessons which the School can enforce.

We might raise a further question here. Everyone is agreed that the school ought to teach virtue: not everyone as to the extent to which it ought to teach about virtue. For of course morality is one thing—a thing of trained instincts, good habits, right feelings, clear and upright purposes, sound judgment: instruction in morality is quite another. And it must needs be a problem how far in a school it is profitable to enter upon the latter. This however is a question which may perhaps be left to answer itself when we have discussed in the sequel the educative value of Precept[1].

The question:—how far the School ought to teach about virtue?

Friendship.

When we pass to the influence of friendship, we are at once met by the difficulty that the friendships which are ethically of most importance are precisely those that are least within control. Of all human relationships this is perhaps the one which most

Friendship resists dictation.

hesitate to lay upon him the formidable responsibility of being the incarnation of Moral Law. Cf. *Institutes of Education.*

[1] Cf. pp. 183, 207, 221. The value of School for discipline of character is well discussed by Mr Barnett in his *Common Sense in Education*, c. ii.

jealously resists dictation. For the tie cannot be made: it must grow. Phase must have time to follow phase, as acquaintanceship becomes interest; interest, liking; liking, settled attachment.

Some encouragement may however be drawn from the fact that friendships spring up upon grounds that are so many and so diverse. This one makes a friend to be a hero-worshipper: that one, to have a hero-worshipper. With another pair the bond may be a common past, that "first secret of happy association," and one that often strangely holds together in later years those who have ceased to have much else in common. With others still the initial tie may be simple companionship in some common cause, project, adventure, taste, study, or sport.

It is these last that offer possibilities for guidance. For though a parent may discreetly put far from him the very semblance of dictation, he need by no means remain passive and powerless.

Guidance in formation of friendships.

He can at very least strive to plan the family life so that his children may avoid alike that undiscriminating companionship which exposes the friendly instincts of the young to too great risk of misplaced choice, and that seclusion of life which is apt to leave these instincts perilously undiscriminating by denying them sufficient variety to choose from. He can do more still by the steady encouragement of all sound tastes and recreations in which friendly association is possible. These, it may be granted, will be but a partial security. They will certainly be no panacea against friendships that are foolish and ill-assorted. And indeed one of the lessons that parents have to learn from children is a wise toleration of the undiscriminating attachments and odd hero-worships through which all sociable young souls have to pass. But if these friendships of whim and caprice are duly to be checked, it will not be by wise saws and warning injunctions upon the need of carefulness in forming friends. Better than all such is a single strong and wholesome interest, be it literary, artistic, or practical, round which, as a rallying point for kindred spirits, companions may meet and learn the secret of comradeship.

It is needless, in presence of the many truisms about friendship, to dilate upon what our friends can do for us. It is abundantly recognised that they are the confidants who save us from becoming, in Bacon's somewhat violent metaphor, "the cannibals of our own hearts[1]": that they are the partners and counsellors of our perplexities and deliberations, from whom we can bear to hear (though perhaps not too often or at too great length) of our faults and foibles; that they are the comrades whose tried and welcome presence in all enterprises, from boyish adventure to service of Church or State, not only divides our difficulties and cares, but often comes near to dispelling them together. And though Aristotle does well to warn us that absence dissolves friendship, it is happily none the less true that friend may powerfully influence friend though the two be by no means constant associates. Even far removal in place, or in occupation, or in fortunes, cannot arrest influence. For once any man has true friends, he never again frames his decisions, even those that are most secret, as if he were alone in the world. He frames them habitually in the imagined company of his friends. In their visionary presence he thinks and acts; and by them, as visionary tribunal, he feels himself, even in his unspoken intentions and inmost feelings, to be judged. In this aspect friendship may become a supreme force both to encourage and restrain. For it is not simply what our friends expect of us that is the vital matter here. They are often more tolerant of our failings

(marginal note: What friend can do for friend.)

----

[1] Essay on *Friendship.*

than is perhaps good for us. It is what in our best moments we believe that they expect of us. For it is then that they become to us, not of their own choice but of ours, a kind of second conscience, in whose presence our weaknesses and backslidings become "that worst kind of sacrilege that tears down the invisible altar of trust[1]."

Nor may it be forgotten that friendship is one of the ways by which we may pass out from the private to the public affections. It shews how strong may be the ties that grapple us to those to whom we are bound neither by kinship nor early association. For good friends are not good haters, except in the sense that they are capable of hatreds to which the cold-blooded and the unsociable are strangers. Their sympathies are not a fixed quantity that exhausts itself within their own small circle. Contrariwise. For in all hearts with any generous instincts, friendship warms and quickens the more distant relationships, and checks the cynicism that corrodes the wider ties. Not that it is impossible for the civic tie to be weak or even non-existent where the friendly bond is strong. The Epicurean brotherhood of the ancient world is an instance for all time how friends, associated on the basis of philosophic or other culture, may sit loose to the wider practical interests without seeming to miss their absence. But it is precisely upon this point that they, and all who in the larger or the lesser scale follow in their path, lie open to criticism. For it is not the highest tribute to our friends to remember with gratitude how security in their affection and respect can fortify us against the indifference of the world, or strengthen us in our indifference to it. The greater service is that by their comradeship, and by what they expect of us, they render us the more capable of wider civic interests which

Friendship and the public affections.

Comradeship and citizenship.

[1] George Eliot in *Middlemarch.*

8—2

private friendships can never satisfy. For if the citizen of a free state is to act with effect he must act in association; and it is not to be supposed that any form of association for public ends, from the village club to the political party, can afford to rest upon nothing more than agreement of opinion and community of interest. If it is to stand against attack, dissension, discouragement and failure, it must count upon that tenacious loyalty of comrade to comrade, which seldom ripens except when friendship has sown the seed.

CHAPTER VI.

LIVELIHOOD.

BOYS leave school to enter upon the longer education of later years, and this begins for most, and ends for many, in the pursuit of livelihood. "When a man has a competency," so runs the maxim of a Greek poet, "he ought to begin the practice of virtue"—"Perhaps sooner" is the dry comment of Plato[1]. And in an industrial and commercial nation like England, the comment is truer than the maxim. For of course it is in the pursuit of competency that we both develop virtues and realise the need of them.

Pursuit of Livelihood brings us into practical relations with our country's industrial and commercial organisation.

The central fact that concerns us here is that when a youth begins to earn his living he comes for the first time into direct relation to the industrial organisation of his country, and passes under the iron yoke of that Law of Division of Labour, before which, in a nation of workers, the vast majority of us must bow, or starve. And the question that must be faced is the natural one as to whether this organisation can be regarded and welcomed as a satisfactory school of virtue.

Now of course the Division of Labour has abundant economic justification. It is the recognised condition of all efficient material production. It is thereby the accepted means for providing the economic basis upon which a nation's moral and spiritual life is built. And it is further one of the prime causes of national unity, inasmuch as, in the very fact of dividing work, it knits the workers together in the strong bonds of mutual dependence and helpfulness. All this is

Though this organisation has its justifications,

[1] Cf. *Republic*, III. 407 A.

indubitable. It is when we turn to ethical considerations that there comes a doubt. For when we scrutinise the motives in which this Division of Labour, this organism of Livelihood, has had its origin, nothing can be clearer than the fact that, so

yet it has not been devised in the interests of the moral development of individuals.
far as human design is concerned, it has not been devised in the interests of moral development. It has taken shape for far other, and for lower ends. It is simply a contrivance, marvellously evolved in the long course of national growth, for the adequate satisfaction of material needs, or, as in the higher forms of specialisation, for the effective transaction of the national business in all its infinitely ramified detail. So much so that it has become a truism to say that it recks little of the individual life, and indeed that it advances upon its ends over the sacrifice of the workers in all modes whom it enslaves to its tasks. "Mental mutilation" are the sufficiently emphatic words of Adam Smith in forecasting the baneful

And the specialisation it demands seems hostile to moral growth, because it treats men as means not as ends.
intellectual effects of industrial specialisation[1]. Can we escape the fear that there will be moral mutilation also, when the one condition upon which a man can earn his living is that the best hours of his day, the best years of his life, are perforce given to some specialised task-work, meagre out of all proportion to his potentialities as a moral being? It is not wonderful therefore that the imperious necessities of livelihood should as a matter of fact come to many, not cheerfully as the path to development, but unwelcomely as the cost, sometimes bitter to think upon, at which the opportunities for development are dearly purchased.

The force of this is undeniable. This iron law of specialisation turns men into means for the realisation of ends, especially of industrial ends, which are not, in design and inception, moral. And in a society like our own, where the

[1] *Wealth of Nations*, Bk. v. c. i. p. 365, Rogers' ed.

struggle for livelihood is intense, it follows of necessity that the more purely moral ends are again and again, now by the exigencies of material production, now by the urgencies of other social work, deposed from that preeminence which they would never lose were the social organism planned, maintained, and developed in the interests of the moral life of its members. Social reformers, stung by this fact, plan and work for a better time, and they may perhaps reasonably hope for the dawning of a day when Division of Labour will exact a less merciless tribute. But as social organisation is, and as it seems likely long to continue, there remains a sharp contradiction between the paltriness of the specialised vocation that is the path to livelihood, and the breadth of moral development of which the average man is capable. The compulsory activities of bread-winning, in short, appear, and are often felt to be, very far from an ideal school of character.

Yet happily this picture has another side. At very least, the Division of Labour is a condition under which we can effectively get to work. It enables us to act; and as our wisest from Aristotle onwards have taught, it is in and through action, and not by hopes, wishes, or barren projects, that character is made. It is something more

Division of Labour, however, in certain aspects is a condition of moral development.

that whatever makes for the unity of society must needs have far-reaching ethical results. This is what Division of Labour admittedly does. It may be a rough and unkindly teacher, but the lesson is learnt. For through it, we first come to realise that, with our consent or without it, we must needs stand to our fellows in relations of mutual dependence. As Adam Smith has it : " while our whole life is scarce sufficient to gain the friendship of a few persons, man stands at all times in need of the co-operation and assistance of great multitudes "[1]. It is not of this that men will think first of all when they begin to earn their bread. They will think first of all, and no one

[1] *Wealth of Nations*, Bk. I. c. ii.

will blame them for it, of day and way for themselves and for those who are dependent on them. Yet there is nothing to prevent even the drudge, if only he can summon enough philosophy to his aid, from reflecting that, even when he is fighting simply for honest independence, he is as matter of fact fulfilling a social function of the first magnitude—none other than that of taking his place in the ranks of industry in conserving and increasing those national resources which, but for Division of Labour, would speedily perish before the unresting forces of Consumption[1].

It is more important still to remember that it is in the school of compulsory labour, and nowhere else, that the most of us come effectually to know the stern, but never really hostile, face of Obligation; as the idler, who being "his own master" is seldom his own task-master, can never really know it. We are apt to fall into illusion here. We sometimes picture the youth going forth into life with all the world before him. And it is true, especially in these days when Status[2] has all along the line been giving ground before Choice, that he has a freedom of choice of which his forefathers could not have dreamed. Cannot even the humblest, in an age of democratic freedom, choose his vocation, his place of abode, his master, his friends, his rulers, his church? And yet, when all is said, this "choice" is on a closer view narrowly conditioned. It is limited by parental ignorance or apathy, by inherited rank and station, by want of education, by lack of opportunity, by accident, by a hundred causes not really within the individual's own control. And even where it is comparatively free, the chooser, once the die is cast,

Compulsory work as a school of moral Obligation.

Are we free to choose our career?

---

[1] The phrase "accumulation of wealth" is apt to conceal the extent to which wealth is undergoing perpetual reproduction at the hands of industry and enterprise.

[2] "Status" is that condition of Society in which a man's career is determined for him by the social system into which he is born.

speedily finds himself in the grasp of the Division of Labour, which forbids to most a second choice on penalty of ineffectuality and failure. For there remains perennial truth in that noble image of Plato[1]. Behind the Fates that spin the destinies of men sits the august figure of Necessity. Upon her knees the spindle turns. And he who would fitly act his part must give up the illusion that he can spin his destiny just as it may chance to please him. Even under a social system more ideal far than that we live in, it must remain but one part of duty that consists in the exercise of "free choice," because the other part must lie in the acceptance of inexorable limitations.

Rightly regarded this need be no evil. Practical compulsion to work within limits neither of our making nor of our unmaking, need not by any means be bondage. For moral bondage is to be discriminated from moral freedom, not by the presence or absence of limitations, but by finding an answer to two questions:—the *first*, what in origin and nature are the limitations thus inevitable; the *second*, what manner of life within these remains possible for the average man.

It is the nature of the limitations under which we work that determines whether we be morally free or not.

On the first of these questions it is not possible, in a practical enquiry like this, to dwell. It would manifestly lead too far into social and even metaphysical analysis. It has been already remarked that there are certain ethical, as well as economic, justifications for the organism of Livelihood with its supreme law of Division of Labour. And to this we may add the suggestion that, though this organism has certainly not been deliberately devised as a school of virtue, it may nevertheless, in the large scheme of social evolution, be more in harmony with moral progress than might at first sight appear. The ends which industrial and

Though not devised as a school of virtue, the economic organism may subserve moral ends.

[1] *Republic*, Bk. x. pp. 616—17.

commercial institutions subserve are never to be circumscribed by the range of motive that called them into being.

It must, however, here suffice to turn to the second point, with the reminder that it is very easy, in impatience with the thraldom of specialisation, to forget the real worth and fulness of the moral life which even drudgery cannot preclude. There is a passage in which Carlyle tells us that Madame de Stael found that the place of all places ever known to her she had enjoyed the most freedom in was the Bastille[1]. We need not press this rhetoric to definition. It will serve at any rate to carry two matters of fact which are as nearly incontrovertible as may be. One is that, even in the obscure service of men and organisations who may reck little of the individual moral development of their servants, there are large opportunities for the realisation of all the cardinal virtues of the life of livelihood. Is there not room for independence, integrity, thrift, endurance, generosity? If we deplore the usurpation of livelihood upon life, it is well to remember that livelihood has its own strong virtues, second to none. The other fact is that whatever we may think of our limits, it is by the kind of life that is within them possible that we can best judge how far they present a real, or only an apparent, obstacle to the growth of character. Madame de Stael appears to have found "liberty" in the Bastille. Be this fact or figure, it remains certain that as often as we see a character that has come out victorious in this so common, yet so sifting, struggle for livelihood, the attitude that least befits us in its presence is patronage or commiseration. We may wish, for this is natural, that the sphere of action had been less obstructed, and we may

And even under adverse conditions pursuit of Livelihood may yield an enviable moral development.

---

[1] Letters to Lockhart, *Lockhart's Life*, vol. II. p. 237 : "Servitude is a blessing and a great liberty, the greatest can be given a man. So the shrewd little de Stael, on reconsidering and computing it, found that the place of all places, etc."

wonder what such strength of character might have done and been under more favouring circumstance. Yet the result is there, intrinsically valuable, and a living proof that even narrow limitations may be no moral disability, if indeed, as the Stoics and as even the practical Aristotle taught, they be not the opportunities for a higher achievement.

If such results are within the resources of human nature where limitations are peculiarly grinding and obstructive, *a fortiori* we may believe them possible of the average lot. Be the defects of Society as a school of virtue what they may, it can hardly be denied, in the light of what many a man has actually done, that human nature is strong enough to turn to moral account social conditions which may still be far short of the ideal. It is fortunate that our characters have not to wait for their development till economic or political reformers have transmuted society into a perfect school of virtue.

Moral advance may vance may thus be independent of economic reform.

It is however time to recall the fact that, though it is in the pursuit of Livelihood that the vast majority mainly make or mar their characters, this is not the only sphere available. There are in especial two other resources, each of them abundantly fruitful. The one of them is that active participation in the life of citizenship which Democracy practically puts within the reach of all; the other, membership of one or other of those religious societies, which have always made it their peculiar glory that even the most obscure and obstructed of mortals can find within them a deeper and more satisfying life than any secular activities can even at their best afford.

The more so because Citizenship and the Religious life open up further spheres.

CHAPTER VII.

CITIZENSHIP.

When we pass from the life of Livelihood to the activities of Citizenship, there is of course a difference. The latter, with few exceptions (the payment of Rates and Taxes for example), are neither compulsory nor indispensable. Even under Democracy, as before its advent, many a man has realised a sterling character without lifting his eyes beyond the ordinary charities of home, neighbourhood and craft. Yet it is one of the good things of days democratic that they open up a sphere for the manly and man-making duties of local and imperial citizenship.

Democratic citizenship enlarges the sphere of duty.

This tells in more ways than one. As one result, it makes the preparation of the citizen for his duties a necessity. In part this is a preparation in knowledge, some knowledge at least of his country's history and laws, its political institutions and economic system. And the need for this will be intensified should the days come—as the socialists assure us they are coming—when self-government in industry and commerce will be added to self-government in politics. For then will arise the demand not only for educated workmen, but, far beyond present supply, for enlightened leaders of workmen. Thus much we must look for, if government by democracy is not to end ignobly in the fiascoes of mis-government by ignorance.

And thereby necessitates the preparation of the citizen for his duties.

But it is more urgent still that there should be preparation in morality. Knowledge alone, even if popularised to infinity, will not suffice here. It must strike alliance with

those qualities of character without which it may be heedless
or reckless of the common good.   Hence it is
that Democracy adds a new ethical, as well as   Preparation
political, significance to the home, the school,   of paramount
the industrial organisation, the religious society.   importance.
For it is to these it must look for the nurture of its
citizens to be, so that to knowledge they may add love of
country, and to love of country active public spirit, and to
public spirit loyalty to comrades and leaders, and to loyalty
the integrity that abhors corruption.   Telling may do something here : for the family, still more the school, may tell of
the national examples of heroism and devotion, and of the
moving struggles and victories of war and peace that are a
country's heritage ; or they may throw the enkindling lights
of legend and romance upon historic cities, memorable battlefields, mouldering keeps, or storied countrysides.   But telling
is here the lesser part, and Family and School best serve the
State in laying securely the foundations of the energetic, law-
abiding, and devoted character.

Yet all this is but the beginning.   For the fuller growth
of the political virtues we must look to political
life itself.   We stumble here upon the old   Yet it is
discovery.   It is by doing craftsman's work   active citizen-
that men learn to become craftsmen, and it is   alone develop
by active citizenship that they learn truly to   the political
be citizens.   There is no other way.   Hence indeed the
unreason of the contention that no man is entitled to the
enjoyment of political rights, till he is proved fit to exercise
them.   It is an impossible requirement.   Before he has political rights, no man's fitness for them can be proved.
Because, though there are of course various tests, educational
or economic, which may be accepted as securities, there is
but one genuine *proof* of fitness—the experimental proof that
shows how men use their rights after they have got them.
Manifestly there is room enough here for political risk : it

must be so if it be the behaviour of the citizen after enfranchisement, and not the arguments of his friends before it,
that is the final justification of the step taken. And it is
for the political reformer and statesman to set this risk against
the probabilities of advantage. Meanwhile however the moral
reformer may be permitted the reflection that, even if the
raw recruit of Democracy is not likely to be wholly a benefactor to his country at the polling-booth, he can always, if

he be honest, be a benefactor to himself. He
**The ethical
argument for
a wide
franchise.**
can gain indubitably in widened and impersonal
interests, such as the narrow and monotonous
round of private duties can never give ; and he
can seize the opportunity for developing the political virtues,
which are made not otherwise than by strenuous participation
in actual political life. This is the ethical argument for a
wide franchise. It must not of course be pressed too far ;
and manifestly no one who loves his country need consent
to turn it into a whetstone upon which, at possibly ruinous
political sacrifices, incapacity may blunder into a modicum
of political virtue. Yet it is, *per contra*, well to remember
that, after all, our country does not exist simply to furnish
forth a model of political perfection, unless indeed, with Plato
and Aristotle to help us, we construe political perfection as including in it, as main element, the fullest development of the men
and women who in organic union ultimately *are* the State.

This—is it needful to say it ?—does not mean that men
are drawn to civic life by the motive of im-
**The moral
results are
none the less
valuable be-
cause not di-
rectly sought.**
proving their moral characters. Happily not.
They of course vote, canvas, organise, agitate
and so on, for much less lofty reasons—because
they like it, or because the civic impulse is upon
them, or because they do not wish to be beaten by the other
side, or governed by men worse than themselves, perhaps for
no other higher reason than that they cannot be idle when
excitement is in the air. None the less, by the exceeding

cunning of the national Destiny, they usually gain far more
than they consciously seek; inasmuch as, day by day, while
thinking only of politics and parties, committees or election
speeches, they may unconsciously be forming the political
virtues.

It is an inevitably precarious discipline. Where party
organisation is strong and party feeling runs
high, it is the condition of all effective action
that the partisan should develop that loyalty
which can endure much self-suppression in lesser
things for the sake of the larger common ends.
Yet this must be united with the nerve to break
with party and cast party allegiance to the winds, in obedience
to the leading of a patriotism wider than party. Is it not
of the very elements of politics, that the consistency that
clings to party as the effective instrument for the enactment
of political convictions, must reckon with that higher consistency, which welcomes light even from political opponents,
and is ready to face the fact that even a cherished party may
cease to furnish the fittest expression of political convictions?
So, again, where power rests with the majority.
It is much to learn to defer to majorities, it is
an essential lesson in a democratic state; but it
is even more to preserve inviolate that freedom of individual
judgment which, if need be, will withstand the majority to
the face, in the conviction that, in the absence of this, the
verdict of majorities will lose all its value, and degenerate
into verdict by count of worthless heads. It is the very
last tribute to offer to a majority to bow before it as a fate,
and to forget that it is fallible[1]. Nor need it be forgotten
that the sphere for the political virtues may, especially when
School and Family fail to do their duty, become the sphere
for the political vices. For obviously a wide
franchise offers enlarged area for charlatanry in
the leader, and gullibility, possibly corruption, in those who

*The life of
citizenship
has, however,
its peculiar
dangers to
morality, such
as servility to
Party,*

*or subser-
viency to
majorities,*

or corruption,

[1] Cf. *Ethics of Citizenship*, p. 74, 4th ed.

follow. And far short of this, political life, not being organised
primarily for moral ends, may easily beget a
certain energetic secularity of spirit, and a hard-
ness and unscrupulosity which blunt the edge
of honour, habituate the mind to compromise and trickery,
and forget the more distant ends in the short-lived triumphs
of faction.

or secularity
of spirit.

It therefore needs its counteractives. And these are found,
in part at least, in the early nurture of Family
and School. But they may also be sought in
what may become the most powerful of all—
in the religious organisation.

It therefore
needs coun-
teractives.

CHAPTER VIII.

THE RELIGIOUS ORGANISATION.

THE religious organisation is not on the same plane as
other moralising agencies. It claims, not to be
simply one agency among many, but pervasively
to influence all the rest. Amidst all the differences, which fulness of life and of strife
have developed, the smallest sect is, in this claim, at one
with the most universal Church. The claim is not pretentious. For in truth the kind of influence which even the
humblest of religious organisations must, if it be not a failure,
exercise, is such that it cannot be experienced without profoundly affecting every relation, private and public, in which
its members have to play their part.

The Re-
ligious Organi-
sation claims
to leaven the
whole of life.

For in all ages religious organisations have striven, and
if they be alive must ever strive, to bring their members into
personal relation to a larger and more enduring life.   The fact

lies on the surface. The mere outward aspect of some
religious house may suggest it—a grey cathedral   It does this
—a country church caught sight of as we rush   by bringing its
past on the railway—a poor village chapel. In   personal re-
any one of them, the meditative eye can see a   lation to a
   larger and
symbol, homely or august, of that persistent   more enduring
aspiration to grapple human life to what is   life.
eternal, without which, as one of our wisest has said, "no
one generation could link with the other, and men become
little better than the flies of a summer."[1] Emerson has told
us how, on that memorable visit to Carlyle in the Dumfries-
shire moors, the conversation turned upon "the subtle links
that bind ages together, and how every event affects all the
future." Carlyle pointed to distant Dunscore village, as it
lay a tiny speck in a wilderness of moorland:—"Christ died
on the tree: that built Dunscore kirk yonder: that brought
you and me together: time has only a relative existence."[2]
If such thoughts be stirred by the mere shell and symbol,
are they not likely to come, with more penetrating force, from
a genuine personal contact with the inward spiritual life of
a Church? Channels are not lacking, rites, liturgies, sacred
song, preaching, teaching, union in practical work. And indeed it is the simple fact that in these time-honoured ways—
whatever be the scepticisms of the reading and the thinking
world—men have for generations come to feel as if they had
passed into the presence of realities in comparison with which
"the things of Time have only a relative existence."

It is here in fact that religious organisations can bring to
the most unlettered of men the very message   The Re-
which philosophy has striven to offer to the   ligious Organisation can thus
thinking world. "Do you think," asks Plato,   do for the
"that man and all his ways will appear a great   many what
   Philosophy
thing to him who has become the spectator of   can do for
   the few.

[1] Burke, *Thoughts on the French Revolution.* Works, vol. II. p. 367.
[2] Froude's *Life of Carlyle*, vol. II. p. 358.

M.   9

all time and all existence?"[1]   And is it not the central doctrine of Spinoza that, to him who has once learnt to look on
existence "sub quâdam specie aeternitatis" the world, and
the worldly cares and ambitions that bulk so largely, will
shrink to their proper significance—or insignificance.   A
similar result may be wrought upon those who are far enough
from philosophy by all genuine religious experience.   Whatever else this may do, or fail to do, it must needs bring into
changeful human life a background, which will profoundly
alter its spiritual perspective and its estimates of value.

Hence it is that religious organisations can do so much to
bring their members to live for distant and

*It can, fur-
ther, bring its
members to
live for distant
and unseen
ends.*

unseen ends.   All great organisations can do
this.   They have an intersecular life and conti-
nuity, to which the short individual span can
lay no claim; and they point, with all the faith
of persistent practical effort, to far-off results of corporate
action, with the thought of which the individual, though he
knows he will not live to see the day, can forget his nothingness, chasten his impatience, repress his despondencies, steady
his energies, and feed his hopes.   But there are reasons why
a Church can do this best of all.   Like the others, it offers
even to the weakest, membership of a larger whole; like the
others, it speaks through deeds as well as words of distant
ends; like the others, it brings to bear the great twin forces
of comradeship and leadership.   But, beyond the others, it
takes the more spiritual ends for its peculiar province.   It
does this manifestly when it stands witness for a Future Life.
And whatever speculative difficulties beset this conviction,
there can be little doubt that its acceptance has made the
world a different place for millions.   But this is not the only
way.   Perhaps it is even more important that the religious

---

[1] *Republic*, Bk. VI. p. 486.   "Then how can he who has magnificence of
mind and is the spectator of all time and all existence, think much of
human life?"

life, here already in the world of all of us, and apart from the special faith in immortality, has found an antidote against two dangers, perennial in human
life, but especially menacing in a society like
our own.   One is the danger that the indi-

In rendering
this service,
it counteracts
two dangers.

vidual may be crushed under the sense of his personal insig-
nificance or even nothingness: the other, the snare of every great commercial and industrial country, that he may forget or deny the existence of immaterial ends at all, not from the temptation to plunge into license but from absorption in that "virtuous materialism" which is even more deadly[1].

But it is just in presence of these two dangers that a Church finds its opportunity.   To the despondencies of the first, it offers participation in a
corporate life dedicated to noble ends, which
are distant only in the sense that men will be
living for them when centuries are gone as they
are living for them here and now.   And to the
comfortable or gross materialism of the second

For it can
deliver the
individual
(1) from the de-
spondencies of
felt insignifi-
cance; and (2)
from ma-
terialism.

it offers the better way of a more spiritual life.   Churches may
differ. as to what materialism is : they may differ as to the means of counteracting it, from the hair shirt and the scourge, from fast and penance, to the policy of spiritualising the comfortable home and the cheerful intercourse of social life. But they are at one in unslackening hostility to gross pleasures, absorption in creature comforts, and the slow sap of a luxurious and frivolous life.

It goes closely with this that Churches have ever been
among the great quickeners of moral responsibility.   They have worked by many instruments, by vows and penances, by ecclesiastical
discipline and censure, by severance from the
congregation, by keeping of the conscience, by

Church
membership
can also do
much to
quicken indi-
vidual respon-
sibility.

[1] De Tocqueville regards this as the real danger of democratic societies.
Cf. *Democracy in America*, Part II. Bk. II. ch. xi.

consecrating the virtue of obedience, by insistence on the direct accountability of the soul to God.   But all have worked to one end, as bearing witness to the reality of supreme laws of life which must, on penalties, be obeyed.   And all have striven to touch the heart with that moral emotion, be it reverence for authority, fear of sin, or love of God, without which no law, however august, will ever move the will to action.   We may not say that it is only the *religious* organisation that can do this.   The Family begins it; the School plays its part; the discipline of practical life adds its contribution.   But it has always been a task for which a Church has great opportunities; not so much because of its ethical teaching (though this of course is one of its functions), but rather because of the constant pressure it brings to bear upon the conscience throughout the years, and not least at those seasons when the years inevitably bring man face to face with trial, suffering, bereavement and death.

Nor would it be just to place the ethical *teaching* of a religious organisation on just the same level as that of the mere moralist, however earnest.   Being a practical even more than a didactic institution, a Church is bound to illustrate and to commend its precepts by its deeds.   And it is here, one may suspect, that there is more room in our own day than ever for that time-honoured insistence upon the worth and the possibilities of the individual soul which it has been the peculiar glory of Christianity to proclaim. For in the wider outlook of our day upon Nature and life, it is only too easy to come to think that the individual life is worthless.   What is it in comparison with the teeming life of perished generations?   What is it in its insignificance as against the thought of nothing wider than the massed population of a great empire?   No thought is more paralysing than this.   It cuts the very nerve, not only of moral but of educational and social effort. For though those who work for moral and social ends need

It is an additional advantage that the ethical teaching of a Church is not divorced from practical effort.

not be men of many dogmas; there is one article of the faith from which they may not part,—this conviction of the worth and possibilities of those they work for. It would be rash to assert that this conviction could not survive the downfall of Churches. On that we need not speculate. The fact remains that no influence has probably done more hitherto to keep it alive than the message of Christianity, repeated from age to age, that the most flickering, obscure, and even degraded life has worth in the eyes of God.

It remains to add in conclusion that a Church, even when it does not aspire to a casuistical keeping of the conscience, can always, if it be genuinely efficient, do something in opening up channels of social work. When the instinct of social helpfulness asserts itself, it is not good economy that the young should be left to strike out paths for themselves. Better that an organisation should find work for them by discovering the best use for the gifts and aptitudes of its members. Yet one may doubt if it is more than a subordinate part of a religious body's work to find a sphere of action for its members. Its main task is rather to create the spirit in which the work of the world, sometimes called secular, ought to be done. So that thereby the rendering unto Caesar of the things that are Caesar's may become, not the false antithesis, but the true result, of rendering unto God the things that are God's.

[Margin note:] Though the Religious Organisation may open up channels of work for its members, its main concern is with the spirit in which work ought to be done.

CHAPTER IX.

SOCIAL INFLUENCES AND UNITY OF CHARACTER.

WHEN, in later years, a man reviews what Society has done for his character, he will be fortunate beyond most if two convictions be not forced upon him. One is that of all those instruments, through which Society has been making him its own, there is not one but might have been better. And though reverence, and loyalty to his home, his school, his church, as well as an inward voice that tells him he is far from having made the most of these such as they are, may keep him silent, none of these things need hide from him the fact that home, school, and church have had their shortcomings. He is still less likely to think his ordinary working life, or his public life have been a perfect school of character. For this indeed they do not claim to be.

The education of social institutions has two main defects: (1) the institutions are severally imperfect;

The second conviction will probably be that the course of his moral education, even though it may have given him many a quality for which he is thankful, has been beyond denial fragmentary. Something, he knows, has come to him from one influence, something from another, as Family gave place to School, and School to the varied influences of later years; and the virtues thus derived will no doubt have grown together into some kind of organic unity, psychological if not ethical. But there will also be other memories—memories of shocks and disillusionings as he passed from the quiet haven of home to school, and, again, from school to workshop or office. He will be aware, too (for which of us is not?), of incongruities, shall we say of contradictions, between the requirements of the

and (2) the character they produce is fragmentary,

and sometimes inconsistent.

Church and of the world. And though it would be niggardly to grudge to a rational being a natural aspiration after consistency, this will hardly hide from him the fact that he is not the same man in one sphere of action as he is in another, not the same in his moral standards, and it may be very far from the same in his moral practice.

Something of this he may dismiss as incidental to moral development. For it may be accepted that few can pass from the narrower to the wider experiences without discoveries and disillusionings[1]. But much will remain to suggest that Society is out of joint and inconsistent with itself; and that the successive beneficent influences which have done so much to make the good son, schoolboy, craftsman, citizen, have not been working up to a common plan, or aiming steadily at that unity and consistency which are inseparable from the character of the good man.

This is because social institutions are not permeated by a recognised common ideal.

It is not to be denied that, in the experience of most, this is the actual result. When we say, and say truly, that society moulds our characters, we must not fall into the fallacy that lurks under the general term. We must not ascribe to society, even though we call it organism, a greater ethical unity than it actually possesses. The fact remains that within society we have many masters. Some, like family or church, make moral character their prime concern. Others, like the workshop, the counting-house, or the political party, may hardly think of moral character at all. Is it wonderful then that the resulting product is not all of a piece, and, to speak the truth, often grievously lacking in that well-compacted harmony and proportion which is one of the touchstones by which we discriminate the man of character from the man of qualities?

The social organism lacks ethical unity.

[1] Cf. p. 226.

And yet, in moral education, there is no distinction more vital than this. Moral education must not be content to aim at the development of qualities, however shining and effective. It must estimate consistency of life above this or that quality, and thereby take some security against the production of the type of man in whom what at least appear to be sterling virtues in one sphere sadly lack their counterparts in another, if indeed they do not give place to positive vices. It must unify the life as well as enrich it.

It is of more importance to produce a mán of character than a man of qualities.

This does not mean that we can expect even the best among us to be equally strong in all the virtues. On the contrary, men will differ endlessly here, according to their native aptitudes and according to their vocation and opportunities. The important matter is that each man, in whatever spheres he may have to play his part, should carry into these the same principle and standard. Yet this is precisely the result that is *not* likely, so long as the great moralising social influences which we have been discussing work in, at any rate, partial independence of each other, and not under the unifying influence of one all-dominating moral plan and purpose.

This being so, we come in sight of two conclusions. One, that the moral training which any actual society is likely to give, stands manifestly in need of supplementing ; the other, that, whatever form this supplementing takes, its aim must be to bring into human character more of that unity, consistency, harmony, proportion, upon which the Greek philosophers were never weary of insisting as the essence of virtue.

Hence the education of actual institutions needs supplementing, in the interests of unity of character.

The further question that emerges is therefore fairly clear. We must ask how the actual influences even of a well-developed society are to be supplemented in this direction. And to this question there are more answers than one.

It was the conviction alike of Plato and Aristotle that the betterment of the character of individuals is, to any great extent, impossible without the re-organisation of society, the instrument of edu-cation, in the interests of the moral life. They did not of course deny that even in a bad It has been held that this can only be done by a reorganisation of Society. society a good life could be led. There are pages in both, in which they join hands with the Stoics themselves in de-lineating the victory of virtue over circumstance. Yet the doctrine is central to both that character will never come to its best until the day that sees society reorganised as at once a school and sphere of virtue.

There is a characteristic well-known passage, in which Plato falls to discussing what a man has open to him when his lot has fallen amidst adverse and evil social surroundings, and when it seems a hopeless struggle to make the society of which he is a member better. Even The teaching of Plato. then a strong man is not without resource. He can withdraw from the press of life, possess his own soul in patience like one who shelters from the wintry blasts, until the day comes for him to depart with a calm mind to the islands of the Blessed. But then Plato adds, "He will not have reached the best, nor ever can he, unless he have found the fitting social life."[1] Hence the burden of Plato's whole message that the hope for morality lies in the reform of insti-tutions. Commentators have sometimes accused him of sacrificing the individual to the State. Strange criticism! For is not his ideal State expressly devised to evoke in utmost fulness all that he believes to be best and most permanent in human nature? There is nothing more characteristic in Plato, and indeed in what is most valuable in Greek ethics, than this.

We need not reject it as a devout imagination. Many are the generations in which social reformers have been

[1] *Republic*, Bk. vi. 496.

proving experimentally that society is modifiable. And the
evolutionists have come, in these latter days, to

The Platonic view is not wholly impracticable; tell us from a wide survey of things that, by the
very laws of life, society must needs undergo
ceaseless transformations. And though evolution
has more to say about the Whence than about the Whither of
this process, and may even trample ruthlessly upon the
individual and his hopes, it may help us to believe that there

though reform of the economic and political systems, in a moral interest, is peculiarly difficult. is nothing visionary in the reformer who bids us
work, at any rate, for better homes, schools,
churches, than those we know. It is when we
stand face to face with the forces that, in a moral
interest, are more intractable, in other words with
the economic and political systems, that the difficulty comes. For however far we may be from the obsolete
conservatism that would ascribe to these the fixity of Nature's
ordinances, experience, even though now and again illumined
by the fires of revolution, carries the lesson that their modification is a slow process at best, and slowest of all when
it is our aim to transform institutions into better instruments for
the making of the character of their members. They are so
firmly wedded to their own ends, so intent upon wealth-
production or wealth-distribution, or upon the reform or de-
fence of the constitution, or upon the administration or expansion of the empire. Not that there is any reason to despair.
On the contrary, it may be that with the growth of the
genuinely democratic spirit, the belief in the worth and the
possibilities of the individual man, that central article of a
democratic creed, may steadily translate itself ever more into
practice. And if so, it is as certain as any social forecast
can be that men will be less willing than heretofore to be
dealt with as nothing more than means whether for the
creation of wealth, or for the realisation of political pro-
grammes. They will claim to be, as indeed they are, "ends
in themselves." And in proportion as they do this, character

as the ultimate end of all industrial and all political activities will begin to get something more nearly its due, even in the scramble for wealth and the struggle for power. Yet any reconstruction of institutions is slow, arduous, and liable to be in a thousand ways impeded by imperious economic and political exigencies, by the growing pressure of population, by the niggardliness of soils, by the race for markets, by the rivalries of parties, by the passion for national aggrandisement, even it may be by the struggle for national existence. And, this being so, it is natural to ask if anything can be done in the meanwhile. The answer is that something, perhaps much, may be done by using such instruments as are already available, family, school, church, and the rest, in the service of Moral Ideals.

These difficulties drive us to ask if, apart from social reorganisation, nothing can be done.

The answer.

CHAPTER X.

EDUCATIONAL VALUE OF MORAL IDEALS.

IF moral ideals are to help us in education, it will not be by bringing into life elements that are not already found there. This may, it is true, happen sometimes. It happens at those rare intervals when a great prophet or teacher or brotherhood lays upon the world the obligation of some hitherto unrecognised duty. Yet, even then, the duties that find prophetic utterance are sometimes independently discovered by the world, so that the voice that seems to be crying in the wilderness quickly finds an echo in the hearts and consciences of willing disciples. And, as a rule, the ideals we use, and

Moral ideals may diverge from actual morality in various ways.

the ideals we need, diverge from actual morality otherwise than by discovering the wholly new. Thus they diverge by their omissions; and indeed we may always form a quite unattainable ideal by the simple expedient of omitting our frailties and vices. Whence the remark, in which there is at least a half truth, that ideals are but men's actual lives over again with the flaws and failings left out[1].

It is more to our present point, however, that in what they do *not* omit, they imply an altered emphasis. In other words, the duties they embody may be none other than those that meet the most of men in the daily round and common task; but, then, their relative preponderance may be changed, so changed, indeed, as almost to justify the mistake that between ideal and actual the vital difference is one of content.

But, especially, they give an altered relative emphasis to duties already recognised.

It is this last characteristic that is of especial practical importance. For the service of ideals would be a forlorn hope if it were the task of education to impress upon mankind duties and virtues which are only conspicuous by their absence. For this is not what those who have come, as we all have come, under the moralising influences of actual institutions mainly need. It is more important that an ideal should embody, though in juster and fairer proportion, the very virtues and duties which those to whom it is to be applied are already able in some imperfect fashion to fulfil. For it is only then that men can be led to see in the ideal that is held up to them, not a humiliating reminder of what they are not, but a forecast of what they may hope, and have it in them, to be. No moral ideal is needed to evoke virtues

[1] Bonar, *Malthus and his Work*, p. 27. "Writers of Utopias, from Plato to More, and from Rousseau to Ruskin, have always adopted one simple plan: they have struck out the salient enormities of their own time and inserted the opposite, as when men imagine heaven they think of their dear native country with its discomforts left out."

and duties. These come by the normal response of man's nature to the actual influences under which he passes as a social being. The need for ideals only emerges when, as we have seen, these virtues and duties are found to stand in need of a more coherent and better proportioned co-ordination than they find in that imperfect mirror of morality, society as it is.

This raises at once two further questions: the first, how such an ideal (or ideals) may be found by those (parents, or teachers, or moral reformers) with whom rests the initiative in moral education; the second, how, when found, it (or they) may best be made effective.

Two ques-tions raised.

In a sense there is nothing easier for anyone than to find a moral ideal. For such ideals abound. They abound, from the limited and homely hopes which the most average of parents may silently cherish for his boy, up to the ideal of the ethical thinker set forth with the most careful classification of virtues tabulated according to some scale of moral valuation. There are ideals saintly and worldly, ascetic and hedonistic, simple and elaborate, rational and emotional, and so on throughout innumerable varieties. The whole history of moral progress as we pass down the ages is the record of a succession of changing ideals. Nor is there any highly developed society which does not exhibit the spectacle of a multitude of ideals competing with each other for survival and supremacy. In brief, ideals are so easy to find that the problem is, not to find, but to select.

Moral ideals already exist in such pro-fusion that the practical problem is one of selection.

It is here that the ethical thinker can undoubtedly help the educator. For it falls to him, as one of his most important tasks, to pass before him in critical review, not otherwise than the logician scrutinises scientific methods, the various ideals which moral experience has produced. The world is perhaps prone to think him over-ready

Selection, however, must proceed upon some prin-ciple; and here Philosophy can render service.

to evolve an ideal of his own.   But in truth he is far more
concerned to examine and estimate the ideals that already
exist than to add another to the number.   Yet he will be a
poor critic if he have not positive convictions of his own to serve
him as a standard.   If he is to criticise with firmness and
effect, there are certain points upon which his mind must
be made up.   He must be clear as to the nature and authority
of Moral Law; he must glean all that Psychology has to
tell him of human endowment and faculty; he must satisfy
himself as to the fundamental conditions of social life through
which as seed plot, in which as sphere of action, moral
development is alone possible.   And from these data he must
frame his conclusions as to the ideal type of man in whom
the Moral Law can find its noblest and most adequate attainable realisation.   His result of course will be abstract.   It
will remain inevitably abstract even when he does his utmost
to descend to statement about the particular stage and
mode of civilisation in which he is himself an actor.   And if
any parent or teacher goes to him, as a Greek father once
went to Pythagoras, expecting to be told what to make of
his boy, he need expect no more than the advice that limits
itself to generalities.   This is to be expected.
When an ethical thinker formulates an ideal,
it will only be by the familiar device of sweeping
abstraction—abstraction from peculiarities of
individual faculty, and from peculiarities of
social circumstance.   It would however be rash in the extreme
to infer that on this account the thinker's ideal is barren of
guidance.   Individual peculiarities do not swallow up the
whole of human nature, nor peculiarities of social circumstance
the whole of social life.   And this being so, the educator
who turns for light to the ethical thinker will be so far from
going empty away, that he will carry with him, not indeed
the concrete ideal which he will strive to
actualise in his son or his pupil, but the core

*For though
the ethical
thinker's ideal
must needs be
abstract, and
so far empty,*

*it remains of
value.*

round which this concrete ideal will gather. For the thinker's ideal, if it be based on a genuine study of what man is, and what moral law is, will be the truth, and nothing but the truth, even when it is very far from being the whole truth.

And yet, however great the service it can render here, it would ill befit philosophy to be dictatorial in insisting that ideals must have the hall-mark of Theory upon them before they are fit for enactment. Ideals are not born of philosophy alone. They existed when as yet philosophy was not. They have come into being, like the virtues and duties that are their substance, in obedience to the needs and strivings of the ages before theory, and more especially in response to that craving for coherency and unity of life which is inherent in rational beings, whether they be philosophers or not. And when, in the fulness of time, the ethical theorist comes upon the scene, it is not his function to decimate the ideals, however diverse they may be, which have made good their place in the imaginations, the aspirations, and the practice of the world. If he should be tempted in that direction, there are facts to keep him tolerant and comprehensive. For he must know, if he know anything, that philosophy is still at war within its own household as to the manner of ideal, ascetic or hedonistic, individualistic or social, which, as the result of its synthesis, it is to hold up to the world. Add to this that, in proportion as his outlook has a true philosophic width, he must see, however firmly he may hold to his own central convictions, that in the manifold diversities of human endowment, circumstance, and function, there is room and to spare for variety of plan of life. Nor can he fail to know, for none ought to know better than he, how real is the world's need of ideals. These things being so, he may well pause before taking it upon himself to rule out even one ideal, however modest or however fanatical,

Yet it would be unreasonable to require that all ideals be held on philosophical grounds.

Philosophy ought to welcome variety of ideal.

however fragmentary or however incomplete it may be, so long as he is convinced that it makes for any needful uplifting of standard and practice. Rather ought he to rejoice that the competition of ideals is so large a fact. For he will be able to see in it, not only a consensus, all the stronger because a consensus amidst rivalries, that ideals are in demand, but a witness to the vitality of Moral Law, which thus needs for its realisation the service of many minds and many hands.

This toleration of ideals, however, must not be taken to imply that all ideals are on a par, and that selection is other than a matter of the first moment. For between the adoption of an ideal upon philosophic grounds—a thing at most for the minority—and its adoption upon no grounds at all, there are two alternatives.

Two alternatives to philosophical ideals.

One of these is to look to Authority—a Church, a chosen Leader, a Book, possibly a Philosopher—and to take the ideal from it upon trust. It is what is actually done in many a home, school, or church; and it has its justifications. If it would be unreasonable, and even monstrous, to declare that no one is entitled to adopt an ideal and enact it till he has thought it out for himself upon philosophical grounds, one of the alternatives open is to take it upon trust. The risk is obvious. Trust may be misplaced, and deference blind and slavish.

Authority as source of ideals.

Yet there are Authorities and Authorities, and when any one of them can point to a long record of educative achievement as credentials for its dogmatic ideal, he who submits his reason and accepts his ideal in faith, can still claim to be paying his tribute to what has stood the sifting test of experience. "A conscientious person would rather doubt his own judgment than condemn his species," says Burke, putting with even more than his usual emphasis, one of many pleas for deference to

Deference to Authority may imply deference to Experience.

authority[1]. And the plea may always find a reasonable place, if those who fall back upon it are as careful as Burke to discriminate the authority that has, from the authority that has not, the argument from long experience to recommend it.

This however is not the sole alternative. Intuition divides with Authority the suffrages of the non-theorizing world. Needless to say that it too has its snares. Trust in Intuition may be nothing more than a fine phrase for caprice and precipitancy. Hence the "experiments in education" we sometimes light upon in families whose heads are opinionatively set upon following their own lights. This however is but the parody. For it is in life as in all other arts. There is an insight that comes of experience, an intuitive penetration that is the fruit of long and thoughtful contact with moral fact. It does not find its ideal by analysis and reasoning. It is enough that the ideal be presented, it may be in the glowing words of some ethical prophet, or in some commanding figure of fact or fiction. Forthwith it is adopted with an unwavering allegiance.

Intuition as source of ideals.

The insight that comes of contact with fact.

It is in one or other of these two ways that the vast majority of our educators find, and are likely long to continue to find, their ideals. And though there are superiorities—and they are not slight[2]—which attach to the ideal that is held upon reasoned grounds, this is far from justifying philosophy in declaring war upon Authority and Intuition. In respect of his own convictions the philosopher, being a believer in reasoned truth, may refuse to trust to either. But so long as he recognises, with Plato[3], the fact that reasoned truth is

The attitude of Philosophy to Authority and Intuition.

---

[1] *Letter to the Sheriffs of Bristol*, Works, vol. II. p. 39.

[2] Cf. pp. 233—238.

[3] Cf. *Republic*, Bk. VI. 494. "It is impossible for the multitude to be philosophers." This conviction is part of Plato's contempt for the masses. But even the strongest democratic faith must admit that philosophical

beyond the hard-driven practical world, the most fruitful service he can render will be to strive to make Authority more rational and Intuition more discriminating.

The further question is how, once ideals are adopted, they

How ideals are realised. can best be made effective.

This question has already found a partial answer. For the channels of influence are none other than these social institutions which have been already dealt with. This is abundantly recognised in the case of some of them. Family, School, Church are all avowedly enlisted in the service of ideal morality. But this is not enough. Never will ideals really leaven the world if their realisation be

Ideals must enlist in their service leaders in industry and politics. left to those, the parents, teachers, priests, and moralists, who are so to say educators by profession. They must also enlist in their service those who lead in industry and politics.

There are many to whom this requirement will seem Utopian;

Character is the ultimate end of all social activity. and it may be freely conceded to them that men are not to be expected to enter either business or politics with the direct moral aim of making better men. The leaders of commerce or industry will think mainly of competence or wealth, and the politicians will look more to the transaction of the national business, and to the material conditions of national power and happiness, than to the moral development of their fellow-countrymen. Yet it is well within the scope of both, if they have a genuine patriotism, to hold steadily before their eyes the type of man they would wish to see in the workshops, offices, fleets, armies, polling-booths of their country, and to shape their action accordingly. It is precisely in the sphere of industry, commerce, and politics that ideals are most needed to uplift the practice of the world; and unless those who lead there find room beside commercial and political

analysis and construction are, if only by reason of the urgency of practical life, quite beyond the average man. Cf. p. 231.

ambitions, for moral ideals, the life of livelihood and the life of citizenship will inevitably remain the imperfect school of virtue we have seen them to be[1]. The character of the citizen was the supreme political as well as moral end in the eyes of the great philosophers of Greece. And though in the larger and more complex modern State it can no longer be made the direct object of public action to the same extent as in the small self-centred communities of antiquity, it must still stand as the one supreme and satisfying end for which all polities exist.

It is not enough however to describe the contributions which the various natural and social influences, which we have passed in brief review, make to this high enterprise. For there are certain quite specific and time-honoured expedients to which mankind, from the dawn of history, have never failed to turn. And they have been used with so firm a faith and such manifest effect, both by individuals and institutions, that they demand a separate and more detailed consideration. These are the thrice-familiar resources of Punishment, Example, and Precept.

Three expedients for actualising ideals.

[1] Cf. pp. 118, 128, 134.

CHAPTER XI.

PUNISHMENT[1].

WE have seen (with the help of Herbert Spencer) that
Nature has her sanctions. So have institutions.
So have individuals. Many of these sanctions
are of express human contrivance, and are prompt
and definite, like the penalties imposed by parent or schoolmaster or the stern reactions of the criminal law upon the
public malefactor. Others fall no less surely and heavily
though they have never been deliberately planned, and make
themselves felt only after many days, as when a self-seeker or
a cynic, who has done despite to the ties of family and friendship, finds himself in later life alone in the world, or as when
the thriftlessness or extravagance of years has at last brought its
victim to want. For Nemesis is a goddess not to be dethroned.
Swiftly or slowly, and through all degrees of severity up to
beggary, infamy or death, she pays her unwelcome wages.

Many of these reactions, it must be obvious, are little or at
all within control, and many, when they are, are of such difficult
application that both individual and collective want of wisdom
have blundered badly in applying them. But
this would be a poor reason for standing aside
and leaving "Nature" to do the work. The
inference lies in the opposite direction. Mankind have suffered,

*The reality
of sanctions.*

*Suffering
and the art of
Punishment.*

[1] There is a suggestive chapter on *Punishment* in M{c}Taggart's *Studies
in Hegelian Cosmology*, pp. 129—150.

do suffer, and will continue to suffer, so much, under sanctions of one kind or another, that the magnitude of the suffering becomes a challenge to every educator and law reformer to devise methods whereby this bitter, and too often barren, harvest of suffering may be made tributary to the public good and the discipline of character. Nor have they declined the challenge. They have rather turned their thoughts to the theory and art of Punishment.

For it has long been recognised that there are certain large general ends towards which Punishment may be directed. It may be retributive: the culprit must expiate his offence. It may be deterrent: **The ends of Punishment.** it may stay the steps of the offender from offence, or if the offence and its penalty needs must come, it may scare him, and such as can profit by his example, from a repetition of the experience. It may be eliminative (or suppressive): it may, by locks and bars or other method, make further wrong-doing impossible. Above all it may be educative (or reformatory): it may strive to make the culprit, one may not say *perfect* through suffering—for no man since the dawn of time ever became perfect through suffering alone—but at anyrate less imperfect than he would have been had the hand of punishment never fallen upon him.

Not that these principles by any means exclude each other. Reform need not be sundered from deterrence; and there is a sense in which retribution can never be absent if punishment is to do its work, as we shall see. And therefore, if it be said that it is important (and in truth it is of vital moment) to choose between these principles, this need mean no more than that some one principle is chosen as paramount.

There can, however, be little doubt as to which we must wish to be paramount in education. It may, or may not, be the function of the State to better the character of its citizens through the adminis- **Punishment as an educational resource.** tration of the penal Law; on this point publicists may differ; but when the making of the character is the central aim, as of course it is in education, the only question worth asking is whether punishment can be so used as to secure this indubitably desirable result. And, as all forms of punishment work through the infliction, in fear of the infliction, of pain, this question may be resolved into the enquiry if this infliction of pain can be made a means of betterment.

The answer is that it can, or rather that it can *provided one condition be satisfied,* in the absence of which all **Punishment ought to act upon the will of the culprit.** else is of comparatively slight avail. That condition is that the infliction of pain be so used as to produce in the sufferer a consciousness of having done wrong, and, by consequence, a real penitence for his offence. This is central. No genuine progress in character can be achieved by punishing any offender unless we have succeeded in securing that altered attitude to his offence which involves firstly, that he acknowledges his offence (if only to himself: it need not be by open confession), and, secondly, that he repents of having committed it. The whole case for the educative value of punishment turns on this. Short of this, we can of course do something. We can convince even hardened backsliders that there is such a thing as retribution. We can deter by terror from the commission or repetition of offences. We can segregate and suppress, not otherwise than as we can shut up dangerous animals. But we do little for character, even when we may do much for correct behaviour, until we have secured the penitent will.

It is safe to say, however, that this will never be done unless **To secure this result, the authority that punishes must be recognised as moral.** the source from which the penalty emanates be, either before the punishment is administered or after it, recognised as the organ of a moral authority. One often hears it said, and it is too true a tale, that the punishments inflicted under the Criminal Law of the State seldom induce repentance. It is not to be wondered at. For the State, as actually with us, is not recognised, or, at most, imperfectly recognised, as the organ of a moral authority. Thinkers who follow Hegel may so regard it. Nor need it be denied that, to a certain extent, Courts of Justice do voice the verdict of the popular conscience. But unhappily this is a lesson the criminal has still to learn. He knows, of course, that he has broken the law of his country, but all too seldom does he interpret his punishment as a revelation of the fact that he is guilty of moral turpitude as well as crime. His conscience is not touched. Far otherwise, however, in home, or school or church. In them the authority that punishes is, normally at any rate, recognised as a moral authority, and with that the punishment takes on a different aspect. It becomes a way—not the best way but still an effective way—of enforcing a lesson in morality. For the culprit has his eyes opened to the fact that, by heedlessness or sluggishness or self-will or passion, he has lapsed into an offence against a law that has a moral sanction, an offence from which his own conscience ought to have saved him. And when that perception is awakened, it is a short step to remorse and penitence. Nor is it necessary that the punishment be severe. Even a penalty that may at first sight seem trivial in comparison with the gravity of the offence may be enough, if it suffices to shake the culprit out of illusions, to convince him that he is morally guilty, and that a moral obligation is not lightly to be set aside. Nor can one doubt that if only the State, or Society, in its reactions upon offenders, could come to be clothed in the eyes of its members with the same moral attributes that are already freely ascribed to family, school and church, it would wield the tremendous sanctions of public sentiment, and punitive action, and criminal law more effectively in the interests of moral reform, and less effectively for the degradation of such as fall under its heavy hand, than it does in the present imperfect condition of human affairs.

Punishment as a severe lesson in morality.

Nor is it the least of the advantages of Punishment, thus
regarded, that it helps us to put a right construction upon those two repulsive but inseparable
concomitants of all deliberate infliction of pain,
fear and disgrace.

Two con-
comitants of
Punishment.

Wherever punishment exists, it is inevitably shadowed by
fear. Nor is anyone likely to deny that, in a
thousand cases, fear of pains and penalties may
become abject and slavish. But fear of the penalties administered by an authority that is respected is another thing. For
then it is not the mere pain that is feared. The pain that is
feared goes hand in hand with the fear of painful alienation
from what—be it person or institution or law—is recognised as
good. And, so transformed, it may so entirely lose its slavish-
ness as to become a kind of tribute to morality. Better no
doubt that moral motive should be unadulterated by fear at
all. Yet if fear must come, as come it must in the wake of
punishment, the fear that flows even in part from respect for
the accredited representatives and organs of moral law is no
longer abject. One may see this unmistakably in all those
cases—teacher and pupil, father and child—where there are
mutual relations of confidence and affection between the
punished and the punisher. Who can deny that in these the
base fear of pain may sink quite into the background, and
become almost a negligible quantity? The affection of child
for parent, or the respect of pupil for teacher, is not so fragile
a plant as to wither up into slavish fear under the ordeal of
even many a punishment, if only the penalties be just.

(a) Fear.

Similarly with disgrace. Inevitably there is disgrace in all
punishment, and so we often meet the remark
that punishment is degrading. So it is, if our
minds travel no further than the penalty, and the thought of
how subjection to it must appear in the eyes of onlookers.
But if the inevitable disgrace in these ways be indeed the
culprit's price for penitence, it will forthwith take on a new

(b) Disgrace.

character as the way of escape from a bad will, and as per-adventure the beginning of a new life. Disgrace is no longer degradation if it be a step in moral advance. The degradation lies in the offence: the punishment, and its disgrace, are rather to be welcomed as a step out of degradation.

It follows closely upon this that, if punishment is to be reformatory, it must be also retributive. For, if the path to reformation lies through penitence, let no one fancy that there can be penitence without suffering. This is inevitable. The penalty indeed may be light: it may even be remitted altogether, and yet the suffering may remain bitter beyond words. Nor can it ever be otherwise, so long as the backslider can only be brought back into a right relation to the law he has broken by feeling in full measure the shame of the offence of which he has been guilty. In this sense he must drink the cup of suffering to the dregs; in this sense expiate his offence; in this sense make reparation, to the last jot and tittle, to the law he has broken.

The retributive element in Punishment.

Nor, we may add, is it wrong for the authority that punishes, or for the community, small or great, that stands behind it, to cherish that indignation at wrong-doing on which the believers in the retributary principle usually insist. It is good for a nation that it should hate crime with a perfect hatred as well as punish it: it is good for a school or family that it should abhor vice as well as check it: it is good that there should be in both a passionate indignation if outrage goes unpunished, and a felt satisfaction where nemesis overtakes guilt. And this, not because of any vindictiveness of spirit or lack of compassion for the culprit, but for the better reason that, in order that punishment may work reform and teach its stern lesson in morality it is never so effective for these purposes as when it has a strong public sentiment behind it. When Burns breathed over the arch-enemy of the human race the aspiration, "Oh wad ye tak' a thocht and mend!" we may admire the courage

Moral senti-ment can make Punishment more educa-tive.

of his compassion; but if it ever entered into the scope of education to reform that hoary criminal, it will hardly be disputed that those who embark upon the task would have their hands greatly strengthened by a sufficient public detestation of his works of darkness.

This last point is however somewhat speculative, and it may serve a better purpose if, as a parable, it be used to suggest the very practical question: Are there no incorrigibles, and what are we to do with them? This is pertinent, because it is in presence of the incorrigibles that a purely reformatory theory of punishment breaks down. For of course, if our only justifiable principle in punishing were reform, it would follow that we ought to punish our incorrigibles not at all. In other words we should let the incorrigibles go scot free, and punish the rest who have the credit, such as it is, of not being altogether hardened sinners.

The "incorrigibles."

It is everywhere an acute problem; but it is far more acute for the family or the school than for the State. For the State can fall back on Elimination. If it cannot cure, or even deter, it can shut up and segregate, if need be for life. It can do this in the public interest. But we cannot do this in the School. The School no doubt, when the worst comes to the worst, can expel, and so relieve itself of this contagious residuum. But that does not solve the problem: it only turns it over to some one else, be it the truant school or reformatory, or to the home—if indeed these wretched failures have a home to own them. And what are we to say of the family itself? Is it to shut its doors, and cut the ties of nature, and let them go—to penal servitude in the long run, or to worse?

It is hard to say. Nor are we greatly helped by the obvious conclusion that so far as incorrigibles exist, they must be dealt with, if only in the interests of public order, decency and moral sanitation, on some other principle than either reform or

How are "incorrigibles" to be dealt with?

deterrence. There is no escaping the fact that Society must segregate its moral lepers.

But there is another way and attitude. It is to hope against hope, and this is happily not the same as to hope against possibility. For good and evil, despite all their repugnancy, are so strangely blended in human nature that, in many an instance, it is rashness itself to rush to the conviction that good is non-existent because it may seem to have vanished. After all, many of the worst cases are cases of lapse, and where good has once been, it dies hard. Testimony is not lacking from those who have been in life-long presence of even the worst of the criminal classes, which bears witness to the presence, even in infamy and deep degradation, of some lingering forlorn traits of a better life, some sparks of human feeling to which appeal may be made and not in vain. Hence the hopes, not only of sanguine philanthropists but of expert criminologists, that, by a long and careful course of moral hygiene, involving little punishment except the necessary penalty of prolonged compulsory restraint and discipline, many a life, especially of course if it be still a young life, may be rescued which our forefathers would have abandoned as hopeless. He would be a bold man who averred that the science and art of criminology has touched, or nearly touched, its limits.

Not all "incorrigibles" are incorrigible.

Nor must we needlessly darken for ourselves our estimates of the so-called incorrigibles of school or home by viewing them under the shadow cast by the atrocious habitual criminals of Law Courts and prisons. In ten thousand cases, they are manifestly far from wholly bad, and above all they have not had the time to become hardened. And if this be so, it is anything but utopian to pluck courage from the many and ever-increasing resources of education, and steadily to refuse to fling aside the incorrigible upon the ghastly scrap-heap of worthless lives, until patience and contrivance are exhausted.

How much more with the cases which are not "incorrigible," and far from wholly bad. For however
necessary the art of Punishment may be, it is
nothing more than an under-agent in the far
greater art of making character. Even for purposes of repression (as we have seen[1]) it falls
short of that positive policy of development which is the most
effective means of discipline. Nor is it a groundless faith that,
if justice be done to the inexhaustible range of appeal to
example, precept, and conscience, the art of Punishment,
though never likely to disappear from the earth, may take a
place more creditable to human nature than in these days
when castigation is still all too often believed to be the
necessary path to virtue.

The art of Punishment has a quite secondary place in education.

Nor would it be right, seeing that punishment needs must
come, to pass from the subject without suggesting
some of the canons by which the application of
principles to practice ought to be regulated[2].

Some canons of Punishment.

The first requirement here is to be certain that the offence
has been committed. If one were asked how
many offenders ought to be suffered to go unpunished rather than that one innocent person
should be penalised, there is no answer. There is no answer
because the two things are incommensurable.

1. The offender must be convicted.

A second requirement is discrimination between classes of
offences; between sins of omission, for example,
and sins of commission, or between sins that are
primarily against the culprit's self and those
(bullying for instance or slander) that betray a still deeper
selfishness, or between offences against social order and those
which have a more directly moral culpability and contagion.

2. Offences ought to be classified.

---

[1] pp. 48 and 88.
[2] Cf. Bentham, *Theory of Legislation*, Part III. esp. c. vi. *The Choice
of Punishments*, in which, though of course without special reference to
education, the principles of Punishment are formulated.

A third is that the punishment must be proportionate to the offence—a maxim that is soon said but not so soon interpreted, so long as the comparative heinousness of offences, and the comparative grading of penalties, may well tax the wits of the wisest. The difficulties are sufficiently great in criminal Law even though Law, by reason of its inevitable roughness and generality, cannot go far into consideration of individual desert. It is ten-fold greater in school or home, where individual desert can and ought to be so much more closely scrutinised. The best way out perhaps, here and everywhere else, is simply to prefer the penalties that seem most likely to induce repentance.

3. The penalty must be proportionate,

This is indeed the main justification of a fourth requisite— the well-known maxim that the punishment ought to be analogous to the offence. It must be so related to it that it strikes the will, so to say, at the right point. Starve the greedy, humble the insolent, compel the idle to work, or the heedless to retrace false steps with leisurely care. Only thus will the imposition go home to the offender.

4. and analogous to the offence,

It is not less reasonable that punishments should be exemplary. Since they needs must come, it is not enough that they should open the culprit's eyes and give him his due. They may with advantage be utilized as object-lessons for behalf of that large class, the culprits in potentiality.

5. and exemplary,

This however must not be taken to mean that they need be severe. " Make an example of you " is apt to mean that; but in reality it ought to mean rather the opposite; namely, that few things are of more importance than that no penalty should exceed the quantum that is needful to vindicate authority, to stigmatise the offence, to satisfy the wholesome craving that the wrong-doer shall suffer for his deeds, above all to touch the conscience of the offender. In this sense punishment ought to be *economical,*

6. and economical,

or, in other words, never heavier than to secure the end in view, be this simply the preservation of law and order or the betterment of the sufferers.

Not least there is the just requirement that punishment should, in all possible cases, go hand in hand

7. and require indemnity. with insistence on appropriate indemnity, so that the wrong-doer, in things small or great, may be forced to repair, so far as practicable, the irreparable mischief which offence implies.

It is not, however, by the application of maxims about punishment, be they never so carefully formulated, that character is really made. For this we must turn to the great positive resources which are fruitful at once of development and discipline. And amongst these of course is Example.

CHAPTER XII.

EXAMPLE.

IN its earliest phase Example works through literal imitation. What children see done, and almost as
early what they hear of as done, they in-   **Example at
first evokes**
stinctively do likewise. Born actors, each of   **literal imitation.**
them has already in his nursery life played many
parts.

Much of this is of trifling ethical significance, however
interesting it may be to the psychologist. It is interesting to
the psychologist because it is here he finds the beginnings
of those firm associations between impressions or ideas and
actions, which explain how it comes to pass that in later life
the bare idea of things to be done is followed almost auto-
matically by the doing of them. It is thus in fact that the
will gradually, through the alliance of habit, acquires that
large store of motor-ideas which enables it with such facility
to command the requisite neural and muscular movements.
Direct ethical significance, however, emerges only when the
actions born of imitation are such as may develop some
capacity or instinct that, through encouragement and exercise,
may become a virtue. Of such actions there is certainly no
lack, and with their performance, and especially their frequently
repeated performance, the moral influence of example has
really begun. For somehow, even to the very young, the
ongoings of fellow human beings have an inexplicable interest,

and as this example or that comes, in fact or in story, to be repeatedly presented to the mind, imitation becomes habitual.

It is the examples of the home circle that, in the ordinary course of things, are naturally first. But it does not follow that they are therefore the most effective. We can sympathise with children, if they frequently prefer to personate Achilles, or some other of the heroes of Greek or Roman or English story, rather than their latter-day fathers and mothers. It is at any rate no fancy that the simpler life of early times often finds readiest entrance into the simpler minds. But be this as it may, it is not long before the examples of the home circle, whose persistent influence[1] no one need disparage, are recruited from those of fiction.

The examples that most powerfully work upon the young need not be those that lie nearest them.

This is what Plato saw once for all so clearly. For the Platonic education does not begin in the influences of "real" life, but with the tales, religious or other, which children learn at their nurses' knee, and from those who, from earliest years, speak to them of gods or heroes. Fiction there must be. We must educate to begin with by a "lie." But then the lie must be an "honest and noble lie." So that, whatever be the liberties it may take with fact, it must wear, beneath the mask of imagination, the lineaments of a sound and well-considered moral purpose[2].

Plato's insistence on the value of fiction.

This however must not be held to mean that the moral purpose need shine through. On the contrary, children are so quick to detect a moral ambuscade that above all things the moral must from them lie hid. The person from whom it must not lie hid is he who puts the story-book

Fiction must have a moral purpose, though this must be concealed.

[1] See p. 103.
[2] *Republic*, Bk. II. 377, and cf. 414.

into youthful hands. And this for two reasons: firstly and mainly, because of the positive influence of wholesome, honest, and really great literature; and secondly, because the best index expurgatorius is not to be found in a catalogue of the books that are not to be read. Contrariwise. It is the carefully fostered love of good fiction that will in the long run do tenfold more to oust the tales of scandal, frivolity and crime than a thousand repressive Thou-shalt-nots.

Nor is it to be forgotten in this connection—who that knows the *Republic* of Plato can ever forget?—that the purveyor of literature for the young, however large and catholic his own appreciations may be, is not in the same position as the genial lover and critic of books who thinks first of literary form and art, and little or not at all of the play, the novel or the poem as instruments for the nurture of the moral character. There is a good deal in the permanent literature of the world, as well as in the literature that is happily not permanent, which is hardly appropriate to the school-library or the family circle.

The broad fact however remains that we do well, in a spirit far removed from a strait-laced puritanism, to enrich the roll of examples from Epic, Romance and Ballad, so that boy or girl may learn to live in the habitual company of those creatures of the imagination who, though they never saw the light of the sun, may so profoundly influence life. One can understand what Robert Chambers meant when he declared that he "raised statues in his heart" to the story-tellers who first gave him views of social life beyond the small circle of his natal village[1]. And indeed it is not doubtful, as many a schoolmaster who has followed the later lives of his pupils can vouch, that the career of many a boy has been overmasteringly shaped for good, or for evil, by the sort of fiction that has been the companion of early years. It cannot be otherwise so long as

Examples who never lived may powerfully influence life.

[1] *Memoir of Robert Chambers*, p. 64, 2nd edit.

imitation is one of the earliest, deepest, and most tenacious
of human instincts. Nor need we limit these influences to
boyhood. It was Diderot who, to the surprised enquiries of
friends who found him in tears, replied that he was weeping
for his friends—his friends Pamela, Clarissa, Grandison[1]. And
every reader of Wordsworth knows how he found unfailing
refuge from the trivialities, or worse, of gossip and "personal
talk" by betaking himself to the society of Una and Desdemona, and to the nobler loves and nobler cares bequeathed
to him by the poets[2].

And of course we need not limit ourselves to fiction.
Almost as soon as the story-book comes the biography, and
with the biography, the history, which for the young, at
any rate, is still mainly but a gallery of biographies. And
Appeal to
example more
persuasive
than exhor-
tation. what economy there is in the use of these!
For when we wish to bring home some lesson
of courage, of generosity, of mercy, it is not
necessary to discourse at length about them.
"There! that is courage, that, generosity, that, mercy." This
is enough.

It is not, however, to be supposed that all this will come
of literal imitation. For the literal imitation
Imitation
of the spirit of
an example is
of more im-
portance than
literal imi-
tation. of examples has but a limited reign, and inevitably passes into something higher. All imitation, all imitation at any rate where the imitator
is human, is, in fact, something of a discovery.
It is not the mechanical work of a copyist. For
when imitation passes into act, there comes the experience
of what it feels like to do the act. And, in the light of this
new experience, the example is henceforth regarded with new
and more penetrating eyes. There is imputed to it a similar
inward experience, and thus the world of motive begins to

---

[1] Cf. Morley's *Diderot*, p. 261.
[2] See the four Sonnets on *Personal Talk*, Works, IV. 219 (Moxon).

be revealed to conjecture and interpretation. This goes on progressively and the result follows. Imitation deepens. It does not stop at the actions that are overt and visible. It strives to reproduce what it divines to be the spirit in which the imitated acts are done. So that the "hero," be he the hero of romance or only the common-clay hero of actual life, begins to live a second life not merely in the acts but in the soul of his "worshipper[1]."

This marks an immense onward step. It gives imitation a vastly wider range. For it enables it to profit by many an example whose value lies not in the precise manner of action but in the spirit in which the action is done. We see this in the perennial influence of examples drawn from ages far remote. We have seen already that it is not those who are nearest in circumstances and externals that most powerfully fasten upon the imaginations of the young. Rather is it the Homeric hero, the viking, the crusader, the knight-errant, the voyager, the Indian chief, the castaway. And though these, and many another, have their first tribute in the "make-believe" that needs must reproduce what it admires, the time comes round—one may hope it does not come too soon—when this literal imitation begins to be childish and absurd. But it does not follow that the examples need forthwith be discarded. All that need happen is that now it is the spirit they embody that begins to work in the imitator— the spirit of daring, fidelity, endurance, adventure, valour. In a word, the cherished examples are neither discarded nor reproduced in the letter: they are imitated in their spirit.

Hence the value of examples that cannot be literally imitated.

It is necessary that this should be so, because if it were otherwise our allegiance to examples, however illustrious, would be anything but the path to goodness. The very nature of goodness forbids a slavish literal imitation. For a good

[1] Professor Baldwin has thrown much light upon Imitation in his *Social and Ethical Interpretations in Mental Development*.

man is, above all things else, a genuine man.   He is "original,"
in the sense that he is sincere.   And his every
look, word, gesture, act, so far from being copied
and merely dramatic, are the direct living expression of the moral spirit within.   This is
his charm and fascination.   If, then, we would
imitate goodness, we must not fail to be like it in its essence,
in its genuineness, in its "originality."   For it is the last
tribute to offer anyone we admire—to set ourselves to mas-
querade in his clothing.   Nor will it mend matters though
the examples thus pedantically copied be of the noblest.
Good for us, if we can, to set ourselves in imagination in the
place of the heroes or the saints of other days: not so good
if we try, by a literal imitation, to transplant them into our
own days.   The one loyal tribute is to act, not as they acted,
but as we believe they would act under our altered circumstances.   It is only as thus used that examples can yield up
the whole of their vast influence.   As precise precedents they
are of subordinate value.   For their ways are not our ways,
and in the effort to make them so, we do but make ourselves
pedantic and ridiculous.   This much truth at all events there is
in the startling warning of Emerson, "Never imitate. * * *   That
which each can do best none but his Maker can teach him."[1]

Thus liberally construed, examples tell in at least three
conspicuous directions.

(1)   In the first place, they serve to purify
and to elevate our moral estimates both of men
and actions.   Much moral failing, it is to be
remembered, is due not to inability to see the conditions under
which we ought to act but to inability to weigh
them[2].   A stingy man, for example, or a stingy
boy, may see quite clearly in a given case that
his money will give pleasure or do good.   But,

The highest tribute to illustrious examples is to imitate their sincerity of spirit.

Three aspects of the influence of Examples.

(a) They purify and elevate the moral judgment.

---

[1] *Essay on Self-reliance*, Works, vol. II., p. 67 (Macmillan & Co.).
[2] Cf. p. 207.

even as he sees this, the thought of his five pounds or his five shillings, and what they might procure for himself, rises up before him with such vividness, that it dominates all else, conjures up a strangely distorting medium between him and his kindly projects, and ends by chilling his benevolence to zero. Suppose however it be his good fortune, still on the brink of this mean illusion, to light upon some rare type of generosity. Will it not alter his comparative estimates of things? Will it not bring him even to wonder at the distorted valuations that threaten to make his money bulk so large, and the delight or relief his money might give to others so miserably small? It is in this way that an example, if it lives habitually in our minds, can come almost to change for us the very meaning of propositions. Telling the truth, honouring father and mother, paying debts—they are generalities on all our lips, but they take on a new significance, and carry altered estimates, after we have once really known even a single type who has given them just and unselfish embodiment.

(2) It goes closely with this that an example is something of a revelation to us of ourselves. Not least when it is so far removed from us that our first and fitting emotion in its presence is reverence and humility. For the spectacle of a noble life *(b) They reveal to us the possibilities of our own moral nature.* is never simply a thing to wonder at, as we might wonder at a work of art, or at the strength or grace of an animal. It is the unobstructed manifestation in loftier mode of that same moral spirit of which we are aware as the best thing in ourselves. Immeasurably superior, the example is yet not alien. It is kin. As the phrase goes, we "identify ourselves with it": thereby hazarding the hope that what it is we have it in us at least to strive to be. In the light of it, our failings draw upon them a new detestation. For they begin to wear the aspect of obstructions—obstructions which are frustrating a principle of moral life capable of far fuller realisation than anything it has yet attained in our unworthy best. It is thus,

as even Kant is constrained to admit, that examples serve for encouragement[1].

For, as the Greek philosophers were never weary of insisting, the virtues are one.   They are not mere
gifts, bestowed here, withheld there, by caprice
of fortune.   For however diverse they may appear
to be as we range through the different ranks,
classes, occupations of life, the seeing and sympathetic eye may trace, underneath all diversities, one and
the same moral spirit striving manifoldly to vitalise human
nature.

Reasons why we iden-tify ourselves with the lives of our neigh-bours.

Nor is this mode of influence limited to those cases where
the example is our moral superior.   That same common
humanity, that same common moral spirit, that emboldens
us to see in the saint our own human nature transfigured,
enables us also to put a deeper and a more sympathetic
meaning into the lives of our ordinary neighbours.   They may
differ in their lot, in their fortunes, in their gifts.   But these
things do not cut us off from them.   That poor man, that
rich man, that beggar, that noble—what are they but ourselves, our own moral nature that we know so well, only
under altered circumstances[2]?

It is here that Fiction, building upon this recognition of
man by man, can again render signal service.
For it is one of the prerogatives of the writer
of Fiction to emancipate obstructed human nature from the baffling limitations of fact, thereby
revealing it to us in the transfiguring surroundings of favouring ideal situation.   Cases are common enough
in actual life where a man, after long struggle and obstruction,
has at last "grasped the skirts of happy chance," and won
his way into the life that suits him.   "Now," we say, "he

Fiction may largely con-tribute to this revelation of the moral possibilities of man.

---

[1] *Metaphysic of Ethics*, Sect. II, see infra, p. 173.

[2] This point is dealt with in a chapter on Fraternity in *Ethics of Citizenship*, p. 26, 4th Ed. (Mac Lehose & Sons).

has a chance of showing what is in him." What Fortune can thus do sometimes, the writer of fiction can do always. By setting human nature in the sunshine of visionary circumstance, he can, so to say, give human nature its chance, and show us what it has in it to become. There is an analogy here between Fiction and those physical sciences to which it is often too rashly supposed to be wholly alien. When a chemist, for example, wishes to shew us what an acid or an alkali is, he exhibits it and its behaviour under the enlightening, artificial, conditions of experiment. By a similar artifice imagination, in its laboratory of fiction, reveals to us what the soul of man is by shewing how it thinks, feels, wills, acts, under the carefully devised conditions of fictitious circumstances. William Godwin once wrote a story in which he avowed the intention of "mixing human feelings and passions with incredible situations."[1] We may quarrel with his manipulation: we must not censure his attempt. If a chemist can better exhibit to us the properties of phosphorus by burning it in an artificially devised atmosphere of oxygen, is there not a chemistry of the human passions, concerned with the behaviour of men under circumstances expressly fabricated to call out just those passions which we wish to study? The result is not amusement only. Floods of light have been in this way let in upon moral truth: so that the men and women of Scott and Shakespeare have become to many of us more real than those we know in actual life. Hence the wisdom of the remark that illusion is not delusion. There can be no delusion where genius, by this great artifice of fiction, brings what is best and greatest in man into the very situations that make the revelation most complete. Thus it comes that those creatures of the imagination, though they

Analogy between Fiction and Physical Science.

---

[1] *St Leon.* The story is an attempt to work out the effects upon human ties and relationships which might be expected to follow from the possession of the philosopher's stone and the elixir vitae.

never lived "under the canopy" themselves, have helped
others to live, thereby giving to men what they themselves,
retainers only of a poet's or novelist's mind, never had.

(3) In these ways examples avail to enlighten. But
they likewise quicken.

(c) Examples can quicken the moral spirit.

It is the trite difficulty in moral education
that these two things, light and stimulus, may
be divorced. To arguments, precepts, exhortations, people listen. They assent. They promise. They do
not perform. It is otherwise when the appeal is to example.
For a type being concrete, kindred to ourselves, impressive,
easy to be apprehended, comes home to us and stirs the
feelings that lie close to action. The precept is less easy to
hold and to bind. Hence the need of devices to retain it,
vain repetitions and the like. But the image tarries with us,
and by its prolonged presence touches the springs of action
when a definition, or a precept, or a command, may stir

The claims of "hero-worship."

never a pulse. Hence "hero-worship" has been
magnified as a more powerful lever for the uplifting of mankind than all the wisest words of
all the sages[1]. Not without reason. It is one test of a moral
force to confront it with the difficult, and indeed the desperate
cases. If it be these that test the physician's art, it is not
otherwise here in the larger art of life, when we ask how the
coward is to be made brave or the profligate pure. And the
answer of the apostles of "hero-worship" is that the spectacle
of a devoted or a pure life can awaken the passions by whose
expulsive power even these dire vices can be cast out. Philosophy itself, after a fashion, bears its witness to the same
truth. Did not the man Socrates inspire his followers, and
this even in spite of the fact that he strove above all things

[1] Cf. Carlyle, *Sartor Resartus*, Bk. III., c. vii. (Libr. Ed.). "In which
fact, that Hero-Worship exists, has existed, and will for ever exist, univer-
sally among mankind, mayest thou discern the corner-stone of living-rock,
whereon all Politics for the remotest time may stand secure."

by his well-known 'irony,' to sink his personality, and teach as one *not* having authority? And have not Cynicism, Epicureanism, Stoicism, wrought themselves, more even than the wisdom of Aristotle, into the imaginations and the lives of men? The reason is plain. To doctrine they added type—the Cynic type, the Epicurean type, the Stoic type. And the type has found entrance when precept or argument might have knocked for admission long and in vain.

> "For Wisdom dealt with mortal powers,
>   Where truth in closest words shall fail,
>   When truth embodied in a tale
> Shall enter in at lowly doors."[1]

"Example," says Burke, "is the school of mankind, and they will learn at no other."[2] And the exaggeration—for exaggeration it is—may at least be pardoned. The facts are so strong. "Perhaps the truth is that there has scarcely been a town in any Christian country since the time of Christ" (and may we not add, "or before it"?) "where a century has passed without exhibiting a character of such elevation that his mere presence has shamed the bad and made the good better, and has been felt at times like the presence of God Himself."[3]

Limitations of Example.

Yet to the influence of Example there are most specific limits—limits inevitable because bound up with what, in its very essence, an example is. For an example is concrete, a real or fictitious person with personal characteristics, and as such subject of necessity to the limitations of time, place, and circumstance.

The most typical of examples has inevitable limitations.

---

[1] *In Memoriam*, xxxvi.

[2] *Letters on a Regicide Peace*, I., Works, V. 223.

[3] Seeley's *Ecce Homo*, c. XIV. *The enthusiasm of humanity*, p. 161 (20th ed.).

This holds even of those we canonize as types. Socrates,
St Paul, Marcus Aurelius, St Louis, St Bernard,
Erasmus, Luther, Loyola, Washington, Gordon
—are they not all great types just because
Time can extinguish neither them, nor their limitations?
There is danger here; and it is greatest in proportion as
our imaginations and our allegiance are carried captive. The
type is always limited. It is Greek, Hebrew, Roman, me-
diaeval, English. But, by its mastery over us, it may come
to hide the fact that the moral life is a larger thing than any
single type can embody.

1. It is more or less concrete.

This risk obviously becomes more serious in proportion
as the chosen example is of a humbler kind. Who has not
seen boys and girls devote themselves to " hero-worships,"
which in six months' time were over-worn? And with what
feelings would most of us face the sentence to return to old
allegiances? They have had their day: they have ceased
to be. And this, not because we have proved fickle, but
because they have proved finite.

Hence it comes that a life patterned wholly on examples,
especially if these be not conspicuously typical,
is apt to come short in either of two ways.
Either it may, in fragmentary fashion, live
through a series of inconsistent admirations and
imitations: or, if it be more tenacious of its attachments, it
may find itself in the plight of striving to entertain a company
of guests diverse to incongruity. Nothing, at all events, can
be more obvious than that the more examples a man admires,
the more must he realise the limitations of each. And indeed
it is thus that the morality of example suggests its own limitations never so much as when it is most catholic.

Consequent defects of the life patterned wholly on examples.

A second qualification has its source in the limitations not of the example but of the admirer. For there is
a large class of persons so constituted that whatever makes
demands upon the imagination, as Example does, can find

access to their minds only with much difficulty. They are
the unfortunates to whom the whole great world
of fiction is closed. "Art," it has been said,
"would need no commentators, if it were
thoroughly competent to tell its own story."[1]
But it is not Art that is incompetent. It is that
large section of the world who, by lack of
imaginative sympathy, can so feebly apprehend artistic crea-
tions, that they must needs be taken by the hand by
these middlemen of the intellectual world, the critic and the
expositor. Some of them refuse to follow even then. Nor
need the example be born of fiction to be thus unintelligible.
It is enough that it be removed from us in time, place, and
circumstance. And there is many a teacher of Christianity
itself who could tell us that, notwithstanding all the resources
of poetry, painting, sculpture, allegory, it remains one of the
hardest of tasks to bring the world to enter, with a real insight,
into the record of the life of its Founder. This is enough to
suggest that we must look beyond Example—unless, indeed,
we are prepared to say that people need have no morality if
they have no imaginations.

2. It makes demands (which are not always met) upon the imaginations of those to be influenced.

A still more fundamental limitation remains; none other
than the central fact that Example finds its
true place as an instrument for evoking moral
possibilities, and must not therefore be exag-
gerated into a means, still less the sole means,
of implanting these. We must here follow Kant.

3. It pre-supposes in those appeal-ed to a respon-sive principle of moral life,

"Respect for a person," says that greatest of all decriers of
Example, "is properly only respect for the law (of honesty, &c.)
of which he gives us an example."[2] The dictum is startling;
and indeed it is manifestly false, if it be construed as meaning
that we withhold respect for persons till we have come to a
consciousness of laws, whether of honesty or veracity, or

---

[1] Thomson, *Outlines of the Laws of Thought*, p. 33.

[2] *Metaphysic of Ethics*, Sect. I., note.

courage, or of any other of the duties. Is it not a commonplace that the laws of morality usually make themselves known
first in a concrete and individualised embodiment? Yet a
substantial truth remains. All respect for persons involves
presuppositions; and the types, even the most splendid, which
appeal to our admiration, do their work upon us because they
evoke the response of a moral spirit that is already implicit
in our consciousness. In Platonic phrase there must be "an
eye of the soul" to recognise the example when it sees it.
in the absence
of which the
example could
not be inter-
preted aright. Else might all the beauty of life pass unseen before blind eyes, and all its music go wandering
unheeded past deaf ears. Ordinary experience
illustrates this. For is it not matter of observation that even the cleverest of scoundrels is but a fool, when
he tries to read the character of an honest man, and blunders
like any simpleton by putting his own mean and villainous
constructions upon it? And do we not know, contrariwise,
that an honest man, even when he has no exceptional intellectual acumen, is quick in discerning good in his neighbour?
The reason is manifest. It is because the one has, and the
other has not, the clue within himself—the clue that is found
in the presence of the indwelling moral spirit from which goodness finds spontaneous recognition and welcome. For goodness is not a thing that can be seen in other men. Its
presence, or absence, is always matter of interpretation, an
inference from what they do or say. Nor can we ever hope
to interpret aright, unless there be within our own breasts,
as feeling or idea, that same moral spirit from which we believe
the interpreted word or action to proceed. Hence a certain
justification even of Kant's sweeping assertion that "imitation
finds no place at all in morality."[1] It is a needed reminder

---

[1] *Metaphysic of Ethics*, Sect. II. "Nor could anything be more fatal
to morality than that we should wish to derive it from examples. For
every example of it that is set before me must be first tested by principles
of morality, whether it is worthy to serve as an original example, i.e. as a

that, much as example may do for us, it cannot implant the moral spirit, because its efficacy presupposes in the onlooker that capacity of emotional and intellectual response without which there can be no real perception of moral quality in that which he beholds. There is an ancient principle in philosophy to the effect that "like is known by like." It is true here. If there be human beings without any potentiality of moral life already within them, the spectacle of even

> "that one society on earth
> The noble living and the noble dead,"

would not avail them. It would only bring to light more unmistakeably the extent of their moral incapacity.

Rightly regarded, this is not a discouraging doctrine, though at first sight it might seem to be so. It of course suggests the final limitation to the educative influence of Example. Yet this is a limitation to which we may well reconcile ourselves, because we can find in it evidence of the strength and independent vitality of the individual life. After all it would be a poor service, if the great examples of the earth could only hypnotise us into a blind and involuntary devotion to them. We have more to give, as they have more to ask. And we give this when, in the very act of loyal surrender, we assert that independent principle of moral life which constitutes our ultimate claim to an absolute moral worth[1].

Hence this final limitation of Example may furnish a proof of the moral strength of the individual.

pattern, but by no means can it authoritatively furnish the conception of morality. Even the Holy One of the Gospels must first be compared with our ideal of moral perfection before we can recognise him as such. * * * Example finds no place at all in morality, and examples serve only for encouragement." (Abbott's trans.)

[1] Cf. Kant, *Metaphysic of Ethics*, Section I. "Nothing can possibly be conceived in the world, or even out of it, which can be called good without qualification, except a good will."

A similar line of remark applies when that which is held up to us is not a single life, but an imaginative ideal of social relations, such as great minds have sometimes pictured, or such as most of us picture to ourselves at times, even though it may only take the form of more cheerful surroundings and more congenial occupations.

The superiority of a social type lies in its comprehensive-

Though a social type can better than an individual type embody the many-sidedness of duty,

ness. It can better embody the many-sidedness of duty and endeavour. It exhibits the duties of life sketched on a larger canvas. And if a type of this kind come from the mind of genius, its value does not really turn upon the question whether it is ever likely to be literally realised in

this world. The duties which it will embody—self-control, or courage, or love of truth, or justice—will remain of permanent value and applicability under social conditions wholly different. It is in this aspect it ought ever to be regarded, and not in the vain hope of finding in it a map for the guidance of the details of conduct. For this would be just as unreasonable as to estimate an individual example by its nearness to ourselves in time, place, and circumstance.

Yet the same limitations cling to the social type which

it is subject to similar limitations.

we have seen to be of the essence of the type that is individual. It is still concrete, and as such partakes inevitably of the limitations of

the place and time that produced it. Even Plato is an instance. He fashioned an ideal state on which men were to pattern their lives. He wrote of it as if it were a universal type. But even he who runs as he reads can see that it was Greek to the core. But the greater limitation is the other. No man ever yet drew in the first life-breath of the moral spirit from the spectacle of the greatest Utopia that it has entered into the heart of man to imagine. There must first be within him that which no ideal can implant. And it is for this

reason that even faultless outward conformity to the noblest of
social ideals would be a miserable substitute for the freely
given admiration, and the spontaneous loyalty, which are
at once root and fruit of the moral independence of the individual.

It may be added that this admiration of social Utopias has
its own peculiar dangers. One of them is
pedantry. Again and again in the history of the
world men have set themselves to mould their
lives after some social pattern far removed from
their day. It was so with our own Puritans and
Covenanters, who carried into their councils and battlefields
the precedents of the Old Testament, reading their Bibles,
as Sterling said, in the flash of their pistol shots. It was so
also with some of the enthusiasts of the Renaissance who
laboured to pattern themselves upon the Classical model;
and with the French Revolutionists who must needs set themselves to re-enact, under far other skies, the achievements of
Roman "freedom." The same thing happens in lesser ways,
as often as men or women fall in love with some plan of life
drawn upon the clouds of the past or the future, and brood
upon it till they are betrayed into follies or fanaticisms. Such
persons know well how to insist; the lesson they never learn
is when to desist.

The admira-
tion of social
Utopias may
also be per-
verted (a) to
pedantry;

The other danger is day-dreaming. There is an indolent
and improvident cheerfulness which is content
to feed on a diet of visionary schemes; and it
is a faculty (or a failing) which often serves to
carry its possessor lightly through much that is irritating, dull,
or hideous in the actual life around him. At least it is an
anodyne. But its weakness is disclosed in the hour of action.
It is so easy, when the first sod of a difficult duty has to be
cut, to turn aside and indulge in easy imaginings of some
fresh project. And so these builders of castles in the air grow
old, cheerful to the end, cheerful—and ineffectual.

(b) or to day-
dreaming.

When all is said, the conclusion must be faced that education through type, whether individual type or social, is by
Education through type, whether individual or social type, finds its limitations in the very nature of the faculty of imagination.
the very laws of imagination doomed to limitation. Let us not conceal it from ourselves that, in all its work, the imagination is engaged in something of an unconscious intellectual fraud. By its very nature it presents and can only present what is in some measure concrete, finite, limited. Such are the very conditions of imaginative presentment, even when it is presentment of the truth. And there is no fraud in this. The "fraud" only comes when the concrete, finite, limited picture is regarded as if it were the whole truth. And from this "fraud" it is hard to escape. The artist in biography, history, or fiction, is never more entirely honest, never truer to himself, than when he is guiltiest. For just as he is true to himself must he paint his picture with such charm and finish, such warmth and glow, that as we look at it, we are prone to forget all else besides. We forget, in other words, that his picture is but a fragment
The dangers of mistaking a part for the whole.
of life rent away from its context in the larger world of experience. For though (as we have seen above) he may tell us the truth, and nothing but the truth, he will not, he never can, tell us the whole truth. Hence, from the nursery tale to the epic, his strength and his weakness: his strength in glorifying aspects, phases, elements of human life and human nature: his weakness in doing this in such a fashion, "marrying gracious lies to the mind of him who reads them," as Cervantes has it, as to beguile us into a forgetfulness of how much else there is in the world beyond the limited completeness of his fascinating picture.[1]

---

[1] The aspects or elements of Life which Imagination selects and gathers up in its synthesis may, of course, be many. They may also be supremely important and inspiring. Thus Imagination may lead us towards truth,

For this, if for no other reason, we may suspect that there is room enough to supplement the morality that rests upon actual or imaged Type by that which looks to Precept.

because it may involve a great advance from the limitation, the onesidedness, the abstractness which ever cling to ordinary or common-sense views of life. Fiction may, in this sense, be far truer than so-called Fact. Yet there remains room for the criticism in the text. Spinoza hit the point exactly when he urged that errors, or rather limitations, due to "abstraction" (i.e. onesidedness and incompleteness of view) are never so hard to avoid as when they enlist the alliance of imagery.

CHAPTER XIII.

PRECEPT.

IF the morality of Type has been treated first, it is not because the morality of Precept appears at a later stage. For though it may not be till a later stage that precepts truly take effect, nothing is more certain than that infancy is not long past when they first make their appearance.

At an early period in a nation's life men begin to moralise. Their epics are no longer divided between war, love, and feasting: here and there, as in the pages of Homer, deep intuitions interspersed show that reflection has begun. So with their histories: the unreflective detail of annals is broken by the moralising vein. And, then, there arise these moralisers by profession—lyric poets who give expression to feelings that have begun to struggle for utterance, priests to reprove or direct, "wise men" whose oracular words pass from lip to lip. And so the growth of precepts goes, till every child born into the world comes into a great heritage of saws, proverbs, reflections, commonplaces, which have become part and parcel of the national mind; and which, being nothing if not practical, come ready to hand to moralist and educator. The result is familiar. Under all variety of circumstances, in season, and often out of season, we are fed on a diet of line upon line and precept upon precept. Children find precepts

Precept plays a con- spicuous part in life.

on the walls of their nurseries, and boys and girls in the
headings of their copy-books. When the country girl leaves
her home, it is with a precept her mother bids her farewell;
and it is with a precept that the father sends out his boy
to make his way in the world. In precepts the old man sums
up his lifetime's experience; and not seldom a man's last
legacy to those near him—when all other legacies are far
enough from his mind—is the legacy of a precept.

(1) *Unsystematized Precept.*

With facts like these in mind, it would be absurd to deny
that precepts help to shape men's lives. They do
so powerfully, even in the lowest of three phases
which they may assume—that phase in which

I. Un-
systematized
Precept.

they form a current popular morality without any pretensions
to system, or even arrangement. Lines of the poets, epigrams
of the moralists, words of the preachers, above all that multitude of proverbs whose origin no one can trace, and whose
authors no one can name—these are the forms in which the
moralist may find them now, just as the Platonic Socrates
found them in the Agora at Athens, when he went about discussing Justice. The value of proverbs is itself
proverbial. Proverbs have, at lowest, that currency which counsels that are commonplace so

Proverbial
morality.

readily enjoy. They move, for the most part, on a plane
which is only too level to the comprehension, "the wisdom
of many" if "the wit of one." And it is not to be forgotten
that "the wisdom of many," if foolishness in matters scientific,
is not likely to be so where the interests are moral. In a
sense we can do no better thing than turn a precept into a
commonplace. Wisely was it one of Spinoza's counsels that,
if men wish to come to the hour of action fully prepared, one
way in which they can do so is by rehearsing to themselves

in meditative hours the best and noblest maxims about life:—
"Wherefore the best we can compass so long as we have not
a perfect knowledge of our emotions, is to lay out a method
and settled rules of life, to commit these to memory, and
constantly to apply them to such particular cases as do
commonly meet us in life, so that our imagination may be
penetrated therewith, and we may ever have them at hand.
We laid down, for example, among the precepts of life, that
hatred should be conquered by love or high-mindedness, not
repaid in kind.   Now that this command of reason may be
always ready for us at need, we should often think upon and
consider the wrongs done by men, and in what manner they
are warded off by a noble mind.   For thus we shall knit the
image of a wrong done us to the imagination of this precept,
and the precept will always be at hand when a wrong is offered
us."[1]   One may go a step further, and maintain that it is
just because a precept *is* commonplace that it is likely to
go home.   For the commonplaces of morality
do not appeal to us on their own merits alone.
By reason of their currency they are more likely
than the most brilliant epigram to come enriched by association with events and experiences under which they may have
on memorable occasions been spoken.   It is this that wings
the shaft, and many a time sends a moral platitude home
to the feathers.   Here is a man whose conscience records
a lie: to cut him to the quick nothing unusual is necessary.
Some well-worn aphorism about telling the truth will suffice,
if spoken by an honest man.   Here is another taken unawares
by sudden temptation—what keeps him right?   Nothing epi-
grammatic certainly: only a few trite words said, it may be
years ago, by some one who loved and trusted him.   And
there is one memorable instance, beyond which nothing can
go as proof how words in themselves commonplace enough

The value of
moral com-
monplaces.

----

[1] Cf. Spinoza, *Ethics*, Part V, Proposition x., Scholium; cf. Pollock's
Spinoza, p. 285.

may gain from their setting. "Lockhart," said Sir Walter
Scott, when he was dying, "I may have but a minute to
speak to you. My dear, be a good man—be virtuous, be
religious—be a good man. Nothing else will give you any
comfort when you come to lie here."[1]

And yet, with or without adjuncts, even a hoard of precepts
is but a poor outfit. For they have a bewildering
way of contradicting each other. We have a
dozen to tell us that honesty is the best policy:
a dozen more to say that the children of this
world are wiser than the children of light. Some to declare
that like draws to like, and others that extremes meet: a
host to persuade us that to hesitate is to be lost, and we
are almost persuaded—till we remember that second thoughts
are best. As many to decide that it is never too late to
mend; and as many more to pronounce that as the tree falls
so it must lie. And when precepts are divorced from context
—as all proverbs are—what is to settle priority, when ten or
twenty thus conflict?

But proverbs often contradict each other,

Add to this that, while undoubtedly proverbs popularise
morality, they have an unfortunate tendency at
the same time to plebify it. They gravitate towards motives that are second-rate, and at best
respectably prudential. There is a risk that every one incurs
who betakes himself to the man of precepts. He may get
advice, or he may find that he has made himself a target for
platitudes. Nor does anything more certainly arrest the influence of "good advice" than the suspicion that it has been
made up as a general prescription. It is but human that
the passionate egoism of personal trial should revolt against
this exasperating procurability of moral commonplaces.

and become platitudes.

Some of these defects however can be remedied; and
as they spring in part at least from want of systematization,
the direction in which the remedy lies is clear. The desultory

[1] Lockhart's *Life of Scott*, vol. VII. p. 393.

saws and sayings of proverbial morality may be systematized into some sort of moral code.

(2) *Moral Codes.*

The great superiority of a code is that it implies selection; and, though mere ceremonial usages may at times be dignified as moral laws, selection of the best and most authoritative. In obvious ways this implies advance. There is a dignity, deliberateness, and breadth in the precepts of a code; and, as there is some attempt at unity, they cannot be so contradictory. This is not all. Once precepts are committed to a code, they acquire an educative value which neither severally nor collectively they possessed before. For codes are not framed lightly. They come from the hands of persons much in earnest with life, to whom a code is meaningless if it be not enforced; who therefore set themselves, in all ways possible, to back it up with legal, or social, or it may be supernatural sanctions, and who make it their life's work to teach and to preach it, until the world can hardly act at all without the commands, and the terrors, of the Law ringing in their ears. And so it comes to pass that a moral code may enter, like iron into the blood, into the lives of men and nations—like that primitive Hebrew decalogue which is the accepted code of the Western World. Moreover, a code of this kind, and with such a history, ends by being more than a code. It becomes the symbol of a time-honoured morality, and of a great religion; and as such it evokes, even to superstition and worship of the letter, a reverence and obedience far beyond the reach of any code without such associations, even though this were put together by the wisest heads.

The Moral Code.

Its superiority to unsystematized precepts.

Codes become symbols.

And yet, when all is said, there are features in the best
of codes which are profoundly unsatisfactory. Defects of
In the first place, a commandment, however the moral
impressively worded, is a weak instrument, un- code.
less the virtue it enjoins has already made good its place in
the feelings, the habits, and, in some measure, Nurture of
in the ideas of those to whom it is addressed. the virtues is
There is nothing easier than to use the words: needed to give meaning to
it is almost, though not always, as easy to listen precepts.
to them. The really hard task is to secure the states in the
soul, and the consciousness of these states, in absence of
which the words will signify little.

This was one of the truths that Pestalozzi, with his random
insight, saw so clearly. He did not give his pupils many
precepts. He tried, so he tells us, to create the feeling of
a virtue before he spoke much about it[1]. This is only what,
after a fashion, we often recognise. There are those of whom
we say: "The man does not know what honesty means."
And when we say so, we know that telling will not mend
matters, because the thing we are speaking about does not
really exist within a dishonest man's breast. What does he
know of honesty, its temptations, its struggles, its resolves?
Yet this is just what is so often forgotten. The commandment is gravely administered on the naive assumption that
nothing more is needed; when it might as well have been,
and indeed, so far as actual understanding of it goes, is spoken
in an unknown tongue.

It is well to remember this in making up our minds as
to the practical value of teaching about the Difficulty
duties of life, especially in home and school. of imparting
The difficulty that has to be faced is not that moral know- ledge.
of bringing conduct into line with precepts that
we can assume to be fully understood. There is the prior

[1] De Guimps' *Pestalozzi* (Russell's translation), p. 159. "I strove to
awaken the feeling of each virtue before talking about it."

task of bringing boy or girl, not to say man or woman, really to understand what we are speaking about. For moral knowledge is not on the same plane as scientific knowledge. When our talk is of triangles or plants we have no difficulty in conjuring up in the listening mind the things referred to. We can, if we please, draw the one upon a board, or produce the other from a herbarium. But we may expatiate about virtues or duties at great length and all in vain. Because, in the absence of the virtue or duty in our listener, our words will call up but a ghost of the fact we wish to convey.

Herein lies the weakness of all exhortation, especially in
Weakness of mere exhortation. dealing with the young. "Be honest, be industrious, be generous, brave, forgiving"; it is good advice; and the manner of those who give it may often encourage. But let us not fall into the illusion that miracles are to be wrought by exhortations. We must take a longer, more arduous, more effective way. We must first, by all the agencies at our disposal, by nurture of instincts and formation of habits, by "natural reactions," by the constant benevolent superintendence of family, school, church, and not least by appeal to examples, create the virtues. So that when the time comes, as it does come, for recourse to precept, it may find the thing of which the precept speaks already deeply rooted in the feelings, habits, thoughts, consciences of those to whom it is spoken.

There is the further defect that codes are seldom systematized enough. They select precepts, but
Codes fail to answer the question:— Which is the greatest commandment? they afford slight clue to the relative importance of the several commandments selected. They do not so much as seem to have contemplated cases where it is not only impossible to attach equal weight to each, but impossible to keep one without breaking another. Here, for example, are two precepts:—"Thou shalt not kill": and "Thou shalt not steal": the one enjoining the sacredness of life; the other of property.

These may conflict. Have they not often conflicted? To protect property do not men take life? To preserve life have they not, in dire straits, taken property? Yet here the code fails us. We need some principle of arrangement; in default of which we are driven to ask that most natural of questions: "Which is the greatest commandment?"

It is an even greater drawback that a code has so irresistible a tendency to become stereotyped and inelastic. All the instincts of moral and religious conservatism become bound up in it; *Rigidity of the moral code.* and the direst penalties are denounced, it may be executed, on the head of him who dares to take from or to add to it one jot or one tittle. But meanwhile life does not stand still. It flows on in ever increasing volume, however we may fossilize our formulas. Fresh experiences arise; unexpected situations develop; difficulties disclose themselves, unforeseen and unforeseeable when the code was framed. The problems of life, in a word, become so complex that it is no longer enough to fall to dutifully repeating the tables of the Law? "Thou shalt not kill": *The enlargement of experience discloses the ineffectual generality of commandments.* good! but there are many things in life, not usually called killing, which yet seem to kill. The stinging word, the pitiless act, the betrayed trust, the broken pledge—these shorten men's days. And what of the prison, the scaffold, or the carnage of the battle-field? They all kill. And when we say "Do not kill" which do we mean, all—or some—or which? Similarly, with "Thou shalt not bear false witness." It includes clearly enough the libellous perjury and the downright lie. But what of all the degrees of distortion or suppression of the truth, down to the significant look, the meaning shrug, the smiling insinuation that takes away our neighbour's good name? So throughout. It is vain to hope that the most pious reiteration of the generalities of a code can solve these difficulties of detail. When in the thick of actual life, time short, action urgent, issues momentous, men find themselves face to face with concrete problems, the rehearsal of moral generalities however sound, however venerable, will not avail much more than a repetition of the multiplication table. Impotent are the counsellors, who in the hour of our need can contribute nothing but a recital, however earnest, of moral generalities.

These difficulties bring us to a parting of the ways. Once

The inef-
fectual gene-
rality of pre-
cept may be
met in two
ways.

the ineffectual generality of precepts has made itself felt, two courses lie open. One is to see in this fact a final proof that a morality of precept is unequal to the demands of life, and to turn from it to a morality that centres its hopes in the training of individual judgment[1]. The second is to refuse to give up the morality of precept without a struggle, and to set resolutely to work to make it adequate to those facts of concrete moral experience by which the morality of code is tested and found wanting. These alternatives imply a fundamental divergence in educational policy. The fear that dictates the first is the production of the weak and self-distrustful character that leans for ever, and often in vain, upon guidance from without : the remedy is the nurture of the self-reliant conscience. In the second, the fear is that not only the youth but the grown man will prove unequal to the difficulties of life, and the remedy, the prolongation of authority and leading-strings throughout the whole of life.

It is the adoption of the second course that leads to the third phase of the morality of precept, that supreme effort to make moral dogmas adequate to life which gives rise to Casuistry.

CHAPTER XIV.

PRECEPT (*continued*).

Casuistry.

INJUSTICE is done to Casuistry because it is so often taken

Casuistry
defined.

to imply no more than the practice of making casuistical objections to moral rules, or possibly

---

[1] See p. 202.

of finding ingenious arguments for justifying the unjustifiable. But these are only incidents. Casuistry proper is a thing much more ambitious, because much more constructive; being indeed nothing short of an attempt to work out a body of authoritative moral precepts in detail, so as to show that every case of conduct, actual or possible, may consistently find its place under one or other of such precepts.

It is like a jurist working out a code of Law. Taking his fundamental laws to start with, the jurist goes on to anticipate the sort of cases which may be expected to present themselves to be dealt with, and by providing for them beforehand in the pages of his code, he enables perplexed enquirers, when the anticipated cases arise in actual life, to find their solutions ready to hand. So with the casuist. He is the jurist of morality. As the other takes his laws as he finds them, so he his body of moral rules; and this done, he goes on to do his best to specify, even to the uttermost detail, the cases to which these rules apply. And for such cases he is never at a loss. Experience furnishes many—and it is one merit of casuistry that it has so keen an eye for experience—but it is not even the widest actual experience that can satisfy him. He has, besides, all the resources of the fertile casuistical imagination.

Casuistry and Law compared.

Once more the legal parallel may help. Sir Henry Maine has told us of a primitive Irish Code of Laws, the Brehon Laws, which present two characteristics hard at first sight to reconcile. The one is that the experience of the men who drew them up was limited. Were they not monks? The other is that this code is celebrated for the singularly full and mature development into detail of its leading principles. But the explanation is easy. What though these monks had but a limited experience: they could none the less sit in their cloisters and invent cases far beyond their personal experience; invent them and solve them by applying to these creatures of their own imagination the principles of their code. With the result

The Brehon Laws.

that these Brehon laws are a monument of early Irish law singularly developed into all the ramifications of detail[1].

What these Brehon lawyers did in their department, the casuist does in his. Not content to wait on slow-footed experience, he takes the initiative and manufactures cases of conscience, invents difficulties, states fictitious problems; and then sets himself, with the help of his accepted code, to solve these cases, even when, for aught he can know, they never existed nor ever will exist in an actual world of men. And so it comes, as cases swell to chapters, and chapters to volumes, that, by this union of actual and fictitious experience, the great library of Casuistry is built up.

As thus built up, it has two characteristics :—(1) It is
Two charac-   dogmatic. It starts with a body of rules which
teristics of   it is its business to uphold. There is no ques-
Casuistry.   tion here of reforming moral rules, or of recasting
them to fit the facts of life. It is quite the other way; the facts of life are to be made, by devices shortly to be mentioned, to bend to them. (2) The second characteristic is that it is logical. Its precepts once accepted (whatever be their source), the next step is to show that the most exceptional case, even the most ingenious vagaries of the casuistical imagination, may be dealt with and solved with perfect consistency. This is the essence of casuistry; which indeed is nothing other than the most elaborate and unfaltering of all attempts to make life adapt itself to system.

It is this which makes it, in the domain of morals, a
Comparison   close counterpart of what Scholasticism is in
between Ca-   speculation[2]. When Scholasticism was at its
suistry and
Scholasti-   height the scientific and speculative spirit of
cism.   modern Europe had already begun to stir.

[1] Maine, *Early History of Institutions*, p. 44. "The Brehon appears to have invented at pleasure the facts which he used as the framework for his legal doctrine."

[2] Cf. Caird's *Kant*, 1st Edition. p. 25.

New discoveries, new thoughts, were, in the gradual revolution of experience, entering men's minds, and the task
of Scholasticism, as has often been shown, was to do its best
to show that no new expansion of experience could arise
which could not be shown to be consistent with the dogmas
of the Church. What Scholasticism thus tried to do for the
growing intellectual life of the West, Casuistry, when at a
later time it made its supreme effort in the hands of the
Jesuits, tried to do in regard to conduct. The Protestant
Reformation had taken place. Business, politics, private life,
were all disclosing new aspects, and there was a felt need of
a morality adequate to the wants of the day. It was then that
the Jesuits, with equal dogmatic confidence and intellectual
subtlety, set themselves to show that, no matter what cases of
conscience experience or suggestion might present, there could
be no case which the authoritative morality of the Church could
not cover.

Nor need we go so far afield for illustration. There is a
scholasticism which knows nothing of the Scholastics, and
a casuistry that has never heard of the Jesuits. When we
meet those who are convinced that in speculative formula
they have reached finality, such persons are in spirit (whatever
they may call themselves) Scholastics. Because, in true
scholastic spirit, their first question about anything which
science or speculation may have to reveal, is not the en-
quirer's question:—" Is it true ? " but the dogmatist's question :
—" How can it be squared with my preconceived system ? "
This is the scholastic, and the casuist of all times and places
is like unto him. For he in his turn is no less firmly
convinced that in respect of ultimate moral creed he has
nothing to learn and nothing to alter. And in like fashion
his first question about action, project, problem is not :—
" Is it right ? " or " Is it honest ? " It is the dogmatist's
question :—" How can this be covered by my infallible moral
code ? " Though the name be not there, the essence of the

thing is there—the dogmatic unbending spirit which is convinced that there is no difficulty of the moral life, however
unique, which cannot be shown to fall under its scheme of
life.

It follows that, be their shortcomings what they may,

Boldness of the casuistical aim. casuists are entitled to the credit of boldness.
Their task is not easy. It needs some confi-
dence to maintain that actual experience will
accommodate itself even to precepts of high authority. Here
is a man who shoots his wife to save her from falling into the
hands of mutinous Sepoys—can we call it murder? Here
is another who, aghast at the situation, tells a crowded
audience in a theatre on fire that there is no danger—is it
to be branded as lying? Here is another who knows that
the one chance for some fugitive slave is to send his pursuers
on a false scent—will honest men condemn him? It is so
that even actual experience furnishes cases which seem to
tie men up either to violate a moral law, or to become parties
to wrong and outrage. If fact furnishes cases like these, what,
we may well ask, is not within the power of casuistical imagination? The very pity of it is that men are sometimes so
perilously able, by comparatively easy combinations of the
complex elements of human conduct, wantonly to imagine
cases that (to use Burke's terse phrase) turn our very duties
into doubts. Where is the moral code, be its precepts drawn
with never so much care, which can stand the action of
solvents like these?

And yet the casuists were not daunted. For they had

Casuistical stress upon intention. an unfailing resource. They conjured by the
help of intention. If what from one aspect is
cut-throat slaughter is from another honourable
war; if what to one eye is assassination is to another patriotic
insurrection; if what in one estimate is wanton waste of costly
product of labour is in another the hyperbole of loving sacrifice,
we know well how the transformation comes. It comes by

reason of the stress we lay on the intention of the agent. Do we harshly condemn Desdemona when she told the fatal lie? If we do not, the reason is plain. We bear with the act for the sake of the intention.

This was of course the instrument which the great casuists wielded with such power. We need not wonder at their success. There are but two things needful: one, a body of well accredited moral precepts; the other, a fair measure of that imaginative subtlety that can manipulate intentions. Let but a man have these, and it will go hard with him if he do not make some progress towards bringing what ordinary men call robbery and murder under one or other of the precepts that are not to be questioned.

Hence the well-known doctrine of "directing the intention" which encountered the deep and delicate sar- casm of Pascal. "Know then," says the monk   "Directing the intention." in the *Provincial Letters*[1], "that this mar- vellous principle is our grand method of directing the in- tention. * * * For example, when I was showing you how servants might execute certain troublesome jobs with a safe conscience, did you not remark that it was simply by di- verting their intention from the evil to which they were acces- sory, to the profit which they might reap from the transaction. * * * But I will now show you the grand method in all its glory, as it applies to the subject of homicide—a crime which it justifies in a thousand instances." * * * "I foresee already," said I, "that according to this mode everything will be permitted, nothing will escape it." "You always fly from one extreme to the other," replied the monk. "For, just to show you that we are far from permitting everything, let me tell you that we never suffer such a thing as the formal intention to sin with the sole design of sinning; and if any person whatever should persist in having no other end but

[1] *Provincial Letters*, **VIII**. p. 147. (McCrie's trans.)

evil in the evil that he does, we break with him at once; such conduct is diabolical. * * * But when the person is not of such a wretched disposition as this, we try to put in practice our method of directing the intention, which simply consists in his proposing to himself, as the end of his actions, some allowable object. Not that we do not endeavour, in so far as we can, to dissuade men from doing things unlawful: but when we cannot prevent the action, we at least purify the motive, and thus correct the viciousness of the means by the goodness of the end."

This of course is satire; but it indicates where the effectiveness of the method lay. If there be no action so unmitigatedly evil in intention but that some extenuating plea may be put in, how much easier, when a project seems not bad but only doubtfully good, to bring it into the desired category of things permitted, by pointing out that it may be done with good, or, at very lowest, with respectable intentions. Nor, if Casuistry deserved the whip of Pascal, was it because it emphasized the intention as the main consideration in morality. It is in the best of company when it does so. All the greatest ethical thinkers, not excluding the utilitarians, agree that it is the inward aspect of conduct, and in one sense or other the intention of the agent, that makes an act moral at all. Nor can it be denied that many a violation of specific moral laws can still be kept within the pale of morality by the adoption of some well-directed intention. "We cannot prevent the action," said the monk. He said rightly. Hardly can such actions be wholly prevented. If they do not come in fact, they will come in suggestion. "We at least purify the motive," he added: and in so saying he did not necessarily become the apologist of immorality. He only specified a resource which by many an one, not casuistically minded at all, has been used in all honesty to justify unwilling departure from the letter of received morality.

This recognition of the importance of intention is not to be condemned.

It is on a similar ground that something may be said for the other resource of the great casuists—the more dubious doctrine of " Probabilism"[1]. This doctrine after all only formulates on a great scale what many men do many a time. They

The casuistical doctrine of Probabilism.

take advice and act on it; thereby making probable opinion the guide of their lives. Who will blame them? The baffling complexity, the inevitable urgency of the issues, force them to it. What more reasonable than to seek advice; what more unreasonable than to suspend action till advice perfectly satisfies our reason? Far short of this a man of sense, if the hour of action is not to pass, will ask no more, and, on the best advice he can get, take a leap in the dark.

If this be so, the casuists are not to be blamed if they counselled mankind to betake themselves to advisers; not even if they went so far as to hold that it was something if a man could justify his conduct by citing even one authority of

In certain aspects, this doctrine is reasonable.

standing which he had been at pains to consult. And then, such authorities were so accessible, in the persons or in the pages of these casuistical doctors themselves. Why should men reject this resource? They do not, in business life, dispense with legal advisers, or with practical experts. It is much if they can find even one trusted counsellor on whom to lean. Why then should they neglect the services of that moral lawyer, that moral expert, the casuistical adviser or the casuistical father-confessor? And yet, in one aspect, the

---

[1] Cf. Sidgwick, *History of Ethics*, p. 151. "The theory (of Probabilism) proceeded thus:—A layman could not be expected to examine minutely into a point on which the learned differed; therefore he could not fairly be blamed for following any opinion that rested on the authority of even a single doctor; therefore his confessor must be authorised to hold him guiltless, if any such 'probable' opinion could be produced in its favour, nay, it was his duty to suggest such an opinion, even though opposed to his own, if it would relieve the conscience under his charge from a depressing burden."

doctrine of Probabilism is nothing more. Assume the existence of accredited moral advisers; grant the
urgency of practical issues; realise how often
men are driven to act on the opinions of
other persons—it follows that any man who has, under these
circumstances, taken advice, whether from casuistical doctor
or from private friend, has followed a course which the world
would characterise as ordinary prudence. As long as there is
lack of the rapid grasp of fact, the swift judgment, the moral
nerve needed by every one who is to grapple for himself with
the complexity and urgency of life's issues, so long will experience furnish an argument for the doctrine of Probabilism.
The rule of life which Casuistry suggests is therefore simple,
however deep moral perplexities may be. "Go to your
casuistical volume and turn up chapter and verse to find
your case anticipated and solved." Or should it happen that
we cannot well find our way in these authorities, any more
than we can in the pages of a law book, what simpler than
to go to our lawyer in morality? He too will have his cases
at his finger tips, our case among the rest, and out of his
resources he will in due time produce the opinion which is
to set our doubts and difficulties at rest.

The need for advice in moral action.

If this be a true account of Casuistry, it would be idle
to deny that it has merits: it is at any rate a
practical protest against the weakness that rests
content with moral generalities. Getting advice
or giving advice, it is with too many of us a
matter of "transgressions," "backslidings," "sins,"
"shortcomings," "temptations," all in the same strain of comfortable vagueness. Will these suffice? Would the most
ordinary of fathers, giving advice to his son as he sent him
out into the world, be content with this? Would he not rather
think of specific sins, concrete temptations, and by thus
anticipating the actual guise in which evil might come, be
enabled to say something as to the precise way in which,

Casuistry is thus a protest against recourse to moral gene- ralities;

when it did come, it could best be met? Bare prudence tells
us that a man is wise to come to the hour of
difficulty with his battles already half-fought. It
is, in point of fact, what is already done by a
large part of mankind, who are all confirmed
casuists at least in this—that they spend many
an hour in anticipating with astonishing minuteness possible
situations in which they may be placed, and in inwardly
resolving what they shall do or say, should these possibilities
come to pass. It is thus, that, as age fights its battles over
again, youth and manhood may fight them beforehand, so
that, by these private (often very private) rehearsals for the
drama of life, they may make sure, when the time comes,
that they will not fail to play their parts. Yet this is just
what Casuistry attempts to do on a larger scale. It anticipates
concrete cases of conscience only that it may solve them
beforehand.

and does justice to the concrete difficulties of moral problems.

It is precisely here however that issue may be joined.
Casuistry has the merit of trying to be practical,
but for that very reason it lands itself in what is
impracticable. For be the casuist never so
subtle in the suggestion of cases, he will often
fail signally to fore-figure the precise difficulties which arise
in fact. The casuistical treatise is unequal to the subtlety
of moral experience. So too is the casuistical
expert. Those who consult him, if their case
be one of genuine perplexity, will be apt
to go away—as patients with some intricate
malady often leave the consulting-room—feel-
ing that the casuistical adviser had not, and indeed could
not have, their case before him in all its details, and that
after all they have undergone in vain the humiliation of trying
to lay bare their soul before another's eye. For it is not
egotism to think our troubles unique. The egotism lies in
exaggerating their magnitude. In their character they are

Yet, in the effort to be practical, it becomes unpractical.

Can the casuistical expert have the whole concrete case before him?

13—2

unique. Else were there not so many persons who are never satisfied with advice however copious, and who return to the charge with an importunity that makes them the torment of their advisers. This is the fatal weakness of "Probabilism." It rests on the assumption that we can find an adviser able to see eye to eye with us in concrete matters which in their fulness are known to ourselves alone.

A further criticism follows. For it is inevitable that in

Casuistry is, further, apt to suggest diffi- culties that never arise.

this vain effort precisely to forecast experience, Casuistry will squander energy upon issues that are gratuitous. This goes on even in ordinary life. How much force is wasted, especially by nervous persons, upon issues that never arise, upon rehearsals for plays that are never performed! If suddenly called upon to save life, how should we act? If asked for this favour or that, how treat the request? Idle questions! The hour never comes to put us to the proof. Similarly with the casuist: in proportion as he is zealous to develop his system into detail, for one event that comes to pass he may forecast fifty that never exist out of his imagination. This is bad economy. It wastes resources. Men cannot afford in life to burn too much powder upon sham fights.

It is a more serious consideration still that the casuist may

And may turn duties into doubts.

easily produce a result the opposite of that which he proposes. Sincerely bent upon turning men's doubts into duties, he may end by turning their duties into doubts[1]. And in his eagerness to uphold his moral dogmas, he may find that he has succeeded only in habituating the minds of his disciples to the idea of their infringement.

This was a point acutely realised by Burke in regard to Casuistry in politics. Every reader knows how Burke dreaded

---

[1] Cf. Burke, *Appeal from the New to the Old Whigs*, Works (Bohn's Ed.), Vol. III. p. 81. "But the very habit of stating these extreme cases is not very laudable or safe: because, in general, it is not right to turn our duties into doubts."

and denounced the politicians, or political theorists, who were
for ever debating the right of insurrection or Illustration
the legitimacy of revolution. It was not that he from Casuistry
held all talk of revolution, or even revolution in politics.
itself, to be wrong. He had read history too well. He knew
that there are dire occasions on which Revolution, "the last
bitter potion of distempered states" needs must come. But none
the less it was in his eyes nothing short of a crime that the
discussion that knows no reticence should lightly stir questions
which threw doubts upon the authority of the laws upon which
the commonwealth stands. The same holds in the casuistry
of morals. There too it needs must be that the dire emergencies come. But for that very reason a man of sense will be
chary of making them every-day topics with all comers. It is
the bane of all casuistical discussion that it gives to exceptional
cases a currency which, as exceptional, they ought never to
possess. When such issues arise a man does well to face
them : he no longer does well if he cries them aloud upon
the housetops. For then he need not be surprised if (to para-
phrase the words of Burke) he has turned the extreme medicine
of life into its daily bread, and thereby made the moral constitution of his fellow men dangerously valetudinary[1].

This danger is never so great as in the education of
youth and innocence. It is so easy, in the Danger of
interests of morality, to put questions that Casuistry in
become the first revelation of the possibilities of the education
of the young.
immorality. For the casuist is a moral patholo-
gist. He brings with him a large knowledge of the thousand
shapes in which perplexities and temptations may come ; and
the risk is that, by the suggestion of the pitfalls that beset the
feet of those he wishes to help, he may instil, first, suspicion
of themselves, and then suspicion of those they meet, where
there was previously the innocent and wholesome illusion that
there was nothing to suspect. For it is not in this way, by

---

[1] Cf. Burke, *Reflections on the French Revolution*, Works, Vol. II. p. 335.

warnings however well meant which suggest that they are capable of evil, that we can best help the young. It is by persuading them that they are capable of good that we can hope to make them good in reality[1].

Difficulty of warning against vice without corrupting the mind.

Men argue sometimes that a knowledge of evil is sure to come in any case. Does it not come through books, through newspapers, through experiences which unhappily cannot be avoided? And they insist, not without reason, that it is better that such knowledge should come from a responsible father or teacher who brings the antidote along with it, than be left to the disclosures of irresponsibility and accident. Be it granted that something of this is necessary. Inoculation with the virus of disease is sometimes, as we know, an antidote to disease in a deadlier form. Yet the central fact remains untouched : the best moral antidote lies not in warnings however particular, but in that positive nurture of character which is the real source of strength in the hour of temptation.

Beyond this there is the effect of Casuistry on the casuist himself. The man who keeps the consciences of his neighbours will need all his strength to preserve his own. He will soon cease to be easily shocked. For he will be so familiar with all degrees of moral lapse, and so adept in the art of justifying case upon case which involves a wider and ever wider deflection from ordinary morality, that even in his own despite, he may end by holding a brief in the name of morality for what is usually regarded as lying, theft or murder, and thereby lay himself open to the indignant protests of the popular conscience.

Effects of Casuistry upon the casuist.

It is not however by the popular conscience that Casuistry is finally to be judged. The popular mind is too rough in its categories, too vague in its definitions, too robust in its judgments, to do justice to the perplexities of the genuinely tender conscience. And the same holds true of that other

[1] Cf. p. 88.

anti-casuistical appeal to criminal justice. It has happened before now that, by the casuistical manipulation of intentions, men have found themselves within the clutches of the law. And where there has been an easy or a sinister self-sophistication, the onlooker may be pardoned if he feels a glow of satisfaction at the shattering of a fool's or a knave's illusion. It is in fact just one of the results that Pascal knew how to suggest :

Yet Casuistry is not to be judged by appeal either to the popular conscience or to criminal justice.

"You have certainly," continued I, "contrived to place your disciples in perfect safety so far as God and the conscience are concerned ; for they are quite safe in this quarter, according to you, by following in the wake of a grave doctor. You have also secured them on the part of the confessors, by obliging priests, on the pain of mortal sin, to absolve all who follow a probable opinion. But you have neglected to secure them on the part of the judges ; so that, in following your probabilities, they are in danger of coming into contact with the whip and the gallows. This is a sad oversight."

"You are right," said the monk ; "I am glad you mentioned it. But the reason is, we have no such power over magistrates as over the confessors, who are obliged to refer to us in cases of conscience, in which we are the sovereign judges."

"So I understand," returned I ; "but if, on the one hand, you are the judges of the confessors, are you not, on the other hand, the confessors of the judges? Your power is very extensive. Oblige them, on pain of being debarred from the sacraments, to acquit all criminals who act on a probable opinion ; otherwise it may happen, to the great contempt and scandal of probability, that those whom you render innocent in theory may be whipped or hanged in practice." [1]

Yet, again, the appeal is not conclusive. Law is a rough engine : and laws are, moreover, enacted not to emphasise moral distinctions but to secure political order or progress.

---

[1] *Provincial Letters,* Letter VII., Mᶜ Crie's trans., p. 145.

And as, in pursuit of its own ends, Law is mainly concerned with overt acts, and only indirectly with motives, it will sometimes happen that a convict may find himself among criminals in comparison with whose moral infamy he is innocence itself. It therefore does not follow that because Casuistry may have brought men to the gallows, it stands condemned.

For criminals in the eye of the Law may not be moral offenders.

The truth is that such appeals do not go to the root of the matter. The real weakness of Casuistry is not disclosed in those casuistical apologies that outrage the popular conscience. The vulnerable point lies, not in the suggestion that a lie must be told or a life taken, but in the dogmatic spirit in which these repulsive possibilities are treated. For Casuistry be it remembered is the peculiar product, neither of an age of easy faith nor of an age of easy scepticism. It comes when moral difficulties have made themselves felt; but when, as yet, there is no thought of setting aside the traditions of the elders. The result is the struggle to fit new cases into old forms at all costs, which produced the great casuistical systems—a struggle the whole aim of which was to show that the refractory exceptional cases were consistent with that dogmatic version of morality which the orthodox casuist still insisted on receiving at the hands of authority. But it is not in this fashion that a real case of conscience is to be solved. When one of these dire emergencies has come in which, with the command of the law "Thou shalt not lie," "Thou shalt not kill" still ringing in his ears, a man feels bound to lie or to kill, his one and only justification must be sought in the conviction that he is setting a lesser moral obligation aside in obedience to a higher. It is not—as Jacobi has it in an often quoted passage—that "the law is made for the sake of man and not man for the sake of the

The central defect of Casuistry is due to its dogmatic character.

Casuistical cases needs must come;

and must be solved by appeal to moral law.

law."[1] If man is not to be the creature of caprice, he must be made for law. The choice is between two kinds of law and two kinds of obedience—obedience to the law of which the last word is "Thus it is written," and obedience to that other law which is more enduring and more imperative than anything that can ever find adequate embodiment in any code of precepts. The final mistake of the casuist is, that of these alternatives he chooses the first. His hands are tied by his own code, and when he should have boldly asked the strong question :—" Is this moral ? " he asks that how much weaker question :—" Is this consistent with formula ? " And if to the nerve to put his question, for which he deserves all credit, he add the dogmatic determination to find an answer in the affirmative, he must expect that, in the effort of a subtle mind to force a false and narrow consistency, he will torture actions till he provokes the scorn of the honest man, and the laugh of the satirist.

The casuist's weakness lies in making his final appeal to precepts based on Authority.

For the casuist's error lies not in " directing the intention." There is no higher aim for the moralist than to "direct the intention." The great matter is, *whither*? It is there that failure comes, because it is there that instead of appealing to the one imperial court of Moral Law, the casuist knows no higher morality than that which moves within the provincial jurisdiction of formulated precepts. Casuistry will always render the world great services ; but perhaps the greatest of them will be that, by attempting the impossible, it may prove the inadequacy of a morality of precept even when consecrated by authority, and thereby send mankind in search of something deeper.

This weakness of Casuistry discloses the need for the training of the individual moral judgment.

---

[1] Cf. an interesting note in Caird's *Kant*, Vol. II. 216.

PART III.

SOUND JUDGMENT.

CHAPTER I.

SOUND MORAL JUDGMENT.

THE shortcomings of the morality of Precept may, however, be met otherwise than by following the casuist. Instead of developing general precepts into detail, there is the alternative of training the individual to decide concrete issues for himself, and in this case effort will be concentrated upon the education of what may most fitly, because most comprehensively, be called sound individual judgment.

Educational systems, however, differ widely as to the encouragement to be given to this supremely important faculty. Some, fearful of premature freedom, strive to prolong even into adult years the guidance of authority (as we have seen in Casuistry). Others dread the creation of the limp character that to the last leans helplessly on good advice. Yet, sooner or later, even under any system, the need for a sound judgment will make itself felt. From early years young people must needs be left free to exercise some choice in their own small realm of School or Pastime. And, as time goes on, weightier decisions will come

Educational systems differ as to the place and value of individual judgment.

Yet the various resources of moral education all point to the ultimate need of it.

with the inevitable temptations and perplexities that are laid often enough on shoulders still young. In the long run nothing else will suffice. The unsuspecting confidence of instinct goes, not to return again. The hardly less unsuspecting confidence of habit gets many a shake in the face of changing situations. The examples an expanding experience offers disclose their limitations, and begin to bewilder by their very multitude. Precepts, however valued, can no longer disguise their mutual contradictions and their ineffectual generality. And if Casuistry steps in to develop them into detail, this is but a postponement. The day comes when the individual is brought face to face with his own peculiar difficulties, so commonplace yet so unique. He must learn to judge his own judgments, or confess himself pitifully unequal to the demands of life.

It is good that it should be so. For of all human faculties there is none which more enriches our lives than a sound moral judgment. Genius is rarer and more wonderful. But this surpasses even genius in the fact that it is not only in itself a virtue but the fruitful mother of virtues. It is as Aristotle said, "Given a sound judgment and all the virtues will follow in its train."[1] Place its possessor in business; and, as the years go round, he will by many a shrewd decision develop the merchant's virtues. Cast his lot among friends, and he will prove himself considerate, faithful, generous. Ask him to enter public life, and even on that slippery foothold he will choose the path that leads to the civic virtues. So all round the wide circle of human interests and duties. For a sound judgment has a twofold efficacy. By choosing right acts it further carries on, and confirms, the

Supreme value of a sound judgment.

It is not only a virtue, but the parent of virtues.

---

[1] *Ethics*, Bk. VI., c. xiii. 6. "The presence of the single virtue of prudence implies the presence of all the moral virtues." (Peters' translation.)

habits of the days of tutelage; and, by its emancipated out-look and open-eyed deliberate choice, it lifts its possessor clear of the automatism into which Habit, even at its best, is prone to fall. Hence it brings an independence which nothing else can give. For, once a man has it, he can never be nonplussed and baffled. No matter how his sphere of action may vary—and it may vary from cottage to palace—the manner of his decisions will never vary. In all places and at all times, by dint of what some will call moral in-sight; some, conscience; some, moral tact; or some simply, good sense, he will know how to pitch upon the very action which, under given circumstances, is the action which ought to be chosen. And should he err, as he well may, he will be the first to recognise his error, and amend it.

Mutatis mutandis it is what we often find in the arts, whether they be the fine arts or those humbler practical arts to which the Greek philosophers were forever likening the moral life. With the sagacity of the craftsman in the greater art of living, and without the pedant's entanglement in precedents and cut and dried rules, the man of sound judgment, sometimes after de-liberation anxious and prolonged, sometimes by a swift insight that appears to take in end and means at a glance, will from competing alternatives pick out just that one which the occa-sion demands. "Prudence," says Burke in the true spirit of Aristotle, "is not only the first in rank of the virtues, political and moral, but she is the director, the regulator, the standard of them all."[1] And, then, this possession is enduring. Ac-complishments may rust for lack of encourage-ment or lack of opportunity; and gifts, even the greatest, may come to nothing by long-lived pressure of urgent duties or sordid cares. But practical wisdom brings the self-sufficing consolation that for

The analogy of the arts.

A sound practical judg-ment is an in-alienable pos-session.

[1] Burke, *Appeal from the New to the Old Whigs*, Works, III. p. 16. (Bohn's Ed.)

it the sphere can hardly, if ever, be denied. For its achievements men find opportunities every day they live; and the fate which may take money, position, friends, cannot rob them here. Once truly theirs, they yield it up only with life itself, and even in the last scene of all they have often enough borne witness to its vitality by meeting their end with becoming fortitude.

It is just here, however, that we find ourselves confronted by an educational difficulty of the first magnitude. For if a sound judgment be thus invaluable, it seems to be likewise incommunicable, and this to an exasperating degree. Social tact cannot be communicated to the victim of awkward manners. Artistic skill is not to be taught to the spoiler of canvases, or to the bungler in arts and crafts. And, at first sight at all events, it appears not otherwise with sanity of judgment.

But is it not beyond the educator's art?

This is what many a man of affairs has felt to his cost, when forced to entrust some delicate negotiation to a subordinate whose good sense he could not trust. It is what the self-distrustful, conscious of past wrong-headed estimates, have known only too well, when, face to face with a critical decision, they would give all the world for that sagacity to which not even their dearest friends can help them. "If you want learning," once said a Scottish divine, "you may get it from books. If you lack grace you may pray for it. But if you lack judgment, God help you!" So incommunicable is this supreme virtue. And indeed it is just for this reason that there is a widely diffused conviction that what is variously described as "mother-wit" and "common sense," and "sagacity," and "shrewdness," and "practical wisdom," is after all a gift of Heaven, and as such quite beyond the educator's art.

Seeming incommunicability of sound judgment.

Happily, however, it is not so incommunicable as appears. A sound judgment is in point of fact a highly complex product.

It is resolvable into elements. And, though in the mature type of man these elements have come to be so organically knit that in exercise they work like a single faculty, it is not beyond analysis to detect what they are, and to scrutinise the manner of their union. It is in this direction that hope lies. Grant that the greatest master of moral training cannot directly impart this soundness of judgment: it still remains to ask what he can do in securing the presence, and the union, of the elements out of which it is fashioned.

Moral education can, however, do much to secure the elements of sound judgment.

These elements appear to be three in number. If the moral judgment is to be sound it must presuppose *character, faculty to deliberate,* and *enlightenment*[1].

What these elements are.

It is of the very essence of our moral, as distinguished from our scientific, judgments that they are profoundly dependent upon the character of the person who frames them. It is indeed one of Aristotle's greatest merits to have seen that character tells vitally upon the decisions of our daily lives as it does not and cannot tell upon the judgments we frame about scientific matters of fact. The cleverest of men, he tells us, will be but a clever scoundrel if cleverness be not allied with virtuous habits; and vice, while it leaves unaltered our perceptions about lines or triangles, is swift to corrupt our decisions upon matters of life and conduct[2]. A high authority tells us that "things hidden from the wise and prudent are revealed to babes." Absurd as applied to science, and worse than absurd if twisted into an apology for ignorance, it has its truth in morality.

1. Dependence of soundness of moral judgment upon the character.

---

[1] I may perhaps refer to my *Ethics of Citizenship,* where this subject has been treated in its relation to political consistency, c. vii. 3rd ed. (MacLehose & Sons.)

[2] *Ethics,* Bk. VI. v. 6, and VI. xii. 10. "Vice perverts us and causes us to err about the principles of action."

The reason is that, in these decisions of our daily lives—acceptance of a situation, spending of money, advice given to a friend, and so on—it is never enough for us simply to *know*. We must also *weigh.* To see with clear eyes the conditions involved in plan or suggestion is much: to lay a just emphasis upon each condition is more. Thus, if it be a question of giving, a man must not think too much of money and too little of mercy; too much of his own thrift, too little of others' needs; too much of the manner of his gift and too little of its urgency or end. For our difficulties in such matters would be light in comparison with what they are, did they end with the mere knowledge of the circumstances involved. The harder, yet no less imperative, task is to weigh this condition as against that, so that, in face of possible exaggerations, possible under-estimates, which in truth are as numerous as are the circumstances involved, we may preserve that delicate equipoise and balance in our valuations which is the central condition of all wise decision[1].

We must not merely k n o w, but w e i g h the conditions of our actions.

Hence that familiar experience that it is so hard to bring our friends to see eye to eye with us, even upon some comparatively simple issue, if the issue be moral. It is a much harder task than the teaching of physics or mathematics. For, while of course we may expect that our friends will, up to a certain limit, understand our words, it would be rash to hope, with anything like the same confidence, that their weights will be our weights, their perspective our perspective, their emphasis our emphasis. To the type of character, for example, in which there is a congenital proclivity to pleasure, or shrinking from pain, not all the words of all the sages will prevent pleasure or pain from tending to bulk too large in every project and every decision of his life. Only by effort and self-discipline will he keep these things in their due

This helps to explain the divergencies of opinion upon moral issues.

[1] Cf. p. 76 and p. 164.

place. For the worst of such predispositions is not said
when we acknowledge that they lead astray in *action*. The
taint goes deeper. Horror of pain or greed for pleasure will
distort the just proportions of things, and render their victim
incapable of that fair and unprejudiced outlook upon which
sound judgment, the parent of action, ought ever to rest. As
Burns has it :

> "If self the wavering balance shake
> 'Tis rarely right adjusted."

Herein we may see the flaw in that old Socratic doctrine
that virtue can be taught. If we construe it
to mean that a teacher in morality can, by the
contact of mind with mind, bring his disciple
to see eye to eye with him in the decisions of
life, as for example we certainly can in mathematics, it is
not true. One mind can teach another facts, and, given a
modicum of aptitude to work upon, can bring the learner to
follow scientific arguments. The terms used (triangles, re-
sultants, vibrations, acids and so forth) will here mean the
same to the mind that gives and the mind that takes. Not
so in morality. The simplest maxims are enough to disclose
the difference. "Honour your father and your mother,"
"repay that obligation you incurred last year in money
or service," "help your friends in their troubles"—there is
not one of these simple injunctions, be it expounded with
never so much care, but will convey different shades of
meaning, fluctuating according to the temperament, instincts,
habits, experience, of the person in whose ears they sound.
For as soon as these and all similar injunctions are applied, forthwith the possibility of
the widest divergence in the estimate of actualising conditions will emerge. So much so
that what to one man will rank as the sacred and cherished
duty of honouring father or mother by supporting their old

Hence the difficulties of moral instruction,

especially where the issues are concrete.

age, may to another (who still owns the obligation of the fifth commandment) be no more than a claim thrust down by coldness of heart to the rank of an unwelcome tax.

It is in this aspect that justice is by no means always done to the value of goodness of character. Popularly, goodness is not especially associated with wisdom. It is often even credited as a set-off against the lack of wisdom. "A good man," they say, "but not a wise one." Nor need we deny that the verdict finds a certain justification in the many mixtures of virtue with folly that human nature can present. Yet, in strictness, the antithesis is false. Wisdom in the affairs of life has no more indispensable ally than goodness of character. Goodness of character alone can purge the mind of that distorted, if not sinister, outlook upon life which betrays our steps by working havoc with all sanity of judgment.

The popular antithesis between goodness of character and practical wisdom is false.

A second condition of soundness of judgment is deliberative faculty[1].

Roughly speaking, the actual decisions of our lives are concerned with the discovery of means to ends. The larger ends at any rate are past deliberating about, and the thesis, "Shall the material universe be dissolved?" — propounded once by a northern debating society—is hardly more gratuitous than the question, "Shall we serve our country?" or "Shall we pay our debts?" or "Shall we tell the truth?" These larger ends are, in short, thrust upon us by the clear requirements of our station in life. What remains, and it is task sufficient, is to discover how best these ends may be compassed.

2. Soundness of judgment involves ability in Deliberation.

Deliberation is concerned with means to ends.

---

[1] Perhaps I may again refer to my *Ethics of Citizenship*, pp. 97—101, 4th ed., where Deliberation is briefly discussed in some of its political aspects.

Now it may not be said that there can be no choice of
means without deliberation. Two facts show
that there can. One is the existence of the
impressive faculty of intuitively divining means,
as soon as the end is so much as mentioned.
The other is the thrice familiar adoption of
precedents. For, of course, in a world where experiences
repeat themselves, there are so many accepted ways of
marching to familiar ends that few have time or desire to make
them serious matter of deliberation or discussion.

Intuition, and recourse to precedents may take the place of Deliberation.

Yet the need for deliberation remains. Intuition, one may
suspect, especially when men call it conscience,
gets more than its due. In many of its most
striking achievements it is intuition only in
appearance. For the masters of decision do not care to lay
bare the workings of their minds in their hours of indecision,
which might by their critics be construed as the hours of their
weakness. And so it comes that many a judgment that passes
with the world as intuitive, may really cover up the brief
wearing tension of swift deliberation. And though it may not
be denied that deliberation is often dispensed with, this does
not touch the fact that, without it, there can be no security.
For though the intuitive choice of means is wonderful as
clairvoyance, like clairvoyance it is often wrong, and none the
less wrong because it so easily mistakes its own self-confidence
for a proof of infallibility. Hence the derisive diatribes of
Bentham against Conscience and Moral Sense
and Common Sense, with their dogmatic and
self-sufficient claim to solve moral problems by
the easy short-cut of intuition. "Another comes and the
phrase changes. It is no longer the 'moral sense,' it is
'common sense' which tells him what is good and what is bad.
This 'common sense' is a sense, he says, which belongs to
everybody; but then he takes good care, in speaking of everybody, to make no account of those who do not think as he

Yet neither of them is adequate.

Bentham's attack on Intuition.

does¹." Hence too Bentham's substitution of a purely utilitarian Calculus or moral arithmetic for intuition in all its forms.
Not that we need pin our faith to Bentham either. His own
onesidedness was certainly not less than that of the objects of
his peculiar detestation. And it may reasonably be argued
that the imperious urgency of life's problems, if nothing more,
forces intuitive decisions even upon the utilitarian mind. Yet
these Benthamite sarcasms may stand. Nor is it the least of
the services of Utilitarianism that it was never weary of remind-
ing the world that it is one thing to judge, and another to find
securities that judgment is justified. There is less security still
in the easy resort to precedents. They may suffice for those
whose lives run in ruts. But they find their limitations in the
fact that, in the changeful scene of human activities, so many
decisions are hard just because life does not repeat itself.
With deliberation, on the other hand, comes security, such
security as is attainable only when chosen means is, intelligently
and by actual calculation, linked to adopted end.

This is however a harder task than might at first sight
appear. For there are two aspects under which
the means to an end may be regarded. It may
be viewed simply as a means and nothing more :
the sole question then to settle is if it leads to
the end by the directest path. But it may have
a second aspect: as a thing to be done, it may have in itself
more or less of moral worth. These two aspects may of
course coincide. The shortest cut to an end may be also the
most moral means towards it. But they may also conflict—
conflict so sharply that the line of action which one man would
welcome as the straight path towards an end, may have to be
set aside by his more scrupulous neighbour for one that is less
direct but more moral. Hence the soundness of the well-
worn dictum that in moral action—as contrasted with artistic

Deliberation in things moral is complicated by considera-tions of moral value.

¹ Cf. Bentham's *Theory of Legislation*, c. III. Section I, "The Arbitrary Principle."

production—the end does not justify the means. It cannot
justify the means, because, beyond that mere
conduciveness to the end, in which moral and
artistic means are alike, the means to a moral
end ought not to be chosen till it satisfies the moral judgment
of the chooser.

*End does not
justify means.*

It is this that complicates deliberation in things moral. It
is not the same as asking how to grow a crop or
how to turn out a commodity. These are cases
to be met by straightforward calculation, qualified
only by considerations of material cost. Conscience or moral
valuation plays at most but a subordinate part. But it is
otherwise in matters of conduct. The means has there to be
weighed in moral scales; and thereby come divergencies of
estimate to which there is nothing adequately parallel in the
province of the arts. And it is this, this moral valuation, that
is the most perplexing part of the problem.

*Comparison
with delibera-
tion in the arts.*

From this it becomes evident that what has been specified
as the first condition of soundness of judgment
is closely interwoven with the second. Training
of character will of course not of itself enable its
possessor to deliberate well: he may still lack
the calculative faculty: he may not be clever enough. But,
by the moral estimates which it has engrained in feeling and
habit, it will save him from cutting short deliberation by the
unscrupulous choice which brushes aside moral misgivings, if
only it is once satisfied that means will lead to end by the
shortest path.

*Hence a
well-trained
character helps
Deliberation.*

For it is important here to remember that the adoption of
a good end will not, as human nature is constituted, secure us in the choice of corresponding
means. Many a man, firmly resolved to serve
his city or help his friends, has dropped woefully
down the moral scale when it came to the actual
choice of the means whereby these excellent

*Even the
sincere adop-
tion of a good
end may not
ensure the
choice of the
best means.*

ends were to be gained. His failure is not intellectual. It lies in some weakness of response to what is better, some facility of response to what is lower, and this again has its root in incapacity of instinctive or emotional or habitual reaction to moral stimulus.

There are, in fact, two misconceptions as to deliberation in things moral which must here be carefully excluded. On the one hand, it is not to be regarded as if it were a process of intellectual calculation like the working out of a theoretical problem. As we have already seen, it is not so purely calculative as even the working out of a practical problem in the arts. For at every suggested step there enters a practical moral valuation, dependent upon the whole previous training of the character. On the other hand, it must not be resolved into a mere competition between isolated objects of desire carried on till the strongest appetite is liberated by finding its appropriate object[1]. For so far is this from being what actually takes place, that suggested actions which appeal to the most imperious natural desires may be rejected in a moment. And the reason is that, despite the strength of their attraction, they do not find a welcome in that context of character which has been woven together by the nurture and discipline of moral training. The final preference, the choice that immediately precedes action, is determined by the whole complex psychical disposition which is the result of moral education and experience. In other words, the less worthy means to an end, however it may tempt us in the hour of weakness, loses its effective attractiveness and its power over us, because it is alien to the settled context of a virtuous life. Hence the supreme importance of education from earliest years in preparing

[Marginal note: Deliberation is not a process of mere intellectual calculation:]

[Marginal note: nor a competition of desires.]

---

[1] Cf. Hobbes' definition of Will. "In Deliberation, the last Appetite, or aversion, immediately adhering to the action, or to the omission thereof, is that we call the Will." *Leviathan*, Part I. c. vi.

us for those deliberative efforts that come later on. Our

Early educa-
tion is of su-
preme import-
ance in pro-
viding the
conditions of
sound De-
liberation.
preferences have their beginnings in childhood, and in the objects we are then taught to seek or to shun. And though our childish preferences are modified in a hundred ways as the circle of our interests expands, and the larger outlook upon life relegates this preference or that to its due place of insignificance, still it is the system of sympathies and antipathies, of attractions and repulsions, which grows steadily with our growth, that to the last profoundly influences our moral valuations. Under favouring auspices, the conditions of healthy and sound deliberation are thus forming many a year before we are called upon to deliberate.

There remains a third condition : a sound judgment must, further, be an enlightened judgment.

This follows. Deliberation cannot be at its best unless it

3. A sound
judgment
involves
Knowledge.
is resourceful ; and it will never be resourceful till, from one source or another, it has gathered a sufficient store of known ways in which ends may be attained. And this implies knowledge. A few men may be resourceful on slender knowledge : they are

Resourceful-
ness in respect
of means to
ends.
fertile in suggestion, ingenious, inventive. But the average man may not count upon this. If he is to escape the poverty of resource that rings the changes on a meagre stock of trite expedients, he must learn either from his own experience or from instruction. All profitable deliberation therefore implies this enlightenment in respect of resource.

It follows further—for indeed the very possibility of deliberation implies it—that there must be knowledge of the ends, be they near or be they remote, upon which deliberation is directed. And it is here of especial moment that this knowledge be definite and vivid.

The importance of a definite conception (or picture) of an end is that it imposes an instant check upon irrelevancy in deliberation. Haziness of purpose wastes endless time over suggestions, plans, possibilities, which are swept aside in a moment by the man who "knows what he would be at." And if the end be not only definite but vivid it brings into judgment the invaluable quality of promptitude. This is especially needful in dealing with two types, diverse enough but alike in their seeming impotence to bring deliberation to an end. The one is the plausible procrastinator. He is fertile in expedients—so fertile that when he has brought himself to the brink of a decision, he is, to the torment of his friends, arrested by the thought of yet some other way of setting to work. The other is the weaker type who is so fearful of any self-committal at all that, even when there is no alternative open, he clutches at delay with what seems, and indeed is, infatuation. There is no better remedy in either case than to furnish a clear and a vivid picture of the end to be achieved.

[marginal note: Importance of clear and vivid ideas of ends.]

[marginal note: For this is an antidote to procrastination.]

It is here that Imagination can do so much to make us practical. Popularly, Imagination is opposed to practicality ; and set down as the mother of day-dreaming[1]. But it is not oftenest so. A vividly imaged end is the very antidote to indecision. It fills the mind. It stirs the feelings. It brings something of that quickening of desire which comes from actual sight of what we covet. It begets the temper of "now or never." "The inferences of these men," says Burke of the impatient revolutionists, "lie in their passions." And there the inferences will always be apt to lie, when the passions are inflamed by vivid imaginings. The risk indeed is that deliberation may be prematurely cut short, and the die cast, before the moral judgment has come to a real decision upon the course to which it finds itself committed.

[marginal note: Imagination creates practicality.]

[1] Cf. p. 175.

It remains to add that if the judgment is to be sound, the
ends thus conceived, or imaged, must be good

4. The
ends thus con-
ceived (or
imaged) must
be morally
good.

(whatever this common perplexing word may
ultimately mean[1]). It has been already suggested that absence of moral worth in an
adopted end need by no means find a pro-
portionate reflection in the choice of means. If a man's life,
for example, be on the slope of declension, his conscience
may long continue to reflect his better days in a lingering
preference for the less immoral means of compassing his ends.
He may embark, for example, on a doubtfully honest commercial enterprise while yet his manner of pursuing it may be
influenced by the traditions of more honourable days. And
similarly, if a career be on the upward slope, the old mean
selfish estimates may strangely survive, even long after the
ends have been purified and elevated. Such things must be
accepted as part of the inconsistencies of man. The leaven of
good or of evil does not all at once leaven the whole lump.
Yet the central fact remains: the moral imperfections in an
end will always be as a steady force fighting against any
scruples of conscience that tend to dictate a choice of means
better than the end requires. And though a lingering tradition
of moral values may long restrain from the barefaced selection
of what is simply the shortest cut, there can be no doubt that
the adoption of a doubtful end will tend in the long run to
lower the means chosen to its own level. Hence this requirement that, if the judgment is to be sound, the ends must be
good.

Such then appear to be the main conditions of a sound
judgment, and the practical question next to be dealt with is
How, and how far, they may be secured.

[1] Cf. p. 237.

CHAPTER II.

THE EDUCATION OF THE MORAL JUDGMENT.

OF the conditions of sound judgment as now specified, the first is certainly not beyond the educator's art. Those great character-making influences, from the Family onwards, which have been dealt with, lie ready to his hand. And where their imperfections have been corrected by recourse to a moral ideal, well-constructed and habitually enforced, it may be assumed that the character, both in respect of emotional susceptibility and habitual proclivities, will possess that sensitiveness to moral values which we have seen to be so essential to all sanity of judgment.

1. A trained character involves sensitiveness to moral values.

We may therefore pass at once to the further question of education in Deliberation.

Something can here be done by opening the eyes to precedents. For precedents, as already said, contribute to resourcefulness. Sometimes they may suggest the action that exactly meets our case, but oftener they will familiarise the mind with a multitude of alternatives amongst which the choice of means to ends is likely to move.

2. The education of deliberative faculty.

The value of familiarity with precedents.

They may however render a greater service still. Rightly regarded, they do not merely furnish materials to the judgment:
they educate the faculty of judgment itself. A craftsman, if
we may revert to this analogy, may bring back from a visit
to studios and workshops far more than specific hints of an
immediately useful kind. He may gain a general insight that
comes of watching men of diverse capacities and methods each
working in his own way. Similarly in life. We can educate
our faculty of judgment by watching those whom we cannot
possibly think of imitating. The civilian may here learn from
the soldier, the student from the merchant. All of these have
light to throw upon the manner in which the practical judgment
works in its endlessly varied tasks of finding means to ends.

Precedents, however, can take us but a little way. When
they have done their utmost, they leave us still
to face the task of learning how to link means to
ends in those concrete problems which are all
our own. In a sense this is not within the
educator's gift. It depends partly upon natural
constitution. For the man who is to use such resources as
experience has given him, must possess that natural intelligence
without which honesty and goodness of heart will grope and
blunder to the end. Mere cleverness of course has its snare:
it loses touch with moral values. But it does not follow that
because cleverness is not enough, it can be ignored. It is
indispensable, if there is to be a shrewd perception of the
effects of actions upon men and things. Plans must be laid,
difficulties foreseen, failures discounted. And these are things
impossible without the alert intelligence that is in part a gift of
nature[1].

In certain respects deliberative faculty is nature's gift.

---

[1] Cf. Aristotle's remarks on cleverness, *Ethics*, Bk. VI. xii. 9. "There
is a faculty or power which we call cleverness (δεινότης)—the power of
hitting upon and carrying out the means which tend to any proposed end.
If then the end be noble, the power merits praise; but if the end be base,
the power is the power of the villain. So we apply the term clever both to
the prudent man and the villain." (Peters' trans.)

Native intelligence is however far from enough. It is not enough, even when united with good habits. It must find its development through practice. For it is here as with our other virtues. It is by living the moral life that men fit themselves to live it, and by judging that they become competent to judge. They learn by their own difficulties, and profit by their own failures. And it is for this reason that the recluse, or the academic type, will seldom attain in full measure that practical wisdom he so often admires in men of affairs. One may discern at times a certain wistfulness in men who have been fated, by profession or circumstances, to be spectators rather than actors in the large drama of practical life, and yet would fain possess that practical wisdom which can never be theirs in its fullness, not because they are lacking in intelligence, sympathy or energy, but for the simple reason that, by the conditions of their lot, they are denied that contact with affairs in which the practical judgment lives and moves and has its being. Yet such are not without their compensations. They escape many an opportunity of blundering. For, if the judgment is to be educated through its exercise, its problems must be real and testing, and, where this is so, there is no escape from many a blunder. The educational difficulty here is therefore manifest: How find securities against the penalties of blundering, and yet concede the liberty that invites them? For it is no absolute principle in moral education to save from blunders. The more hopeful plan is to risk the blunders, and to contrive that they become the purchase price of wisdom.

But its development comes through practice.

Two reminders are however especially needful here. One is that "reactions" may be merciless and insidious[1]. If left to take their course they may have a sequel we dare not face. Left to the freedom of his own will, as a well-known catechism tells us, man fell—and is for ever falling anew—from his high estate. Hence if we would concede liberty—and we must—

[1] Cf. p. 84.

one condition, known to us, though possibly not to those we are educating, must be the taking of securities that, if need be, we can intervene to arrest the disastrous penalties that blunders may draw down. Only then can we concede full liberty with easy minds. It is equally important to take care that the problems with which the inexperienced judgment is confronted be not too hard. Otherwise, of two things, one. Either we foster the reckless confidence that feeds upon the successful event of issues that have not been squarely faced; or we fatally damp by defeat the wholesome self-confidence which needs well-merited successes to develop it. "A pupil from whom nothing is ever demanded which he cannot do, never does all he can," says Mill[1]. He is speaking of intellectual tasks. But if this somewhat heroic rule is to be applied in the moral sphere, it must be qualified by the watchful prudence that suits the burden to the back.

In conceding scope to deliberate, securities must be taken against the consequence of blunders.

And the problems must not be too hard.

It must be added that if deliberative faculty is to be equal to its tasks, provision must be made for training it to do its work with rapidity. Life is so largely lived in an atmosphere of urgency, that suspense of judgment may become as fatal in action as it is admirable in science. Whence, indeed, the pernicious fallacy, only too current, that somehow deliberation had better be suppressed, and supplanted by a trust in those "instinctive" decisions that hesitate not at all. This is the reverse of the true conclusion. In a rational being, quick to look before and after, deliberation can only be suppressed by doing violence to human nature. The wiser plan is to encourage and to develop it to the uttermost, to give it every opportunity of exercise, so that it may become swift almost as intuition by becoming habitual. For the swift deliberation

Deliberation ought to be swift, yet not instinctive.

[1] *Autobiography*, p. 32.

which grasps a situation at a glance is at the opposite pole from the headlong blundering instinct that knows not what it does.

One specific for this, already hinted at, is a clear and vivid conception (or image) of the end to be achieved, and this opens the way to the question how such conceptions are best attained.

3. How we come to know our ends.

Not, we may reply at once, by express moral instruction. When any person is sufficiently matured to learn from moral instruction what are the ends he ought to pursue, the lesson has already in effect been anticipated. He finds himself aware of a multitude of ends which he is already pursuing. He is aware that he is loving kith and kin, serving friends, earning livelihood, preparing for profession, beginning to be a citizen. He does not become aware of these ends by being told about them. He has learnt them by the gradual gospel of daily experience. It is as Aristotle says: he who has once in his early training taken practical ends into his life, will find small difficulty in coming to know what they are[1].

We learn what our ends are by experience more than by instruction.

This is one more proof that moral instruction cannot do so much as the apostles of teaching about morality sometimes suppose. For though any ordinary youth can be quickly told what his main duties are, no one will venture to say that this is worth calling moral knowledge. It is meagrely "notional," not real. "Mere words" we sometimes say; and we say well. For genuinely to know an end, it is not enough to read about it in a manual of duties, or to have it recited to us in a sermon however eloquent. The point has already been touched in the discussion of Precept[2]. The real and effective

Real and notional knowledge of ends.

---

[1] *Ethics*, Bk. I. iv. 6. "The man who has had a good moral training either already has arrived at principles of action, or will easily accept them when pointed out." (Peters' trans.)

[2] Cf. p. 183.

knowledge of our ends comes by pursuing them.   Nor is there one of us who might not in later years smile at the recollection how lightly we had words upon our lips—courage, generosity, public spirit, integrity, independence and a hundred more—the significance of which it has needed many an experience of many a year to bring us to understand.   For it is the institutions that direct and control our actions that are to the end the main teachers of what our duties are.

Not solely however.   For it is the too familiar experience of all but the elect that even our most intimate

Yet moralists and satirists are needed to remind us what our familiar duties really are.

and cherished ends—our zeal for public causes, our service of an institution or a firm, even our care for those we love—sink from their primacy in our imaginations under the deadening influence of familiarity.   Hence the need of voices to tell us in reawakening words what we are doing.   And for these we need not look in vain.   There are satirists enough to lash our shortcomings, cynics to probe our descent upon lower motives, moralists to expound our duties, preachers to touch our consciences, prophets with their burning words to kindle anew the smouldering altar of our duties.   It is not the highest service of these to tell us of things new.   Our debt is greater. For without them we should miss the significance of the duties that are at our doors and amongst our feet—the duties whose meaning we forget in our flagging and obstructed daily efforts to fulfil them.

It is not enough, however, to know our duties, not even when these enkindling influences conspire with

4. Our ends must further be unified in a moral ideal of our own.

experience in keeping them before us.   These duties must be gathered up into an ideal which we have made our own.   We have already seen that no educator can afford to leave those he cares for to become simply what social institutions would make them, but must work up to some coherent plan which he believes will rectify the false and often distorted emphasis and ill-proportioned valuations of all actual societies[1]. What is thus necessary for the educator in moulding the lives of others, is equally necessary for the individual when he claims to think his own thoughts, and judge his own judgments, and take the conduct of his life into his own hands. For then alone will he have adequate security that his ends are good.

For it is thus we know them to be good.

There is a parallel here between the world of knowledge and the world of action. In both, security lies in coherency of view. If we wish to be assured that a perception is real and not illusory, we must ask if it finds a place in the context of systematised knowledge. This is the final test.

We must choose our ends in the light of an ideal.

And similarly, if we would know that an end is good, we must be able to satisfy ourselves that it is in harmony with a settled and coherent ideal of life. This, it is true, is a test that is too often disregarded. Men are content to live from hand to mouth. They trust the isolated intuition or the isolated precept. And there are times when this is permissible enough, or even laudable. When we are dealing with the minutiæ of conduct, it is not worth while, it smacks of pedantry, to invoke anything so imposing as a moral ideal. And there may be occasions when swift decisions, even upon graver matters, are so imperative that there is nothing for it but to fall back upon our own intuitions or someone else's advice. Yet this is not the best. Even when the burden of decision falls upon intuition, there is little safety, if there be not in the mind a well-compacted and habitually-cherished ideal with which each isolated end that claims adoption may be confronted.

We may see this clearly in either of two experiences.

The first is when some end that tempts us is bad. The inherent weakness of a bad end does not of course lie in its lack of attractiveness. It may appeal to a masterful passion; and it may even

How do we know an end to be bad?

[1] Cf. p. 112 *et seq.*

by its glamour sophisticate the reason. The fortunate weakness lies in the fact that it is usually an isolated end, capable perhaps of carrying us captive by sudden assault, but incapable of finding a place in the settled context of a good man's plan of life. Hence the result. Its badness stands detected, not because some mysterious and indescribable moral instinct revolts against it, but because its adoption would bring into the slowly and laboriously knit fabric of the ideal the rift that makes for far-spreading disintegration and ruin.

The second case is when an end has to be discarded, not because it is bad but because some other end is **How do we know, in a conflict of duties, which duty is to be preferred?** better. This happens when there is a conflict of duties. And it is an infinitely harder and more wearing problem than the other, because both competing ends, being good, can claim kindred with our ideal. It stands to the other as evil strife that ranks patriots in hostile camps stands to a war of resistance to invasion. It is therefore a conflict that may be slow of settlement. In truth it is a conflict that will never end, or end only by some random preference, if those who are torn asunder by it cannot decide which end is most consistent with that ideal which, in the long course of moral development, has been taking hold of mind, heart, and will. The conflict may come in many forms. It may be between liberality and thrift, between private friendship and public interest, between modest luxury and the claims of charity, between saying what one thinks and refusing to say what would alienate or wound. But whatever it be, it is judgment in the light of an ideal that alone can loose the knot.

It is therefore of moment to ask how such an ideal comes to take body and shape.

CHAPTER III.

GROWTH OF THE INDIVIDUAL'S IDEAL.

NOTHING is commoner than for a man to have an ideal and yet to be unable to tell whence it has come to him. And this, not for lack of self-analysis, but because the ideals that really dominate our judgments and shape our lives do not descend upon us, as if from the heavens, full-formed. They have a very different history. They grow with our growth from early years, and, if we be morally alive, they never cease to grow even to the last. It is fortunate that it is so. For the task of adjusting our lives to our ideal, and our ideal to our lives, is only possible because it is so tentative and gradual.

The growth of the individual's ideal is unconscious.

It follows that the history of an individual's ideal is, in a large measure, a record of the influences under which he comes, from the Family onwards. These are, in the first instance, influences for shaping conduct. But they also lodge gradually in the mind images and ideas of the ends pursued. The process is, of course, far from obviously uniform and unbroken. There is, for long, much that lightly comes and as lightly goes, as the romantic visions inspired by

The content of the ideal comes through progressive experience,

story-books and youthful hero-worship find their early un-disputed ascendancy challenged by growing perception of the homely demands of daily life and, later, of the sterner calls of

and dis-illusionment.
day and way or public service. From very early years, moreover, illusion brings its shadow of disillusionment. There is disillusionment even in the step from Home to School, as there is a deeper dis-illusionment when the youth, hitherto bred in the seclusion of Home and School, is brought for the first time face to face with the work of the world, with which he has hitherto had but a hearsay acquaintance. It is always an epoch when the largeness and hurrying indifference of the world of business, of social relations, and by and by of political action, begin to dawn upon the mind. Yet all this disillusionment—and it does not cease with youth—is never to be lamented. Really it is a step to discovery. Something no doubt is lost. We may not flatter ourselves that even a thrice-fortunate develop-ment gathers up within it all the true appreciations of childhood and youth.

> " Nothing can bring back the hour
> Of splendour in the grass, of glory in the flower."

Yet the very shocks of surprise that dissolve these dreams of the morning are but signs that experience is bringing into life new ends to be wrought into a richer ideal. For they are possible only because the years bring an appreciation of the magnitude and reality of many aims and interests which constitute the very stuff and substance of human life. Least

Ideals are
not peculiarly
the possession
of youth.
of all is an ideal to be viewed as peculiarly the possession of youth, doomed to be pared down and shorn of its glory by the remorseless years. Such regrets may be left to sentimentalists. A youthful ideal is too devoid of substance to be overmuch bewailed. The really loftier ideal is to be sought at the end of life, not at its beginning. For it can come into full and effective being only when grey hairs have brought home the

knowledge how many and how substantial are the ends for which men have it in them to live[1].

In the light of what has already been said about the educative influence of institutions it is needless to recapitulate the precise elements which each contributes. It will be enough to say that the results are, in the main, two. On the one hand, as the individual comes to be more and more

Two tendencies: (a) Ideals are gradually enriched in content,

conscious of the ends for which these institutions severally exist, there settles down in the mind, never again to be dislodged, a variety of ends which are the materials out of which his moral ideal is made. On the other hand these ends do not lie in the mind loose and apart. There is also at work that striving after

(b) and they gain in unity and coherency.

some kind of coherency and unity which seems to be of the essence of a rational being. Such striving is far from conscious of itself at first. It is also tentative, and it may often be wayward in its constructive efforts. And it falls short in ways to be shortly seen. Yet it is perpetually at work. And though a quite settled and coherent plan of life is far from common, the majority are alive to its value sufficiently to resent even with asperity the imputation of incoherency of purpose. Even the erratic are under illusions as to their own admirable consistency.

Yet the somewhat hap-hazard plans of life which thus shape themselves have definite imperfections, and these may take one or other of two pronounced forms.

In the first place, they may need enrichment. They are rich in possibility just because they are poor in content. But this enrichment they may never find. Under the tyrannous influences of a world

Yet ideals are apt to be narrow,

that wields the whip of compulsory work, and especially under the influence of the Division of Labour which is the accepted iron law of working, the ideal may harden, and indeed shrink,

[1] Cf. p. 243.

15—2

into inhuman narrowness. It remains an ideal : few ideals, in point of fact, exact more than those of the stunted victims of penury, avarice, or ambition. But these are ideals rather of self-mutilation than of self-development. In an industrial and commercial country this is the greater danger.

On the other hand, a contrary fatality may happen. In sanguine types at any rate, especially where free choice is a reality in their lives, expanding experience may disclose so many ends that such unity as the youthful ideal may have had, falls asunder, as life goes on, into fragmentariness of aim. And then we have the multiform product inconsistent with itself, because its ends are so inconsistent with each other that all discernible unity is lost.

*and frag-
mentary.*

These possible disasters, however, have happily each their preventives.

Narrowness may be met by recourse to the larger life revealed in Literature. There is no stronger plea for Biography, Drama, or Romance, or for any imaginative expansion of interests, than that founded upon the need for them as counteractives of the pitiable contractedness of outlook begotten of Division of Labour. The result no doubt may have its incongruities. The ideal outlook may be so big: the working life so small. Hence the notion, not uncommon, that popular education, in a nation ruled by specialisation, is a cause of discontent and embitterment. This is at most a fractional truth. The other side of it is, that from this imaginative contact with lives quite other than its own, the mind may come back with a juster and an enriched view of the manifold ways in which Duty fulfils itself through the diverse capacities and diverse opportunities of men. It is not needful perhaps to be hard upon those who, as they read of achievement that is not destined to be theirs, cannot smother the corrosive thought of

*Narrowness
of ideal—
how remedied.*

*Expansion
of interests
through the
written or
spoken word.*

the poverty of their own lot. But the better, and the more human, reflection is that Moral Law is so great a thing that it needs for its realisation the many modes of many lives; and that it is entirely possible to rise to an intense sympathetic interest in other lives—lives which after all are linked to ours by the organic bonds of social life. Nor need the result be thus impersonal. Many an end really within the individual's reach is never grasped simply because it is concealed by the screen of removable ignorance; and many a man in later years can, with bitter, unavailing regret, see clearly how his whole career might have been different, if only this end or that had been brought within his ken by the written or the spoken word.

And yet it is not by books or words that the outlook is most effectually broadened and enriched. For the ends which are thus disclosed, even when they are eagerly and sympathetically apprehended, are only too apt to remain nominal and notional. To the mass of men ends that are genuinely to enter into their ideals must come in less purely intellectual guise. They must come *For the mass of men, however, the ideal is enriched more by actual contact with political and religious life.* through the strong alliance of idea and practice. And it is for this reason that the wider, more impersonal interests are more likely to take their place in the average man's plan of life through the enlarging experiences of citizenship, and the influence of those religious organisations that constrain their members to live for corporate and distant ends.

Fragmentariness of ideal, again, has its corresponding antidotes. Thus unity may come from a Moral Code which gathers up in its decalogue, or other table of the law, the cardinal duties of life. Or *Influences that make for unity of ideal.* it may come from a type which is the incarnation of these. The most of men may very likely ask for nothing more. For many, the solution of all problems is found in judging as they think their chosen Type would judge. Yet Code and Type

have alike their limitations[1]. And this being so, the question
presses if there be any further resource. It is clear at any
rate what is needed. It is a standard by which the comparative value of ends may be estimated, and which may be
free at once from the rigidity of the Moral Code, and from the
limited completeness of the concrete Type. Such standards

**Importance
of a concep-
tion of the
End of life.**

exist. They are found in those conceptions of
the supreme End of life which philosophy has
been giving to the world since the days of
Socrates. They are diverse as the philosophies
that have devised them; Duty, Perfection, Greatest Happiness, Greatest Blessedness, Self-realisation and the rest. But
they all alike are fitted to render a twofold service. In the
first place, they work for unity because they involve the belief
that all the duties of life are but so many diverse modes of
approach to a single, all-pervading End; and secondly, they
prepare the way for the discovery—so difficult for the man
of Codes—that under the fluctuating conditions of human
capacity and circumstance, the place of prior obligation may
be held now by this duty and now by that. He who looks for
ever to a Code is only too apt to claim for every commandment in it an equal, or in other words an impossible, absolute
authority. He who looks to a Type, even when he goes
behind the letter to the spirit, is prone to exaggerate what is
local and limited. But he who grasps the idea of an End has
risen to what is universal, and will be careful to promote no
duty to the place of absolute authority, except the one supreme
duty of pursuing the End in the highest practicable mode.
This is really an immense advance. It is delusive to suppose that morality requires us in the interests of consistency
once for all to grade our duties in a fixed order of relative
importance. It is not thus that a living unity comes into an
ideal. Living unity follows a firm grasp of the End. For it is
only when this is achieved that the lesser ends of life begin to

[1] Cf. pp. 169 and 183.

be seen in their true light as varied yet kindred ways of working towards one supreme event.

It is here that philosophy has rendered the world memorable service. True to its tradition of seeing "the one in the many," it has, amidst all the controversies of the schools, consistently taught that the inculcation of duties, however shining, will stiffen into formalism, if it be not saved

Philosophy can render the world a service by formulating the End.

from this by a vitalising and unifying conception of the supreme End upon which the otherwise dispersed and scrambling activities of human life may be seen to converge. Nor is it necessary, in order to reap the fruits of such a conception that the average man should himself become philosopher, and graduate in the philosopher's analysis. This would be an absurd, an impossible requirement. The practical world too manifestly cares little for philosophic theories of what it is doing. It does not seem even to miss their absence. The multitude, as Plato said, are incapable of philosophy. Driven on by the relentless urgencies of life —urgencies of livelihood, of passion, of ambition, of impatience—it has not the time, even

Philosophy, however, stands in need of interpreters to popularise its conceptions.

if it had the appetite and faculty, for philosophising about the End of life. Yet what a man may not be able to take from philosophy, he may find in another way. He may turn, he does turn, to the preachers, teachers, moralists, satirists, essayists, poets of his generation. These are the middlemen of the spiritual world. They stand between the philosopher and the multitude. For they know how to translate into terms of imagination and rhetoric those conceptions of the End which appear in the philosopher's pages in difficult analysis and definition. It may be that these " middlemen " do not listen to philosophy enough. It is a grievous fact that some of them so far betray their trust as to become *misologoi* from whom philosophy receives but scant justice. Yet the hope remains that through them the old but never obsolete lesson to look to the End may filter down into the thought and practice of the world. It is all-important that it should. A theory of the End of life may be important; it is not a necessity. But convictions about the End are. For without them, there can never come into our ideal that well-knit yet flexible unity and coherency which make it a serviceable touchstone of the comparative goodness of our ends.

And yet, for those who are equal to it, a theory of the moral ideal has its advantages; and it remains briefly to state what they are.

CHAPTER IV.

PRACTICAL VALUE OF A THEORY OF
THE MORAL IDEAL.

WHEN anyone goes in search of a theory of his moral ideal, it will be mainly under a scientific impulse. For unless he have this, he will probably rest content **A theory** with one or other of those time-honoured rivals **of the moral** of theory, Authority or Intuition. Yet ethical **ideal has** thinkers, and those who care to follow them, **practical value.** need not be here less just to themselves than is necessary, nor deny themselves the added incentive that may be drawn from the fact that there are certain quite specific ways in which a theory of the ideal practically strengthens all who can receive it.

Thus it is theory, and theory alone, that can adequately uphold the moral ideal in the face of criticism. It is of course not necessary to meet criticism **1. It makes** by theory. There is a type who may prefer **it possible to** rhetorical projectiles, and, in Johnsonian fashion, **meet theory** when his pistol misses fire knock down his opponent with the butt end. Another may invoke Authority. A third may appeal to Conscience. They are all effective methods, and we need not, in this so combative world, disparage even the first. Yet he who limits himself to these must pay a price—the price of parting company with the more rational minds of his generation. As a matter of fact it is the perception of the risk of this that has prompted some of the greatest efforts of ethical speculation the world has ever seen. Nor would Plato, Socrates and Aristotle be numbered amongst the conscript fathers of philosophy had they not, in the spirit of moral reformers, set themselves to deliver the better minds of their generation from the Sophistic theories that Might is Right, and individual hedonistic self-interest the measure of morality.

The situation repeats itself. In every developed community there are men born and bred with the rationalising instinct. They cannot shut their ears to theories, least of all to theories that subject their moral ideals to searching criticism. They cannot rest content to invoke in reply dogmas however consecrated, or intuitions however prophetic. They cannot in a word stop short till they have either surrendered to the theories that are negative and subversive, or ousted them by a theory that can justify their counter-convictions.

Akin to this is the further service that theory can do much to sustain belief in the essential reality of the moral ideal in periods of transition and doubt. For it is the theorist's task to analyse experience; not simply his own experience, which may be a little thing, but that larger moral experience of the world that is written in social institutions, and not least in the lives of the reformers, teachers, saints, heroes, of our race. From such analysis he does not return empty handed, and in particular he brings back two convictions. One is the lesson, writ large on the world's history, that it is the fate of all particular modes or forms of moral ideal, from which nothing can save them, to yield to the slow sap of the criticism of the morrow; and the other the complementary conviction that the moral life of which man is capable, and which indeed he feels imperatively bound to realise, remains a far richer and loftier thing than has ever yet found reflection in the imperfect mirror of human life. Not that a man need be a theorist to come to these convictions. Are they not written in the pages of ethical prophets and teachers who, like Carlyle, flout and scoff at theory? For it is the glory of the ethical prophet that he has an eye that can divide asunder form and substance, and discriminate between

2. It can also sustain belief in the reality of the moral ideal.

The ethical theorist and the ethical prophet.

those ideals which are but perishable textures of human imagination, and that imperishable fore-felt and in part fore-seen moral End, for which the imagination of successive generations is for ever striving to weave a worthier vesture. Such advantage therefore as the theorist may have does not lie in his results, but in the fact that, in his case, the results rest, not upon the fitful revelations of intuition, which may so easily mistake the light that leads astray for light from Heaven, but upon the definite and systematic analysis of experience.

It is for this reason that beyond all others the ethical theorist can afford to look on without misgiving at the con-tradictions of moral standards, the conflict of duties, the dilemmas of Casuistry, the negations of the sceptic. Not only will he have discounted these by anticipation. In those very diversities and collisions of moral standards which are so often the terror of the dogmatic mind, and in the spectacle always tragical enough of some cherished ideal crumbling before mordant criticism, he will see but one more proof of the exhaustless vitality of the moral spirit of man which, for ever on the march, does but "strike its tent in order to begin a new journey."

It is a greater service still that a theory of the ideal can bring all who are in earnest with it at least one step nearer that intelligent service which alone is perfect freedom. There is a morality which never asks the reason Why for the ideal up to which it nobly strives to live. And when we meet the men who exemplify it, we call them with Wordsworth the "bondsmen" of Duty, not stumbling at the servile word because the service is so high. The word is however perhaps apter than we think. For bondsmen and no better they still are, and bondsmen they will remain, so long as the grounds upon which service is rendered are unexamined and unintelli-gible. For if Reason be indeed of the essence of man, the

3. Without a theory of the ideal, moral freedom remains imperfect.

service even of a God is but a loftier kind of slavery when it leaves the reason of the servant darkened.

It is here that philosophy brings its message of emancipation. All ethical Schools (unless we except In-
The need
for the moral
emancipation
which philoso-
phy brings. tuitionism which is a kind of despair of explanation) attempt to explain the recognised obliga-
tion to live for an ideal. Their solutions are
different: their aim is one. They ask the reason
Why, in the belief that some answer is possible; and though it
be granted that these answers, if only because they are so
divergent, must needs fail to satisfy, such an admission cannot
alter the fact that, despite all their dissonances, they bring us
nearer that reasonable service to which the bondsmen of duty
must come, if they are to strip off wholly the livery of moral
servitude.

This does not mean that even a perfect theory of the moral
ideal—were such a thing conceivable—would of itself make its
possessors morally free. Of course it could not. Men have
painfully to work out their moral freedom in their lives. They
must make themselves free in their habitual deeds, desires,
feelings and thoughts. And many an unlettered man, incapable of theories, has in this way wrought out, in sweat of
soul, a substantial freedom even under iron limitations which
he could neither alter nor understand[1]. Need it be said that
in default of this actual achievement of the moral life, a
knowledge of all the theories of Obligation which philosophy
contains would profit nothing.

But be this practical moral achievement never so splendid,
theory has something to superadd. It remains
The reason-
able service
that is perfect
freedom. for it to speak the last word of emancipation,
not the "emancipation," spurious and born of
caprice, which shakes allegiance to our habitual
duties, but that far other emancipation that rivets allegiance
the closer by making it open-eyed, intelligent, reasonable. For

[1] Cf. p. 120.

without this there can be no perfect freedom for a rational being.

Nor need we stop here. It is not too much to claim that a theory of the ideal can, in addition, render high service by quickening the moral life. One may venture to suggest that philosophers are here apt to claim too little. Realising truly enough that it is not for philosophy to impart

4. A theory of the ideal can do something to quicken the moral life.

life but to understand the life otherwise imparted, not to make ideals but to explain them, they come to think that theory, as Aristotle said, "moves nothing." "It is not to be supposed," says T. H. Green, "that anyone, for being a theoretic Utilitarian, has been a better man."[1] It is hard to accept this, when one studies the lives of the great Utilitarians, Bentham the founder, James Mill the propagandist, John Mill the apostle. These men might have lived for the public good as they did, without their philosophy. It is impossible to say. Yet one is constrained to think, if there be truth in biography, that as the idea of Human Happiness rose before their eyes, in ever-widening breadth, in ever-growing detail, it kindled a passion for Public Good which would not otherwise in measure so abounding have entered into their lives. Similarly with Green himself. No reader of his "Prolegomena to Ethics" can fail to feel the repressed fervour of its pages, and those who knew the man can never forget the unobtrusive passion for righteousness that shone through a character which shrank from easy expression of itself. It was ethical temperament, habitual moral aspiration, religious fervour. Doubtless. But was it not also, in part, the fruit of a life-long, determined, reasoning reflection upon the moral possibilities and destiny of man?

For it is never to be forgotten that he who goes in search of a theory of his moral ideal, travels by his own analytic path

[1] *Prolegomena*, Bk. IV. c. iii. 331. The context runs "It (the Utilitarian theory) has not given men a more lively sense of their duty to others—no theory can do that—&c."

into a world of august and enduring objects. Is it to be wondered at if the man who has spent his deepest hours of meditation in the presence of Duty, of Public Good, and of the half-revealed and half-concealed possibilities of the individual life, and has habitually looked upon these facts with what Plato called "the eye of the soul," will be something more than the cold-blooded analyst in whom the world too often travesties the theorist? For in his own way he will have been led to see the vision, and as he muses in his silent and solitary hours, the fire will burn within him.

PART IV.

SELF-DEVELOPMENT AND SELF-CONTROL.

CHAPTER I.

SELF-DEVELOPMENT.

IT is difficult, if not impossible, to draw a sharp line between Development and Self-development. On the one hand, all development is self-develop- ment: on the other, what we call self-develop- ment, even when our self is asserting itself to its utmost, will be found to involve the acceptance of many conditions of life which are not of our own making, and sometimes by no means of our own approving.

Difficulty of defining self-development.

Development is self-development in more senses than one. It is the development *of* a self. Across the coming years, a far-off future self sits and awaits us, which, when the years have gone by, we shall claim and cling to as our own. Whether it be a

All develop- ment is deve- lopment of a self,

predestinate self, we need not here discuss. Enough that, from early days onwards, we have a sense of proprietorship in it which deepens as life goes on; and that, although when realised it is greatly the product of circumstances, it is far from wholly so. For from the first there is development *by* a self. Even the seedling and the nestling have a kind of self. They are not

and, in part, by a self.

passive. They co-operate with Nature, of which they are a

part. For there is that in them—that principle of vegetative or animal life—which environment has not given, and cannot give. So that, from earliest hours, they react upon stimulus with an inherent energy that is all their own. Far more is this the case with man. Man, as Spinoza expresses it, has "the power of persisting in his own being"[1]. Hence, if in one aspect, his history is a record of adjustment of internal to external conditions, this is but one aspect of two. From the first, congenital endowment brings him to confront the world with something of an independent life; and this inner life becomes an ever stronger and more stable thing, as these early proclivities are nurtured and organised into settled states under the various encouragements and disciplines of education. Stronger yet, and still more stable, is the self that sees the day when the individual, loosed from leading-strings, lays hold of that ideal which he takes to be his moral destiny, and sets himself, with the help of his own practical judgment, to enact it. It is, of course, inevitable that environment continues to exercise a ceaseless, masterful, and often tyrannous influence, till at last it brings the hour of physical death. Yet it is not to be forgotten that from even early days the immediate environment is in part what the individual, by his own inherent co-operating energy, has made it. And though, in the large impersonal ends in which the adult life is caught up by society and swept along, the self may seem to play the *rôle* of passivity, this is not, at least it need not really be so. For the longer a man lives, the more unmistakeably does he realise that all he thinks, says, and does, even in his most social and self-sacrificing hours and aims, is the manifestation to the world, half-helped, half-hindered, of that inward life he knows and feels to be his own. Has not Leibnitz called man "monad"—a "monad" who, though he may reflect in thought

The self asserts itself more as life goes on.

[1] *Ethics*, Part III. Prop. vi. "Each individual thing, so far as in it lies, endeavours to persist in its own being."

the wide world of experience, is yet in the centre of his being isolated from even his most familiar companions.

> "Points have we all within our souls
> Where all stand single."

says Wordsworth[1]. And the lines never come home more irresistibly than when this "Self" that is the meeting-place of all our interests, the seeming starting-point of all our incentives and projects, has been brought to full consciousness of its own development by long, varied, and reflective contact with Nature and Life.

Development both of a self and by a self may thus be said to be proceeding throughout the whole course of moral growth and education. Yet we may fitly speak of Self-development in a narrower, more definite, yet not less profitable meaning. For we may truly say that Self-development is reached only when the individual tries to regulate his life by his own judgment, and in the light of a moral ideal which he has consciously made his own.

Self-development may, however, be defined in a narrower sense.

This implies emancipation in more senses than one. He who has come to rely upon his own judgment has seen the last of tutelage; and he who has adopted an ideal claims thereby to judge by another and a better standard than that of the world. This is at once his glory and his responsibility. Yet there need be no revolt against society, nor any revolution in the tenor of his life. Innovation is by no means of the essence of self-development. Voices at any rate will not be wanting to counsel him against rupture with the traditions of his past. There will be voices of the men of use and wont to tell him that the world's ways are the world's wisdom; voices of religious teachers to declare that the Author of man's being has providentially assigned to him the part he

It involves emancipation;

but not necessarily innovation.

---

[1] *Prelude*, Bk. III.

has to play in the order of existence[1]; voices too, it may be, of philosophers to point to the fulfilment of the duties of our station as the one solution of our ethical problems[2]. Few are likely to deny that such considerations have grounds in reason; and in proportion as they prevail, the individual will be content to assert himself by accepting, deliberately and of free choice, many a duty imposed upon him in his past life by society, without his having been at all consulted in the matter.

Yet self-development gives a new aspect to old duties.

Yet even then, self-development will imply something of a transformation. For on the advent of free choice regulated by an ideal, the most familiar of duties will wear a changed aspect. It will lose its isolation, and come to be habitually viewed as a clause in a context, a part of a plan, an element in a whole, a path to an end. Results will follow. Each duty may assume a greater, or a less importance than it had before. But never again will it wear the aspect it had when it was but an isolated obligation enforced by authority or commended by example. And as moral growth goes on, every duty will thus in turn be taken up into that moral ideal with which the self has thrown in its lot, and estimated henceforth by its bearing on the moral End[3].

As the self developes, the moral ideal becomes more than ever un-realisable.

Yet Self-development is far from resting here. By a fortunate paradox, it is just when a man makes his ideal his own that he finds it more than ever beyond his grasp. For it is not to be supposed that, whilst he is advancing in moral growth, the ideal that has taken possession of him is not

---

[1] e.g. Burke, *Works*, III. p. 79. "I may assume that the Awful Author of our being is the author of our place in the order of existence; and that, having disposed and marshalled us by a divine tactic, not according to our will, but according to His, He has in and by that disposition, virtually subjected us to act the part which belongs to the place assigned us."

[2] Cf. F. H. Bradley, *Ethical Studies*, Essay v. "My station and its duties." "The belief in this real moral organism (i.e. the community) is the one solution of ethical problems," p. 169.

[3] Cf. p. 230.

advancing likewise. Far otherwise. As reason developes, the idea of Moral Law will rise before his mind as a far greater and more imperative fact than he had heretofore imagined. From an expanding knowledge of moral aspiration, as it is writ large in the upward struggle of men and institutions, he will return with the conviction that the loftiest ideal is eloquent by virtue of its aspirations even more than because of anything it has reduced to definition or formula. Small wonder then if the growth of the ideal may far outrun the growth of the moral life that, with all its striving, can only follow afar off. For it is not the ideals of earlier years that are the most unattainable. "The petty done, the undone vast" is not the thought of the youth; but of those who, having done the most, yet count themselves unprofitable servants, because it is to them only that the experience, the knowledge, and the reflection of maturer years have opened up the far vistas of moral possibility.

Hence when we say that the ideals of age are sober in comparison with those of the morning of life, we must never suppose ourselves to be confessing that they are lower. Their sobriety lies in the recognition that their enactment must be long and gradual, in the clearer perception of their *The ideals of age are both soberer and loftier than those of youth.* relation to fact, in the consciousness of how hard a task it is to realise them even in part, and in the added emphasis they lay upon qualities—patience, toleration, self-suppression, humility, sound judgment—which are too prosaic for the romantic visions of youth. And indeed it would augur ill for the Moral Law that is over all, did not the ideals of those who have lived in its presence through a long life far transcend the first dreams of inexperienced enthusiasm. It is a fact worth dwelling on. For in it lies the hope of a self-development to which we may not set limits. "This is what I am doing"; "This is what I ought to be doing"—in this contrast lies the nerve of moral progress. It is a contrast fruitful of good works : it is more fruitful still of aspiration which works, however good, for ever fail to satisfy.

Such aspiration may find fulfilment in either of two directions.

Aspiration after the ideal may find fulfilment in social activity. In most it will take the form of (as the phrase goes) leaving the world better than they found it. The Self these seek to develop will be emphatically the social self, the self, in other words, that has thrown in its lot with some definite small or large circle of social aims and interests; and their supreme instrument will be that sound judgment which we have seen to be the crowning virtue of the practical man. Such, when at their best, are the types who find their lives in losing them, the men or women whom we call, not without something of a contradiction, "unselfish," so instinct has their self become with the life of sacrifice. It is a consolation to reflect that, by every unselfish enterprise, they give an added worth to the self they sacrifice so ungrudgingly[1]. And such are the men of the world, in the truest sense of that phrase,—the men of action who are unrestingly developing themselves, though, in preoccupation with projects and causes, they hardly pause to reflect that they have a self to develop.

Yet to this line of moral advance there are, in one aspect, very real limits. **But also in a deepening of the moral spirit.** For when society is already highly developed and organised, there is less scope for the individual to strike out in untrodden paths. The ways of action for the vast majority lie along the common beaten highway. And, as result, outward performance may come but poorly to reflect the differences in character between man and man. It would not be difficult to find next-door neighbours, whose lives are to

---

[1] Cf. Aristotle's remark that even in making a sacrifice for a friend a man assigns the greater good to himself. *Ethics*, Bk. IX. viii. 9—11.

a first glance much upon a par, and who are yet poles asunder in real moral achievement.

This is because self-development may find another path, in the cultivation of that inward spirit, that purity and elevation of motive, that sincerity of endeavour, which we find at their best in the life of the saint. The supreme instrument here will be, not so much practical wisdom as habitual self-examination and self-judgment.

There are moralists with a strong bias for action who look askance at this. Fearful that it may run to ultra-conscientiousness and morbidity, they ex- *Dangers of premature self-examina- tion, and self- judgment.* hort the world—often needlessly enough—to turn their minds from all self-scrutiny, and to fix it with the maximum of self-forgetfulness upon the thing they can work at[1]. They have reason. There is a premature conscientiousness that is peculiarly blighting. It is fostered by "melancholic" temperament, by sentimental example, by introspective fiction, by certain modes of religious up-bringing with their anxieties about "the soul." However fostered, it gives a wrong centre to life by turning the eyes inwards, just at that age when, in the interests of self-development, it is above all things important that there should be a healthy outward outlook, and a pursuit of outward interests and ends all but heedless in its eagerness. This is the kind of Self-knowledge that Carlyle seems to have in view, when he beseeches us not to try to *Carlyle's diatribes against self- knowledge.* know ourselves. In one sense, we may echo his warnings. For the fugitive and cloistered self that begins life by self-consciously hanging back from contact with experience will not be worth the knowing. Its conscience is scrupulous only because its instincts and resolves are weak.

But not all self-examination is thus barren. Grant that it is the law of development that men first act and then reflect.

[1] Carlyle, *Sartor Resartus*, Bk. II. c. vii. 159 (Lib. Ed.). Cf. passim, the Essay on *Characteristics*.

Yet this does not make reflection one whit the less human and imperative. Fortunately so. It will hardly be disputed that consciousness of our faults is the first step towards correcting them, and without self-examination how can we escape what Carlyle himself declares to be the worst fault of all, the being conscious of none? It may not seem so necessary for us to be conscious of our virtues. And indeed the same great prophet of Unconsciousness, true to his conviction that goodness is a secret to itself, would have it that of the right we are never, and ought never to be conscious[1]. We need not pause to ask by what means the eye of consciousness, so keen for vices, is to be kept blind to virtues. The more important point is that this whole Carlylian doctrine goes upon an inadequate idea of what self-examination really is. It seems to limit it to a barren introspective fingering of motives. But the self-examination of the saint is a different thing from this. It turns its merciless search-light upon motives only that it may compare the actual attainment of the soul with the moral ideal, so that thereby it may gird itself to fresh resolves and renewed efforts. There is a misreading here of saintly and conscientious lives which does them grievous wrong. Their confessions of shortcoming are construed as confessions of baseness, when they signify no more than that their failings blacken in their own eyes only because they see them in relief against the exceptional elevation and imperativeness of their ideal.

Self-exami-nation and self-judgment are necessary.

And fruitful of moral effort.

Opportunity for self-development is not to be measured by range of experience.

Nor is the self-development that comes of self-examination and self-judgment at all inconsistent with the law that it is only through contact with experience that the character is enriched and developed. Contact with life there

[1] Thus he quotes with approval the dictum: "Of the Wrong we are always conscious, of the Right never."

must be. The recluse who shuts him from his kind will be
only too apt to lose his life in the effort to monopolise it.

> "Then he will sigh
> Inly disturbed to think that others feel
> What he must never feel. And so, lost soul,
> On visionary views will fancy feed."

And this warning, it is well to remember, comes from the self-
sufficing solitary Wordsworth[1]. But it is not necessary that
there should be contact with the world upon any large scale to
furnish opportunity enough. It is sometimes said, even in
face of all the glaring inequalities of fortune, that on an
unprejudiced and discriminating view, happiness is more
equally diffused throughout all stations in Society than
economists or politicians would have us suppose. If we
estimate happiness by moral character we need not doubt it.
The circumscribed lot of an uneventful life is at any rate no
barrier. For sagacity of judgment, consistency
of purpose, purity of intention, depth and sincerity of feeling, persistence of aspiration, all, in
short, that gives action moral as distinguished

The moral
possibilities
of common
lives.

from economic or political value, may be there in measure as
full as in deeds that make the world wonder. This to be sure
is something of a commonplace. But it is not the less significant on that account. For it would never have for so long
held its ground as a commonplace had it not been a common
experience.

---

[1] The whole of the elegiac lines are in point. Cf. *Works*, vol. I. p. 44
(Moxon).

CHAPTER II.

SELF-CONTROL.

ALL development, as we have already seen, involves re-pression. And the same principle holds when
development has become self-development, and
when the repressor and the repressed are one.
The most careful early education will not
obviate this. For the best it can do is to fit its product for
that seemingly never-ending conflict in which the soul is
divided against itself. It is not simply that mankind, by their
own confession, do what they ought not to do. Their malady
lies deeper. It lies in the vitiation of their will. Not a day,
hardly an hour, but they are visited by feelings, desires, ideas,
of which they would thankfully be rid. The best are not
secure against these unwelcome guests. And even the saint,
if there be truth in his own confessions, is to the end of his
days tormented and humiliated by their obstinate resurrection.

The need for self-control even in the best.

Yet it is not the apparition of such things in consciousness
that need be felt as a disgrace. They come
unbidden and unwelcome. They intrude even
upon our best moments with an abruptness that
suggests the ambush of an evil spirit. It is their
presence without the resolute effort to get rid of
them. And the question that profoundly concerns us is,
How?

The problem: how to get rid of evil feelings, desires, and ideas.

A well-known and simple specific is to inhibit their ex-pression in act. Our feelings and desires, it is
truly said, feed upon their own expression. It
is so with the savage who brandishes his club to
bring himself to slaughter pitch: it is so with
the devotee who seeks in ritual the flame that fans his religious
emotions. Hence the policy of weakening the passion by

The policy of denying them expression is reasonable.

denying it expression. Do we not know that the storm of feeling can be checked, if only we can prevent the first word from being spoken, the first gesture from being made. And is it not matter of common observation that persons who begin by being Stoics in demeanour end by becoming Stoics in reality?

This policy is however open to serious qualifications. One is the risk that it will be interpreted too super- *But (a) it* ficially. When a man almost chokes with *may be inter-* suppressed fury, or when his heart stands still *preted too* with cold fear, he must not flatter himself, *superficially:* however impassive his demeanour, that he is really inhibiting the expression of his passion. Little progress will be made if the suppression of overt movement leaves these unexpressed expressions to riot unchecked.

An even more serious qualification is that all strong passion appears to find assuagement actually in *(b) Feeling* and through expression. "She must weep or *and passion* she will die." Nor need we go far afield to find *find as-* the trite "Have it out and be done with it," *suagement* addressed as a general exhortation to all nursers *expression.* of wrath or brooders upon wrongs. There is reason here. Assuagement of passion through expression rests on the fact that all our feelings and desires appear to run down and come to an end when their work is done. They may seem to be feeding on their own expression. They actually do so while they last. But this cannot go on for ever. When they have freely found their natural vent, they flag and die down, and their victim feels again a free man.

So true is this that we might accept this plan of escape from fury by being openly furious, and from *Reasons for* malice by being frankly malicious, were it not *preferring the* for sundry drawbacks of a quite fatal force. All *policy of* passion obeys the law of habit. Timely utter- *that of giving* ance gives it relief. True—and likewise pre- *vent to* *passion.*

disposes it to seek similar relief when the passion recurs. These explosive types go off to ever lighter triggers. Add to this that Feeling and Desire become memorable through expression. Denied expression, they tend sooner or later—emotions especially—to pass: granted expression, they are thereby written, be it in words or otherwise, on a record that we cannot blot.

> "The moving finger writes, and having writ,
> Moves on. Nor all your piety nor wit
> Will lure it back to cancel half a line,
> Nor all your tears wash out a word of it."[1]

For it is the instinct of all strong feelings, joyful or sorrowful, pleasurable or painful, to express themselves in ways that forbid forgetting, and all overt expression works in this direction. So that though a passion may pass, it has its own memorable recorded utterance to feed upon as often as it revives. Nor must we forget that this giving of the passions vent assumes an ugly character, when we reflect that it usually means venting them upon our neighbours. From this aspect, there is no plan possible but that of consuming our own smoke. To shoot the poisoned arrow, and call it peace because we have discharged our last shaft, is not morality. This alone is enough to dip the balance in favour of the policy of inhibition.

And yet this policy is all too simple. Inhibition involves control of those neural and muscular movements which have to be arrested. And it is safe to assume—whatever be the truth about the obscure relation between psychical states and bodily movements—that no man will succeed in performing effective inhibitive acts, who cannot induce the presence of inhibitive feelings, desires, and ideas. Hence we must push the question further back. Granting the efficacy of denying to these hostile and

To inhibit the expression of the passions, we must secure the psychical conditions of inhibition.

[1] *Omar Khayam*, LXXI.

hateful states their expression, we must ask how we can command the presence in the soul of the required inhibiting antecedents.

We need not here raise the question whether, when a good passion ousts a bad, or contrariwise, passion acts directly upon passion (the drama in that case being psychical), or whether this interaction of the passions is in all cases, as in a psycho-physical being like man we might expect, mediated by bodily movements. The point of practical importance is that, for the performance of the work of inhibition, the presence of a counter passion is essential. If this be granted, we may pass at once to the assertion that it is of utmost moment that this counter passion should be more than merely negative, more, that is to say, than the mere desire, however intense, to suppress. For it is poor strategy to wage against evil feelings or propulsions a war of mere repression. We have seen that this is so in educational control of others[1]. It is not less so in control of ourselves. If we would really oust our evil pro-clivities, we must cultivate others that are positively good. It is not enough to hate our failings or our vices with a perfect hatred. We must love something else. In other words, we must contrive to open mind and heart to tenants in whose presence unwelcome intruders, unable to find a home, will torment us only for a season and at last take their departure.

It is not enough to hate our vices.

Evil passions are ousted by good ones.

We may however aim at securing this result in various ways. One way is to practise a moral hygiene[2] by guiding our lives into places of moral health. There are social circles in which malicious feelings wither, energetic pursuits in which contact with a larger life swamps petty irri-

Ways of repressing feelings and passions. " Moral Hygiene."

[1] Cf. Part I, ch. VI.

[2] Cf. Höffding, *Oulines of Psychology*, p. 333. "There is a mental just as much as a bodily hygiene."

tabilities, natural scenes of peace where we can no longer anchor by one gloomy or sordid thought. And Browning has told us how even vice and crime can be rebuked by the mere sight of innocence[1].

The effectiveness of this resource rests upon a characteristic of our feelings and desires which is educationally of the first importance. They do not always lord it over us with equal mastery. They wax and wane. Our policy therefore is clear. It is "to utilise the intervals between strong emotions."[2] If in the flood-tide hour we can make little way, we can strive to take these hostile passions at the ebb, and then let "moral hygiene" do its work.

Its effectiveness.

Our success will manifestly depend on our past. If we have habitually lived in these places of moral health, they will not fail us when we betake ourselves thither in the hour of our need, and our evil humours or evil promptings, taken unawares, will depart at least for a season. It is here that a contracted development finds its nemesis. By the narrowness of its outlook and its interests, it has done something worse than stunt its development. It has shut itself out from the curative influences of nature and life. How different when a generous upbringing has filled our lives with healthy interests. For then it is little that is exacted of us. A favourite haunt, a tried friend, a congenial business, a well-loved book, perhaps even a chosen pastime—they are enough. A wise passiveness will do the rest.

The nemesis of a contracted development.

There is however, and fortunately, a more strenuous way than this. We have seen that it is of the very nature of man that in him feeling and desire are not blind, but on the contrary consciously knit to their objects and ends[3]. This indeed is the very secret of the awful, or ridiculous, tyranny of

As our passions depend upon the nature of their objects,

[1] Cf. *Pippa Passes.*
[2] Cf. Höffding, *Outlines of Psychology*, p. 334.
[3] See p. 37.

the passions over us. They enslave us because their vividly·
imaged objects usurp our minds. This is so with ambition,
love, hatred, jealousy, fear, hope, despair, with all the passions.
And not seldom the passion is masterful just in proportion as
its object is illusory. Here is a man who is mastered by the
evil spirit of revenge till his most patient counsellors cease in
despair to speak to him. And why? Because the image of
his enemy, of his fancied wrong, of his longed-for vengeance,
so fills his imagination that he can think and dream of nothing
else. Life, the apocalypse of a God, has shrunk to a poor
melodramatic theatre for petty personal revenge. Here is
another over-mastered by despondency. It is because some
picture of misfortune to be encountered in some fancied
future has so possessed his mind that it has already begun to
produce the very suffering from which, spectre-ridden, he, in
anticipation, shrinks. It is needless to multiply illustration.
There is not a passion in the whole fearful and pitiful list that
does not thus feed upon its object. Nor can man, so long as
he claims the dangerous prerogative to think, and especially to
think in images, escape this threatened bondage. But there is
a remedy. It is thrice fortunate that our passions
thus feed upon their objects. For then we can
attack them through their objects; or, in other
words, get rid of the passion by deposing its
object from its usurped primacy. This however
is not to be done—let us never so delude ourselves—by
simply thinking the object away. "Try not to think of it" is
the familiar well-meant advice of the miserable counsellors,
who are fruitful of exhortation and barren of expedient.
Would they but vouchsafe to tell us how!

    It is here that Spinoza has offered to the passion-tossed
and passion-driven world a well-known emancipation. Convinced, like the Stoics, that the
despotism of the passions is due to the fraudu-
lent pre-eminence with which the imagination invests their

(margin note: we can get rid of the passion by deposing its object.)

(margin note: Spinoza's way of emancipation.)

objects, he bids us set to work to dispel this enslaving illusion by bringing ourselves to know what the object of the passion really is, when seen in the dispassionate light of the under-

The peace that comes of under- standing.

standing. "A passion," so runs his memorable aphorism, "ceases to be a passion as soon as we form a clear and distinct idea of what it is."[1]

And to do justice to the profound insight of the remark, we need but think of any passion, vengeance or love or ambition, and then ask two questions about it. What was it in the stormy hour when it so possessed us that it was the one thing worth living for, the one thing that blotted out all the rest of the world? What is it now—now that the rolling years, that bring the wiser mind, have opened our eyes to the real finitude, possibly the insignificance, of the object which loomed so large, so extravagantly large in a world where there is so much else to live for? It is only needful to face these two questions in order to see how a strenuous effort to understand the object of a passion, and in understanding it to relegate it to its true significance or insignificance in the context of experience, must needs vastly change it from what it seemed to be in the days of our passionate ignorance. Nor is it doubtful that as the object thus changes, as it shrinks to its real proportions, its influence upon our feelings and desires must diminish accordingly. The ultimate result will be different in different types. It may be the resignation of despair, of trust, of humour, or of melancholy[2]. But in any case the passion will be subjugated[3].

This however is rather a counsel for philosophers, or at any rate for the minority who can unite the resolution and the faculty to think over their experiences with the deter-

---

[1] Spinoza's *Ethics*, Part v. Prop. iii.

[2] Cf. Höffding, *Outlines of Psychology*, p. 335.

[3] The last two pages (with some alterations) have been taken from a paper by the writer in *The International Journal of Ethics* for October 1899.

mination to understand them. For the most of us the more hopeful plan is to overcome our passions by thinking of something else.

This something else need by no means be a serious thing. For it happens sometimes that ideas that do not soar above trivialities may nevertheless have sent down such roots into a man's life, and become so fruitful of suggestion, that they prove more effective allies than more imposing and pretentious resources. Whence it comes that a sport, or a pastime, have before now weaned many from cares and sorrows which seemed proof against even the consolations of religion. Be it granted that, severely construed, this is a proof of the frivolity of human nature. But it is none the less an illustration of the expulsive power of ideas. Let but any idea have once wrought itself into the texture of our lives: its effectiveness is secured. A man may be discouraged and

embittered: it is enough to suggest the hopeful future of his boy or his friend, and the bitterness vanishes: or he may be revengeful and vindictive, till he is brought to remember that there is much else to live for besides the projects in which he has been thwarted or ill-used. So throughout. The serious idea, like the frivolous idea, wins the day; and it wins it, not so to say upon its isolated merits, but because in the course of our past lives it has struck strong alliance with a multitude of associated co-mates, that come crowding in, upon the signal of its suggestion. And the hope is that, against this compact phalanx, our unwelcome thoughts, being often detached and poor in alliances, will be unable long to hold their ground.

There are here however vast differences between man and man. In some all life may have sufficed but to establish one or two genuinely suggestive practical ideas. If these fail them, they are undone. There are others so ready of response in a hundred ways, that when disappointed in one resource, they turn cheerfully to another, so that we can hardly imagine them to have been long at the mercy of unwelcome thoughts.   Yet even with these there is often a difficulty—the difficulty of the first step.   For the healthiest of natures at times succumbs to the dire tyranny of "the fixed idea."   A wrong, a sorrow, a temptation, effects a lodgment, and obstinately refuses to quit.   We may have counter-resources, and we may know we have.   But they seem at times strangely to have lost their power, and to have become impotent to displace the unwelcome intruder.

Difficulty of the first step, especially in dealing with "the fixed idea."

Yet there are definite grounds of hope.   For, even when our ideas are fixed, they are, like our feelings (though not to the same extent), intermittent.   They are not always equally masterful.   Herein lies opportunity.   For it is then that we must bestir ourselves, and cast about us for some rival idea, which we know to be knit in close and comprehensive alliance to a powerful system of ends and interests.   This found, we must forthwith turn upon it the utmost strength of focalised Attention.   This is all that we can do.   Suggestion and association must do the rest.   And they will do enough if, when the hated haunting idea again begins to reassert its malign power, it finds itself face to face with a well-knit system of ideas, feelings, and propulsions, strong enough to resist it. It is thus that many an evil purpose has been routed, many a temptation quenched, many a brooding sorrow deposed from its usurped ascendancy.

Practical value of well-timed effort of Attention.

Fortunately, however, our difficulties are seldom so great as this.   Slavery to the fixed idea is rare.   In most lives the practical ideas that are for ever sweeping through the mind are many and changing.   The good and evil, the trivial and serious, the glad and the sad, pass in many-coloured, never-ending procession.   In other

In ordinary experience, however, there are many opportunities for effort of Attention.

words, there are materials for selection. So that some idea caught as it passes, may by resolute concentration of Attention upon it, grow and gather following strong enough to make a fight for the citadel.

There are fundamental differences among psychologists of the Will as to what is here involved. Some, impressed by the tension, struggle, effort, of which we are all aware when trying, for example, in the presence of a powerful temptation, to maintain a counteracting idea in the focus of consciousness, are ready to see in this momentous concentration of Attention the presence in the individual of a "spiritual force."[1] Others insist, and surely with reason, that effort of Attention, however intense, must needs have its explanation; and these try to find this simply in the felt tension that arises when rival ideas or systems of ideas are contending for mastery of the soul[2]. The divergence here is plainly of educational as well as psychological moment. It would indeed be something if we could believe that we have at our disposal a modicum of "spiritual force," and that it rested with our own "free will" to exercise it, in those crises when we are hesitating whether the idea that is to secure Attention is to be the first step upwards to a moral victory or the first step downwards to moral collapse. It is however beyond our limits to discuss so complicated a question here. Enough that there is general agreement that, whatever be the mental history of this first step, the sequel largely depends, not upon what we can do in the moments when we are striving after self-control, but upon what has been done for us by the long course of our education from our youth up. For it is only through this that our ideas can establish those strong, stable, well-organised alliances

Different views as to what effort of Attention involves.

Whatever be involved in effort of Attention, its sequel depends upon our whole past education.

[1] Cf. James, *Principles of Psychology*, vol. I. xi. 453.
[2] Cf. Bosanquet, *Psychology of the Moral Self*, p. 74.

which will stand us in good stead, when the perilous hour comes in which we are put to the test, either by a conflict of duties, or by the commoner conflict between a duty and a temptation.

Thus it is that the crises that meet us, when we have risen to that stage of moral enfranchisement at which we claim to hold our destinies in our own hands, become the occasions that first truly reveal what has been done for us in days long past, when as yet our lives were controlled by other hands. Nor will our triumphs of Self-control, if we be fortunate enough to achieve such, be the less welcome, if in the moment of conscious victory, we think with gratitude of the men, the institutions, and the slowly-fashioned, deeply-cherished ideals, that have given our resolves and aspirations that habitual well-compacted coherency, that deep root in our moral being, in which lies the open secret of their power.

INDEX.

CPSIA information can be obtained at www.ICGtesting.com
Printed in the USA
LVOW11s0919290515

440144LV00005B/1/P